E-MAIL ESSENTIALS

E-MAIL ESSENTIALS

ED TITTEL
MARGARET ROBBINS

AP PROFESSIONAL
Boston San Diego New York
London Sydney Tokyo Toronto

This book is printed on acid-free paper. ♾

AP PROFESSIONAL
955 Massachusetts Avenue, Cambridge, MA 02139

An Imprint of ACADEMIC PRESS, INC.
A Division of HARCOURT BRACE & COMPANY

United Kingdom Edition published by
ACADEMIC PRESS LIMITED
24–28 Oval Road, London NW1 7DX

Library of Congress Cataloging-in-Publication Data

Tittel, Ed.
E-mail essentials / Ed Tittel, Margaret Robbins.
p. cm.
Includes index.
ISBN 0-12-691397-8
1. Electronic mail systems. I. Robbins, Margaret. II. Title.
HE6239.E54T57 1994
384.3'4--dc20 94-19966
CIP

Printed in the United States of America
94 95 96 97 98 ML 9 8 7 6 5 4 3 2 1

Contents

Appendices

FOREWORD

INTRODUCING THE *ESSENTIALS* SERIES

Welcome to networking! You may be new to the topic or have some experience with computer networks; either way, we want to help you learn more. Maybe you've looked for a reference on electronic mail and found that while there is a lot of information out there, not much of it is aimed at assisting with the day-to-day operation of your network and your e-mail system. There are a great many books available that can explain the mathematical theories behind networking or discuss the engineering principles behind the hardware over which networks run. But unless you're building network hardware or writing network software, those books won't do much good for you—the network administrator who needs a reference book to help in setting up a network and keeping it running.

The *Essentials* series aims to fill the gap between theory and practice for networking. It offers solid, practical networking information, without jargon or unnecessary detail. It explains networking topics in clear, concise language, and plainly defines terms that may be unfamiliar. The series is divided into the topics that are most likely to be of use to network administrators, from setting up a network, to finding problems with it, to more specialized topics such as mobile computing and electronic messaging. Each book takes a gentle, lighthearted approach to the material that focuses on the basic principles an administrator needs to know to master the topic, with plenty of tips and proven techniques gleaned from the authors' wealth of experience in putting theory into practice.

Two books in this series will be of interest to anyone operating a local area network. One, *Network Design Essentials,* covers everything the reader needs to know to put a smoothly running network in place, including the maintenance tasks that will keep it running. The second book, *Network and Systems Management Essentials,* will discuss in practical detail how to identify, diagnose, and solve problems on a local area network.

The remaining books in the series are intended to expand on networking topics that should apply to most, but not all, network administrators. This book, *E-mail Essentials*, will be useful to anyone who uses message-based applications over a network. The recent explosive growth of that huge network of networks, the Internet, will make *Internet Access Essentials* a must-read for anyone wanting to tap into that treasure trove of information. And if your computing needs extend to large, far-flung networks, you'll definitely want to refer to both *Internetworking Essentials* and *Wide Area Networking Essentials.*

The authors want to hear from you about these books. Please write to us, care of the publisher, or contact us through the electronic mail addresses we provide in the About the Authors section. We'd like to hear more about what you liked and didn't like about these books, and on your ideas for other topics or more details that you need for your networking life. Thanks for buying this book. We hope you find it worth the money and the time it takes to read!

ACKNOWLEDGMENTS

Together, we have lots of people to thank for helping us with this book and for making this series possible. First and foremost, we'd like to thank Dave Pallai, the editorial director at AP PROFESSIONAL who has kept us around, even after we finished the first book in the series. We sincerely hope that the project lives up to his expectations and repays him for the time, effort, and attention he's lavished on us. To Karen Pratt, the editorial supervisor: thanks for getting us set up and working so smoothly and quickly! To Reuben Kantor and Mike Lindgren: thanks for working out all of the details with us, for being there when we needed you, and for making this project so easy to finish! If there's anybody else at APP we haven't mentioned, we want to thank them for their help and to apologize for omitting their names.

Finally, we'd like to continue our effusive thanks to our production person, graphical artist, and print professional extraordinaire: Susan Price, proprietoress of Susan Price and Associates, and the fastest keyboardist on the planet. We couldn't have done this project without you, Susan, especially the typesetting. We also appreciate your sterling sense of humor, especially when the deadlines loom large. Two down, four to go!

Ed Tittel

I'd like to begin my acknowledgments closest to home, where I now work, with fervent thanks to my family: bless you, Suzy, Austin, and Chelsea, for putting up with all the time I've spent working on this and other books. Thanks also to Dusty, our seven-year-old Labrador retriever, whose frequent need for bio-breaks kept me from ossifying at my desk. Once again, thanks to the whole Waterside team—especially you, Carole—who made it possible for me to quit my day job and realize my dream of becoming a full-time freelance writer. And of course, thank you, Margaret Robbins, for making this project so much fun and for carrying the bulk of the work for this book. Finally, I'd like to thank my sixth-grade English teacher, Mrs. Harris, and my twelfth-grade English teacher, Mrs. Adams, both of whom taught me how to put words together to what I hope will be every reader's good use!

Margaret Robbins

On the professional side, I'd like to thank Cheryl Currid for helping me get started in this field. A big thanks to Ed, for his quick sense of humor and amazing resourcefulness; he's a pleasure to work with. I also owe thanks to all the friends who helped me during this project and others, and I hope they know I couldn't have done it without them. In particular I'd like to acknowledge Kathy Mitchell and Roy Christmann for many unfailing years of encouragement, support, and patience; and of course, my family, without whom I wouldn't be here at all!

About the Authors

Margaret Robbins

Ms. Robbins is co-author of three other books. She wrote the first two, *Networking with Windows for Workgroups* and *Novell's Guide to NetWare 3.12 Networks*, with Cheryl Currid. Her most recent book, *Network Design Essentials*, is the first book in the *Essentials* series, of which this book is the second member.

When not writing, Margaret works as a software developer and has spent over a decade programming software involving various aspects of networking and telecommunications. Most recently, she spent four years at Vtel Corporation helping develop easy and fun user interfaces for its line of video conferencing products. You can reach her on CompuServe at 75730,1451, or via Internet at mrobbins@wixer.bga.com.

Ed Tittel

Mr. Tittel is the author of numerous articles for the computer trade press and of several books on computer-related topics, including *NetWare for Dummies* (IDG Press, 1993) and a series of PC shareware books, co-written with Bob LeVitus. He's recently concentrated on computer networking, for which he is best known, and has written extensively on that subject for the likes of *MacWeek*, *MacUser*, *ComputerWorld*, *Byte*, *WindowsUser*, and other publications.

Most recently, Ed worked as Director of Corporate Marketing at Novell, Inc., where he was responsible for technical content of trade shows and Novell-sponsored conferences, which is how he learned about networking. You can reach Ed on CompuServe at 76376,606 or on the Internet at: etittel@zilker.net.

Introduction

Welcome to *E-mail Essentials*

Welcome to the *Essentials* series from AP PROFESSIONAL. *E-Mail Essentials* is the third book in the series and is dedicated to telling you everything you need to know about setting up your own electronic mail system—from selecting the software to living with an e-mail system from day to day. Like the rest of the *Essentials* series, this book concentrates on the real-life information a network administrator needs to install electronic mail and to keep it running smoothly and efficiently.

About This Book

This book will take you through the process of setting up an e-mail system, from the initial planning and selection of that system, to the actual installation and construction involved in getting e-mail running, through the crucial but oft-overlooked phases of maintenance, expansion, and even disaster recovery. This book covers everything you'll need to know about installing e-mail, from creating the original design to putting that design into action, and also has tips about what to do in special circumstances, including problem situations.

How to Use This Book

We've designed this book so that you don't have to read it from cover to cover. If you like, you can just pick it up at any point and start reading, or you can begin wherever you find a topic of interest. The cross-references, along with the index and table of contents, will help you build your own thread through this material in whatever way makes sense for your particular situation. Of course, if you want to read it straight through from front to back, that works too! It's a tool, though, not the "great American novel." We want you to find it valuable enough to carry it with you as you work, and we hope it ends up dog-eared and stained from constant use.

About the Reader

Is this book for you? We assume that you, our gentle reader, have some familiarity with personal computers—you probably know a little of the jargon and most likely have a PC on your desk. You're probably not a complete beginner, but just in case, we define most terms so that you can get around without trouble. You know a little bit about e-mail and what it can do for you, and you want to know more.

Here's what we think might be driving you to read this book: perhaps you have a network in your workplace already and have been asked to administer it, and you have an e-mail system to run. Or perhaps you don't have one yet, but have been charged with installing one (or have volunteered to install one). Whatever your reason for wanting to learn, *E-mail Essentials* will supply you with everything you need to know to get the job done.

How This Book Is Organized

This book is divided into four sections. The first section of the book contains orientation information. Scan this introduction, along with the table of contents, to get your bearings about what's in the book and where to go to find what you need.

Part I: Introducing E-mail

This part of the book covers all the background you'll need to set up your e-mail system. We discuss what e-mail is, what it does, and how it works. We go over the fundamentals you'll want to apply when you sit down to design an e-mail system, as well as some key concepts to make the whole process easier (such as mapping). Also, we'll look at some strategies for getting the most for your money.

Part II: Making E-mail Happen

In this part we get into the real nuts and bolts of e-mail selection and installation. Here we describe how to set up an addressing scheme and get the software running. We include crucial strategies for keeping e-mail running, in terms of both routine maintenance and (perish the thought) problem solving.

Part III: Rules of Thumb

This is your reference section. Here, everything in the previous parts is distilled into easy-to-read checklists and charts. If you're looking for a specific point or a quick tip, check here first. If you need more background on why you should do what we say, please refer to the relevant explanations in Parts I or II.

Part IV: Case Studies

Here we give you some real-life examples. In this part we look at three different networks, one small, one of medium size, and one quite large, to examine their e-mail installations in terms of the principles covered in the first three sections of the book. We discuss what worked for them and what didn't and how these organizations are trying to fix their problems. These examples may help illuminate some pitfalls in your own operation, or suggest potential trouble spots for you to avoid. In addition, they may point you at some design elements and strategies you might otherwise not have considered. Either way, it represents what we hope is a valuable opportunity to learn from the experience of others!

Reference Materials

Next you'll find the E-mail Resource Guide. Here we list all the products and services mentioned in the book, with all the vendors' names, addresses, and phone numbers so you can contact them. We also give you sources for publications, if you're inclined to pursue the networking industry's news and information.

Finally, if you run across any unfamiliar terms, or need to cross-reference something, we've provided a thorough glossary and index at the back of the book to assist your search. Happy hunting!

Reading the Road Map

Remember, there are no rules about how to read this book. Start at the front and go straight through to the back if you like; you'll absorb everything you need to know about electronic mail that way. Or, if you have a specific topic you'd like to investigate, start anywhere that interests you. Use the cross-references, along with the Index, Glossary, and Table of Contents, to jump to other sections of the book and move through the book in whatever way makes the most sense for your needs. Each chapter is designed to be complete by itself, so dive right in. Whatever you do, enjoy it!

part I

Introducing E-mail

Overview

Welcome to the fast-growing and exciting world of electronic mail! This first section of the book covers all the basics of e-mail, from the major concepts to the design issues, and offers some practical tips to consider before you install your e-mail system. It also goes over what types of things you can do with e-mail and discusses some features you will want to consider when shopping for an e-mail system. When you finish reading this section you'll have a good idea of what e-mail can do for you, how to set up an e-mail system, and how to make sure you get the most out of your network budget, without sacrificing quality or reliability.

The nine chapters in this section will fall into three categories. The first three chapters cover the basic concepts of electronic mail, the next three discuss design and layout techniques that will ensure a reliable and effective system, and the final three chapters in the section cover the more practical side of things, offering tips on maximizing your networking budget and working with outside consultants.

Basic Networking Concepts

The first three chapters cover the basics. In Chapter 1, The E-mail Model, we lay the groundwork for understanding e-mail systems and define some essential terms that you'll be seeing throughout the book. This chapter introduces the user's view of how e-mail works. Chapter 2, The Pieces and Parts of E-mail, describes in more detail how e-mail systems operate—this chapter offers the system-level perspective on e-mail systems. Then in Chapter 3, What Can E-mail Do for You?, we look at e-mail in the larger context of groupware, discuss what groupware products offer, what e-mail products offer, and what productivity advantages these types of products bring to the workplace.

Implementation Advice

In the three chapters that follow we get down to actually designing your e-mail system. First, Chapter 4, E-mail Design Fundamentals, supplies you with the points you need to consider to make sure that the e-mail system you install is the best one for your needs and your users' needs. Chapter 4 also describes how to lay out your e-mail system to ensure that it is as reliable and trouble-resistant as possible. Chapter 5, Deploying your E-mail System, instructs you on the fine points of making the installation phase go smoothly. Finally, Chapter 6, Building for the Future, explains how to make sure that the e-mail system you install today remains useful and efficient as your organization grows and user needs change.

Spending Your Money Wisely

In the next three chapters we go on to the more practical issues of time and money. It's a fact that setting up an e-mail system costs money, but it doesn't have to break your budget, and in these chapters we show you how to make sure it doesn't. In Chapter 7, Managing Budgets and Installation Plans, we go over the big expenses and point out what types of things need to go into your budget. If you decide not to do everything yourself, Chapter 8 tells you how to get help from outside sources, whether from electronic bulletin boards or consulting firms. Finally, turn to Chapter 9, Smart E-mail Buying Techniques, for specific tips on keeping costs down. That chapter offers lots of hints for installing e-mail systems as inexpensively as possible and also warns you of some potential pitfalls.

chapter 1

The E-mail Model

Welcome to the World of Electronic Mail!

You've probably noticed that people are talking about electronic communication everywhere lately from comic strips to policy speeches. Currently, the most common form of electronic communication is electronic mail, otherwise known as e-mail. You may have been using e-mail for years, or perhaps you have only recently heard of it. Either way, you want to know more about it, and this book will tell you what you need to know to implement your own e-mail system.

In this chapter we introduce you to some key concepts and vocabulary. Let's start with the fundamental question: what is e-mail?

E-mail's Many Uses

The most common example of e-mail is a simple text message sent from one computer user to another over some type of network. E-mail can be much more than text, though. You can use e-mail to send spreadsheet files, word processing documents, programs, images, voice messages, and faxes. Almost anything you can store electronically can be sent via e-mail (depending on your e-mail software). See Figure 1.1 for an illustration.

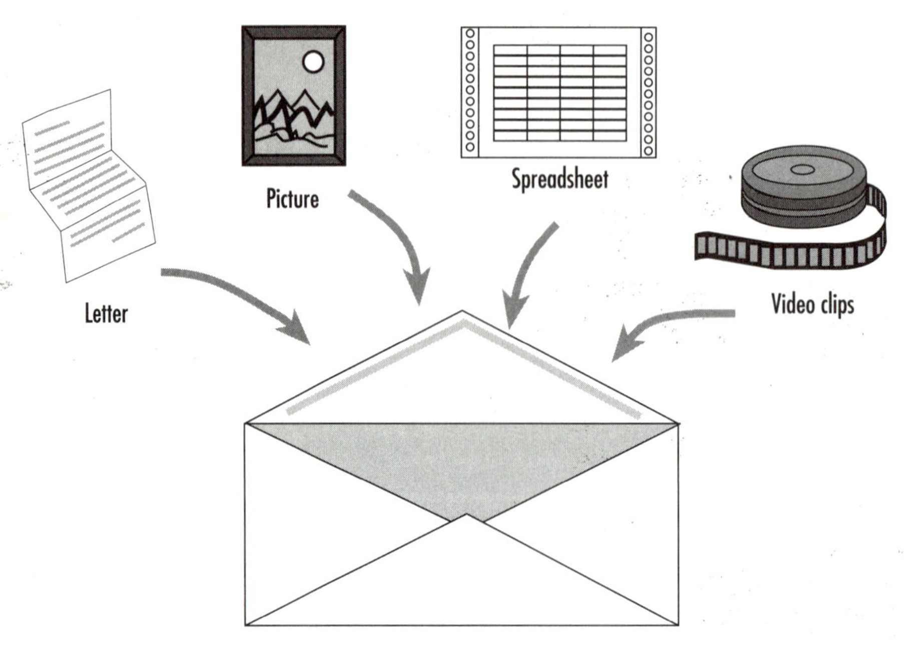

Figure 1.1. *Just about anything can go into an e-mail message.*

People use e-mail all over the world with hundreds of different e-mail systems. The ways they use electronic mail are even more varied. Many users have e-mail systems in their workplaces and use e-mail to exchange information related to the business. Others use it for recreation, to converse about hobbies, politics, travel, culture, and thousands of other topics. We expect that you are primarily interested in e-mail for use in the workplace, but this is far from its only application.

The term "mail" suggests letters and post offices, and this is indeed a useful metaphor for e-mail. Think of an e-mail message as an envelope that can contain a letter of any size or shape. The contents of that envelope could be a word processing file, a text message, or whatever else you might need to send to someone else. You must know the recipient's address before you can send your message, of course, and the receiver must have a mailbox and a local post office to which you can send it. Like any analogy, though, this one is useful for illustrating the basic idea but can't be taken too literally — many common terms have somewhat different meanings in the context of e-mail. So now let's define some common e-mail terms.

Basic E-Mail Vocabulary

Electronic Mail

People also call electronic mail *e-mail* or *messaging*. These terms distinguish it from its paper counterpart in the nonelectronic world (often called "snail mail," since sending e-mail is so much faster). The term "e-mail" refers to packages containing electronic information and the transmission of those packages between networked computer users. These users might be in adjacent offices or halfway around the world.

Message

A *message* is a single piece of electronic information. It might be a memo to your boss or a spreadsheet file you need to send to the accounting department. It might be a program you just finished writing or a chapter of a book. It might also be an electronic instruction from one computer to another, sending or requesting information between two or more computers. A message is not necessarily initiated by a human, nor is it necessarily received by one.

Header

The *header* of a message contains all the information that a networked computer needs to transmit the message. Common fields in a header are the sender's name and address, the receiver's name and address, and the addresses of these two people's computers (see Figure 1.2). The exact format of a header depends on the e-mail system in use.

Queue

Queue is another word for "line," as in, "We queued up to buy tickets for the new film." In computer language, a queue is a repository for information. E-mail systems, for instance, often store messages in a queue, and you will see the term frequently in texts about electronic messaging. Messages stored in a queue are said to be *queued* or *queued up*.

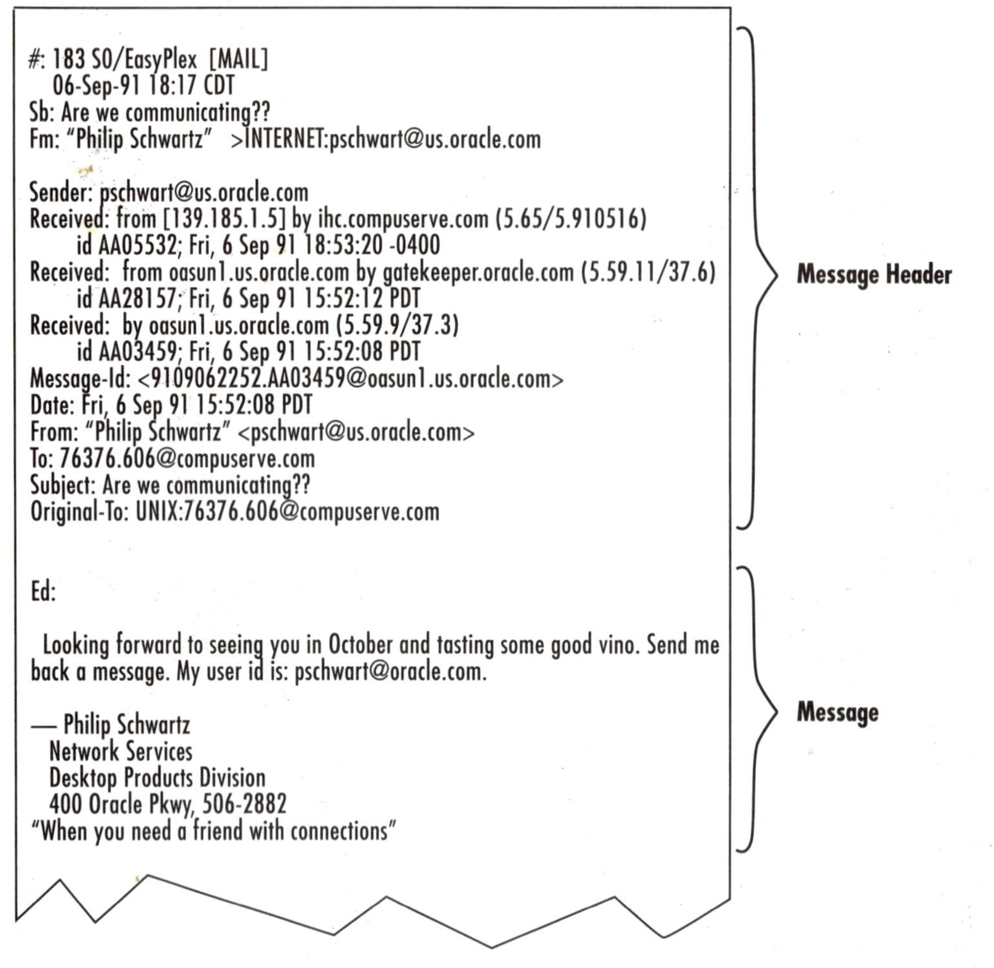

#: 183 S0/EasyPlex [MAIL]
06-Sep-91 18:17 CDT
Sb: Are we communicating??
Fm: "Philip Schwartz" >INTERNET:pschwart@us.oracle.com

Sender: pschwart@us.oracle.com
Received: from [139.185.1.5] by ihc.compuserve.com (5.65/5.910516)
id AA05532; Fri, 6 Sep 91 18:53:20 -0400
Received: from oasun1.us.oracle.com by gatekeeper.oracle.com (5.59.11/37.6)
id AA28157; Fri, 6 Sep 91 15:52:12 PDT
Received: by oasun1.us.oracle.com (5.59.9/37.3)
id AA03459; Fri, 6 Sep 91 15:52:08 PDT
Message-Id: <9109062252.AA03459@oasun1.us.oracle.com>
Date: Fri, 6 Sep 91 15:52:08 PDT
From: "Philip Schwartz" <pschwart@us.oracle.com>
To: 76376.606@compuserve.com
Subject: Are we communicating??
Original-To: UNIX:76376.606@compuserve.com

Ed:

Looking forward to seeing you in October and tasting some good vino. Send me back a message. My user id is: pschwart@oracle.com.

— Philip Schwartz
Network Services
Desktop Products Division
400 Oracle Pkwy, 506-2882
"When you need a friend with connections"

Figure 1.2. *The header contains the addressing information for the message.*

Calling a storage repository a queue often implies that the data items stored there are in a certain order. For this reason, queues are also called first-in, first-out (FIFO) lists. In Figure 1.3, for instance, Msg5 is the message most recently added to the queue, but Msg1 will be the first one processed, since it was the first to arrive. In most e-mail systems, though, this ordering will be invisible to the users. In some such systems, queue ordering can be changed by prioritizing messages or their schedules for delivery.

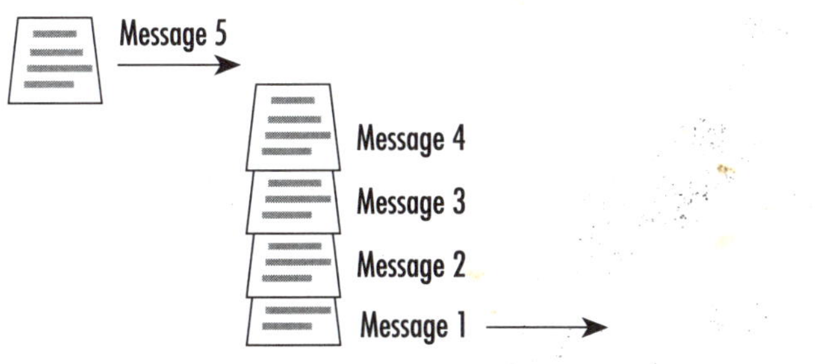

Figure 1.3. *Queues are first-in, first-out storage areas.*

Store and Forward

Some messaging systems, called *real-time systems*, send messages only to users who are currently logged in to the system. This is not so in a *store-and-forward system*. This type of system holds messages in a central repository until users retrieve them. A store-and-forward system also queues mail between different networks (see Figure 1.4) and sends groups of messages in batches, instead of sending each message as soon as it arrives. The delays introduced by intermediate storage are usually invisible to the users. A big advantage of store-and-forward systems is that they are less vulnerable to network problems than real-

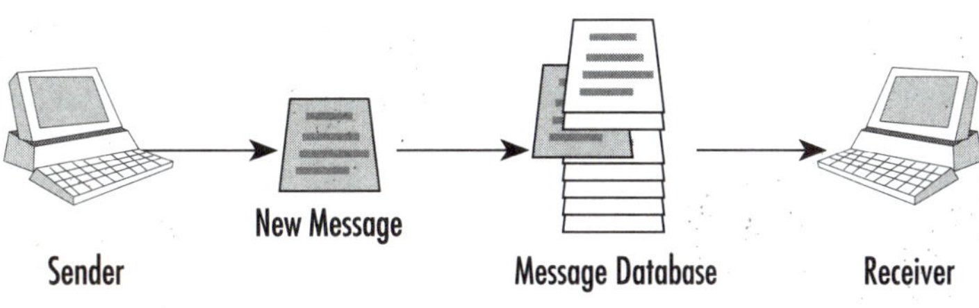

Figure 1.4. *In a store-and-forward e-mail system, e-mail sits at the post office until the receivers retrieve it.*

time systems. If a link goes down in a real-time system, no messages can get through until the link recovers. If a link goes down in a store-and-forward system, the system queues incoming messages and delivers them after the link is back up.

Addressing

Addressing an e-mail message means putting information in the header that will enable the sending and receiving computers to deliver the message correctly. How you address an e-mail message depends on the network(s) and the e-mail system you're using to send it. Unfortunately, this can get complicated, because every e-mail system varies in terms of the information and format it requires in an address. E-mail addressing is expected to get better as software manufacturers begin to adopt a common set of standards. We'll discuss standards sets in more detail in later chapters.

Mailbox

A *mailbox* is a queue for a user, and a place where the e-mail system stores messages for that user. Your mailbox can contain messages you have received but not yet read and messages you have already read but have not yet deleted. You need to clean out your mailbox from time to time by deleting unneeded messages and storing the rest—otherwise your mailbox will be clogged with outdated messages and disk space on the mail server will fill up.

Post Office

All e-mail messages for a particular system pass through a common repository, often called a *post office.* A small e-mail system probably has only one post office, while a large one could have dozens (see Figure 1.4).

Local Machine

This is the computer sitting on your desktop, where you do most of your computing work. It's also called a *client*, a *desktop system*, a *desktop*, or a *workstation.* This is the computer that runs the e-mail client software if you have a client-server type of e-mail system (such as cc:Mail or Microsoft Mail). If you have a host-based e-mail system (such as SNADS or PROFS), your local machine is a *terminal,* or it has to act like one to let you get to your e-mail. In that case, you may have a perfectly functional screen and a keyboard, but if the host is not working, you can't do anything with e-mail.

Host

This is the computer that does all the work in a host-based e-mail system. Users interact with the *host* by using terminals, or by making their PCs seem like terminals to the host (also known as *terminal emulation*). If the host is down, these terminals do nothing. Typically a host is a large mainframe or a minicomputer.

Server

A *server* is also a computer, one that provides services for clients on a LAN. A file server is a central repository for data files; a print server provides printing services; and a mail server gives the clients their e-mail capabilities.

Sometimes people refer to a server as a *host,* but in this book we reserve the word host to describe a mainframe or minicomputer system, and we use the word *server* when we discuss LAN computers.

Local Area Network (LAN)

A *LAN* is a group of PCs that are connected together to share information resources, typically within a single building. The number of computers on a LAN could be as few as two or could number in the thousands, though most LANs today connect fewer than 20 PCs together.

Wide Area Network (WAN) or Internetwork

When a LAN extends outside a building, it becomes a WAN. Think of a WAN as a collection of LANs communicating with each other by telephone, satellite, or some other non-LAN type of connection. A WAN can extend between two adjacent buildings, across a city, or across the world. Because a WAN is a group of networks, it is also sometimes called an *internetwork.* Don't confuse this term with the word *Internet,* though—that's the name of a particular internetwork. We'll talk a bit more about the Internet later in the book.

WAN Mail and WAN Messaging Services

When you send e-mail between different networks you discover that not every e-mail system uses the same addressing conventions. *WAN mail* and *WAN messaging systems* are aware of these issues and provide translation services to ensure correct e-mail delivery, though the systems might have very different addressing schemes.

What E-mail Does

What can you actually do with e-mail? We've discussed the different types of messages you can send to another user. Every e-mail package allows at least this level of functionality, and most offer much more. Next we describe some other features that you might find in e-mail software. In Chapter 4 we discuss what to look for when shopping for an e-mail package, and we'll take a closer look at these features and many more.

Receiving a Message

E-mail wouldn't be much use if you could only send messages but not receive them—you'd get bored pretty quickly. So the flip side of the sending capability is the ability to receive messages, which might be messages originated by other users or responses to your previous missives.

Sending Copies and Blind Copies

The ability to send the same message to more than one person is a useful feature in many e-mail packages, much like the carbon-copy ("cc:") line that dates back to the days of the typewriter when real carbon paper was used to generate additional copies. With this feature, everyone on the list can see who else received the same message.

Another copying feature is *blind copying,* in which you address the message to one or more people but send a copy to someone else whose name the other recipients cannot see. The political usefulness of this feature is probably clear, but the ethical appropriateness is a topic of debate in some circles.

Distribution Lists

Most e-mail packages will let you create *distribution lists* so that you can easily send mail repeatedly to the same group of recipients. If, for instance, you send weekly status messages to your project group, you can create a named distribution list consisting of all the group members' names and just send your messages to the list. It's much more convenient than typing each person's name every week.

Folders

Because it's such a breeze to create e-mail, you will probably get a lot of it. Much of it you can delete immediately (messages of the "Don't forget the 10 A.M. meeting" variety), but other e-mail contains information that you need to store. You don't want to store it in your mailbox, because the volume quickly becomes unmanageable. To address this problem, most e-mail packages allow you to store messages in *folders.* You can give your folders useful names to help you remember what's in them, just as you would if you were naming file folders for a filing cabinet.

Notification of Waiting E-mail

Most e-mail systems can inform you that you have e-mail waiting for you, freeing you from the burden of having to check for it. These notification mechanisms usually flash a message on your screen when you log into your account on that machine or network. Some notification programs will also check your mailbox periodically during your online session and can interrupt you to tell you that a new message has arrived.

Summary

This chapter is an introduction to the form of electronic communications known as e-mail. It's useful to think of e-mail in terms of conventional letters and post offices, but the analogy is somewhat limited. In this chapter we defined terms that are familiar from that world but have different meanings in the e-mail world, and we introduced some terms unique to e-mail. We also touched on a few of the many uses of e-mail and discussed some of the more common features of most e-mail packages, from the user's point of view.

chapter 2

The Pieces and Parts of E-mail

The Inside View

In Chapter 1 we examined e-mail from the user's point of view, describing what e-mail is and what you can do with it. In this chapter we look at electronic mail systems in more detail and introduce the concepts you need to understand how e-mail works, rather than just what it does.

How E-mail Works

When you send a message from your local computer to another user on your e-mail system, what happens? On a LAN-based system, your client software creates the message in a temporary storage space on either your PC or the LAN server. Once you tell the system to send the message, the system transfers it to a *message database* on the mail server. Messages are stored in this database in encrypted format so that casual browsing does not reveal their contents. (On most systems, access to the message directory is highly restricted as well.) The mail system increments a counter in the recipient's mailbox to indicate that he or she has new mail waiting.

The next time that the user checks his mail, he sees that he has one new message. When he issues the command to read that message, the

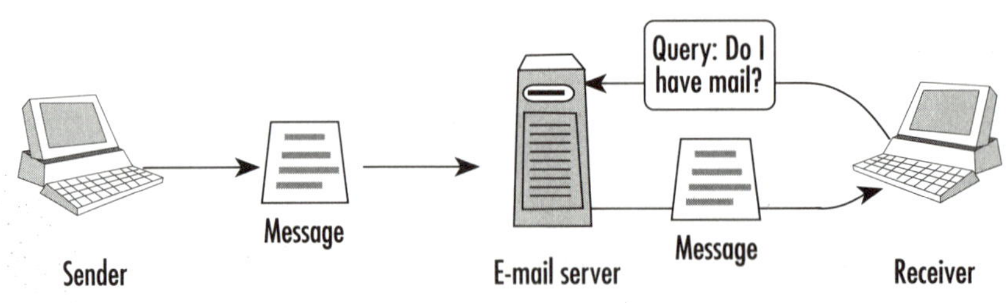

Figure 2.1. *Sending an e-mail message on a LAN.*

mail system decrypts the message and sends it to his PC for display (see Figure 2.1). If he chooses to save the message, it remains in the message database in its encrypted form. If, on the other hand, he decides to delete it, the mail system removes it from the message database and decrements the counter in his mailbox. If he decides to save a copy to his local hard disk, it saves it in decrypted form since it will then be outside the e-mail system's control.

The process is a bit different if you are working on a host-based e-mail system. In the simplest case, host-based e-mail consolidates everything on one computer. The users and system administrator all interact with the system via terminals (or via PCs that are configured to act like terminals), and the message database, temporary files, and user data all reside on the same computer. In a more elaborate host-based e-mail system you might have several large computers networked together—this type of arrangement combines features of LAN-based e-mail systems with those of centralized host-based systems.

Addressing and Standards

So far, e-mail looks pretty straightforward. It would be if everyone in the world used the same e-mail system. Unfortunately, they don't. There are lots of different e-mail systems, each with its own addressing schemes. The addressing scheme a network uses generally depends on what network protocol suite it uses. In this section we look at the major contenders in the WAN arena.

The Internet Standard

Most of the WAN e-mail sent within North America is arranged in this format. Since the Internet is the largest and most well known network that uses this format, it's often called the Internet format, but the actual name of the standard is RFC-822. (You can see why the other name is preferred.) Examples of e-mail addresses that use this format are

```
mrobbins@bga.com
etittel@zilker.net
admin@ramsay.comp.nonu.edu
```

The naming system on the Internet is called the Domain Name System, abbreviated as DNS. Thus, addresses in the Internet format are also called DNS addresses.

Some e-mail observers believe that DNS addressing will be the one standard on which the world will settle, largely because there is already a considerable volume of software that uses it, and because it has been deployed in so many networks throughout the world. Others, however, believe that X.400 naming is the way of the future.

OSI's X.400

X.400 includes an addressing scheme specified by the European international standards committee CCITT, which has also been adopted by the International Standards Organization as a part of the Open Systems Interconnect standards (abbreviated as ISO/OSI, or more simply, just OSI). The Message Handling System (MHS) protocol suite is based on X.400 and uses X.400 addressing.

You will find the largest number of MHS-based networks in Europe and Asia, but at this writing only a small number of networks actually use the protocol. X.400 has strong support among international and governmental bodies, but the relatively small amount of software available has hindered its widespread adoption. The jury's still out on whether X.400 will predominate.

EARN, BITNET, UUCP, and Others

It's impossible to list all of the different networking and related messaging protocols currently in use. Some of the other major contenders are EARN (European Academic and Research Network, mainly in Europe), BITNET (Because It's Time Network, mainly in North America), and UUCP networks (UNIX to UNIX CoPy, linking UNIX computers). Because of the demand for Internet e-mail capability, all of these types of networks have solved the problem of sending e-mail among themselves. They do this by using gateways, which we will discuss further later in this chapter.

What's in an Address?

The address is the most important part of your message, at least until the message arrives at its destination. In this section we look at one type of address, an Internet address, and break it down into its components. This is a very general treatment, but it gives you an introduction to some of the terminology you will need when you start addressing your messages to the world at large.

Within the Domain

Let's look again at the fictitious e-mail address from our previous example:

```
admin@ramsay.comp.nonu.edu
```

In the DNS addressing scheme, everything to the left of the @ symbol is the user name, while everything to the right describes the machine where that user has an account. Our example shows the address of a user called "admin" who has an account on a computer called "ramsay.comp.nonu.edu".

DNS machine names generally get less specific as you go from left to right, often starting with a machine name and ending with a top-level domain name. Thus, our user's account is within the top-level domain "edu". These top-level domain names are usually country codes, but in the United States they often refer to the type of organization to which the machine belongs. Apparently when these schemes were devised, people in the United States did not expect computing to extend beyond their borders.

Appendix B has a list of many top-level domain names in use in the world today. The top-level domain name "edu", for instance, stands for "education," indicating that the machine "ramsay" is probably at a U.S. college or university. We might then surmise that Non U. is the name of the university, and that the machine is in a department whose name is abbreviated "comp," which you might guess stands for something like computer science or comparative literature.

Back to You

If you happen to be using an Internet address, you probably found the previous discussion somewhat interesting. If you're not on the Internet or a network attached to it, though, you may be wondering how this all relates to you. Well, if you never need to send messages to anyone but other users on your own system, you're right, you don't need to know any of this. The issue only arises when you venture outside your own network. Most of the interconnections between networks use Internet-style addressing, so it's helpful if you're familiar with the format. Ideally, you have a gateway that handles the address translation for you, but sometimes you have to address messages by hand. If you know someone's local user ID is 4321, for instance, and she tells you, "Send it to me over the Internet; the domain is mynet dot com" you might be able to surmise that the address is something like "4321@mynet.com". You would be right.

The subject of addressing among different systems is huge. Appendix C describes addressing techniques for some common networks. We show another example in Figure 2.2.

Speaking a Different Language

Please recall our postal system analogy from Chapter 1, in which we thought of an e-mail message as a letter. Now consider what happens when you need to send that letter to another country—you have to make sure the address is in the language of that country, and that it uses a native layout and postal code. Similarly, when you send an e-

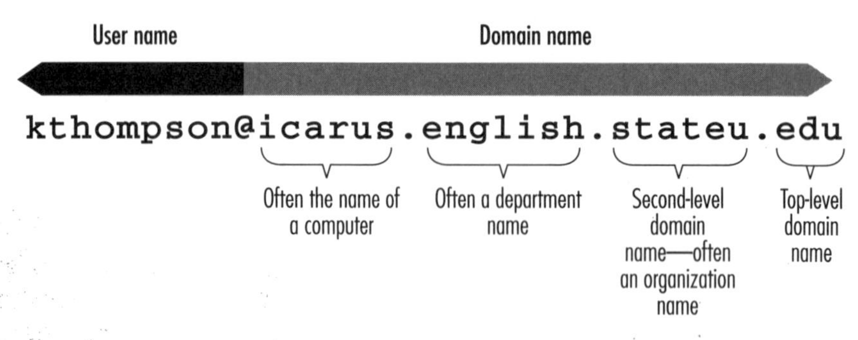

Figure 2.2. *Components of an Internet address.*

mail message to a user on a network or system other than your own, the address of that message must match the other system's addressing format. Otherwise it will not get delivered—or it could be delivered incorrectly, which might be worse!

Standing at the Gateway

In an e-mail system, this translation is performed by a *gateway.* A gateway is a piece of software that reads a message and translates a local address format into the format for some other e-mail system, or possibly even for multiple other types of e-mail systems. The gateway also performs the transfer from the local system to the target one.

In most cases, a gateway is specific to a particular pair of e-mail systems. For instance, you might install an Internet gateway for your cc:Mail system so that your cc:Mail users could send and receive Internet mail in the same way that they do cc:Mail. If they also wanted to send and receive e-mail with a PROFS system, you would need to install a different cc:Mail gateway to provide that link as well.

Gateways are useful and important pieces of software, especially with the large number of different kinds of e-mail systems in use today. The recent explosive growth in e-mail has made the gateway market grow very quickly, and it is likely that you can find gateway software for most pairs of messaging systems between which you need to exchange messages.

Directory Assistance

The e-mail world has grown so quickly, and from so many different directions at once, that finding someone's e-mail address can sometimes be quite difficult. Imagine that everyone in the world had a telephone—and an unlisted number—and you can begin to appreciate the problem. Actually, a more accurate analogy would be one in which there were tens of thousands of telephone directories but all in different languages. None of these directories would be reliably up-to-date; and any directory might not necessarily reflect the fact that someone had moved, changed his phone number, or disconnected his phone.

Sadly, this describes the situation that prevails today for most e-mail directories. Just about every local machine with e-mail has a local directory of its own users, but these directories are not always maintained. Universities, for instance, often give an account to each student but don't always purge their accounts when these students graduate. Or a user might access her account only once per year. In such a case, sending e-mail to her would not be the most efficient way to communicate.

Not only are these directories not updated, they are usually incompatible between systems. Your Banyan VINES e-mail system, for instance, cannot read a PROFS directory, because they are in different formats.

Standards to the Rescue, Again

The computing community has an answer to this problem. The members do the same thing they always try to do when faced with an incompatibility problem: they create a standard. The name of the standard for directory synchronization is X.500. E-mail systems that operate within this standard can all read each other's directories. Software that uses X.500 is not yet widespread, but as more and more systems use it, finding an e-mail address for someone anywhere in the world should become a simple matter.

Summary

This chapter gives you a general look at how e-mail works. LAN-based and host-based systems are both store-and-forward systems, and work in similar ways. We look at addressing and directory issues and discuss the standards that everyone hopes will solve some of the problems associated with so many different addressing schemes.

chapter 3

What Can E-mail Do For You?

What to Expect from E-mail

In this chapter we look at what makes e-mail different from other types of software and examine how it fits into the category generally known as groupware. We look at the capabilities of e-mail and the specific benefits your organization can realize from e-mail. We also discuss the ways that e-mail can change an organization and the way it does business. Finally, we'll look at the lighter side of e-mail with an overview of some of the fun things e-mail has spawned.

Software That Makes Working Together Easy

You're already familiar with the idea of a local application, one that gets information from the user's local drive and from the user. In this type of application, the user fires up an action and the application goes off and performs it. Control returns to the user when the application finishes that task.

Another type of application that is increasingly common is a message-based application. This application gets information from across a network, and its behavior is much more interactive. This type of architecture lends itself nicely to a new type of software called *groupware*. There's not a lot of agreement on a definition of groupware, but you might say it's software that facilitates people working together. E-mail is the most common type of groupware. The differences between e-mail and other groupware products are fuzzy, and they become fuzzier as vendors integrate databases, forms-related capabilities, and scheduling into their e-mail packages.

In order to make an informed decision on an e-mail package, you should know what's available from e-mail packages in general, so in the following subsections we describe the basic types of groupware.

Shared Editing and Drawing Packages

One fast-growing category of groupware is the kind of software that allows multiple users to make changes simultaneously to a single, shared document. These collaborative applications usually run over a LAN or WAN and provide some on-screen means to identify who is making which change (different colored cursors for each user, for instance). With this type of software, a design team can mark up a drawing together, rather than having to mark up individual paper copies and then reconcile and transfer the changes to an electronic version. Similarly, a writing group can make changes to a document together without all group members needing to be in the same room at the same time.

Integrated E-mail and Database Systems

These are the applications that have database capability smoothly integrated into an e-mail system. One such product is Lotus Notes. Satisfied users swear by its ability to handle complex, database-driven information, citing the ease with which they can send e-mail messages that include form data, for instance. It's a bit artificial to list this type of e-mail application in its own category, since Lotus Notes is so often used to form the basis for other types of messaging applications. Action Technologies' Action WorkFlow product, for instance, is built on top of Lotus Notes.

Forms-Based Applications

Another big use of groupware comes from the world of electronic forms, which is the computerized analog of paper business forms. Virtually every large company relies heavily on paper forms to do some or all of its business—it has forms to record employee vacations, to request office supplies, and to perform other internal record-keeping tasks. Most companies also have forms for interacting with external clients and suppliers. For instance, a company might have a particular form for purchases and another for client orders. With forms-based applications, companies can store these forms electronically and call them up as needed. Someone taking an order, for example, can enter all the information on-screen into the order form, then send the order off to the appropriate department. In the right kind of environment, this not only does away with lots of paper but also speeds the flow of information because it's based on e-mail, not a physical movement of paper from one location to another.

Electronic Document Interchange (EDI) is a format many companies use to exchange forms-based data. Ford Motor Company, for instance, will only do business with vendors who use EDI. As a standard format develops, we expect to see more forms-based applications that use EDI or other related formats.

Workflow Applications

Another type of groupware gives users software tools to describe their business procedures in a graphical format, so the software can then provide the users a set of checkpoints throughout the process. Such applications are called *workflow* applications, and they are getting more popular as messaging systems become more advanced.

Scheduling Applications

Think about the last time you tried to call a meeting. You made a list of all the people you needed to have attend and picked out a couple of time slots you thought might work. Then you went to the busiest person on the list, asked her when she could attend, and wrote it down.

Then you went to the next person on the list and did the same. Unfortunately he couldn't meet at any of the times the first person could, so you had to go back to her and set up a different time. Then you went on to the third person on the list . . . .

Wouldn't it be nice if you could call up everyone's schedules on your screen? That's exactly what scheduling applications let you do. You enter the names of all of the attendees, and the software calculates when they're all free on the basis of the schedules each of them has already entered into the system. Many scheduling programs even have provisions for scheduling conference rooms, so you can see which rooms are free at what times. Not only that, but many are integrated into e-mail systems, so once you determine a meeting time that works for everyone, you can send them all e-mail regarding the agenda.

Image-based Applications

Some applications let you work with pictures, or images. You would need to use a scanner to create an electronic image of a document, and these types of applications make it easy to work with such an image. Digitized signature cards are a great example of what this kind of application can do—with the right software, bank employees don't have to search for a paper card in a file cabinet to see your signature anymore. Instead they can call up an on-screen image of your signature card, compare the image to your signature on the check, and complete your transaction quickly and efficiently.

Uses of E-mail

The most frequently used type of groupware, by far, is e-mail. It's usually the most limited type, since it typically doesn't have built-in scheduling or database capabilities, but again, that's changing. Even without those advanced features, you can do a lot with e-mail, as we discuss below.

Notes and Memos

The first e-mail message most people send is a line or two of text to the effect of "Hey, does this work?" Most e-mail is not much more complicated than that. It's usually in the form of a text message, either asking or answering a question, making an announcement, or providing information. All the information you usually disseminate with memos can be easily distributed via e-mail. In most e-mail packages, you can create the memo with your favorite text editor, then import that file into the e-mail message, or send the file as an attachment to a short message.

Word Processing Documents and Spreadsheets

In most e-mail packages it's an easy matter to attach a file to an e-mail message. This file could be a document describing company policy, a spreadsheet with all of the sales figures for the last quarter, or the text of the new advertising brochures. It's important to recognize the difference between attaching a document and importing a text file. If the file you want to send is not simple text, you will probably have to send it as an attachment rather than including it in the body of your message. This is not always the case, though, because some sophisticated e-mail packages can recognize file formats automatically. When in doubt, it's safest to attach the document separately to avoid potential problems for its recipient.

Graphics

A digital picture is just another type of file, so you can attach it to an e-mail message in exactly the same way you would attach a document. Specifically, if your e-mail system allows you to attach documents to messages, you will also be able to attach graphics files. Some packages even allow you to create graphics with their own built-in drawing tools, and allow your recipients to view the graphics without leaving the e-mail program (see Figure 3.1).

Connecting to Other Mail Systems

We've already discussed the fact that there are many different e-mail systems in use and that they do not all use the same type of addressing. This will cause you no problems until you want to send mail to someone on a different type of system. Fortunately, nearly every e-mail sys-

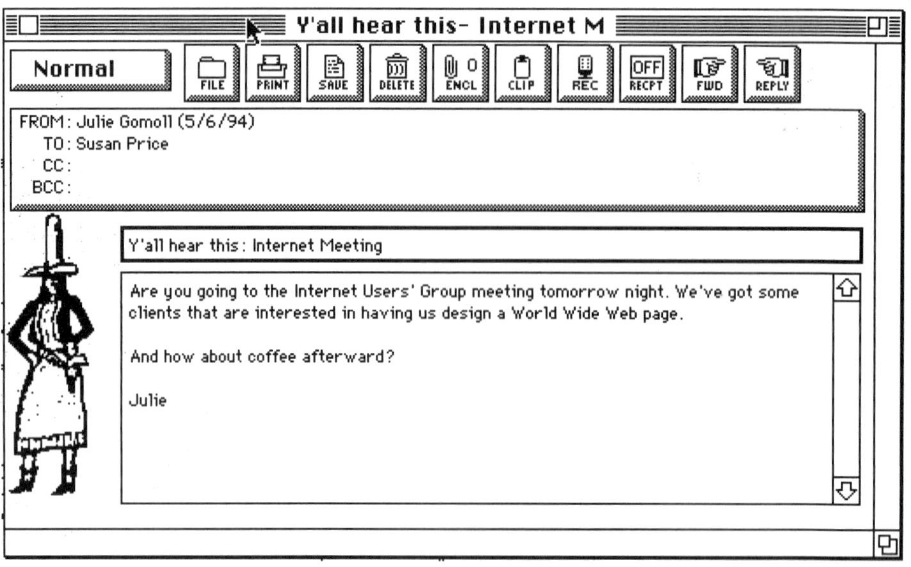

Figure 3.1. *Some mail systems let you send and view graphical messages. This example is from CE Software's QuickMail for Macintosh.*

tem provides some means of sending e-mail to other systems. If the other system to which you want to send a message is an e-mail system, you will need to install gateway software on your system to translate the addresses to the format of the target system, or find some way to use a gateway between the two systems.

On the other hand, if you don't need to send mail to other systems frequently enough to justify installing gateway software, you might be able to work around the issue by hand-addressing messages. How you do this depends entirely on the two systems between which you want to communicate, and you should check with someone who is familiar with both systems, or your system operating guides, for more information.

Note that e-mail addresses are very precise and picky things, not given to ambiguity, and when you combine that finickiness over two different systems the problems tend to multiply. Nonetheless, in Appendix C we give a couple of examples of some of the most common translations. Many of the private providers (such as America Online and CompuServe) charge extra for messages outside their domains, so you might want to check the local pricing structures before you make a habit of sending these types of messages.

Some messaging systems allow you to send messages even to people who are not on e-mail at all. If your recipient has a fax machine or access to a telex machine (these are still quite common outside the United States and Europe), you may be able to send a message through your e-mail system. As a last resort, you can often enter the ground address; some e-mail systems offer a service where someone will print out the message, put it in an envelope, and send it via snail mail. An advantage of sending a message this way is that it often gets printed and sent from an office fairly close to the actual recipient's address, reducing transit time and postage costs.

How E-mail Can Enhance Productivity

More Communication Means Better Communication

Since it's so easy to send e-mail messages, people usually do so more often. Therefore, the overseas representative who used to send in a paper report monthly can now easily send status updates every week or even more often. Similarly, the project team members who have offices in different buildings can send questions and information to each other easily via e-mail, which will improve communication throughout the group. We couldn't have written this book, or any of our others, if it weren't for e-mail!

Reducing Redundancy

In the paper world, if you want to send the same message to a number of people you typically send a memo to all of them. If one person gets left off the list, or someone adds a note in the margin and passes the memo to someone else, the uniformity of information distribution gets lost. With electronic messaging, these problems are easy to handle.

Mailing list capability lets you send exactly the same message to everyone, and if someone adds a comment, it's an easy matter for that person to send it to all of the message's original recipients if needed. Furthermore, nobody has to walk around delivering paper.

The Phone Games

We've all played phone tag. You call someone to ask a simple question, but he's in a meeting. He calls you back after the meeting, but you've gone to lunch. You call back, but he's just left for a three-day business trip. Wouldn't it be nice if you could just send e-mail?

With electronic messaging, you can send a question when you think of it, and your recipient can respond when she sees it, on her own schedule. You are both freed of the necessity to communicate in person. Many business people report that they use e-mail instead of the telephone whenever they can, and that doing this helps them gain more control over their schedules.

Cost Effectiveness

Long-distance phone calls are expensive. With e-mail, even if you have to pay for the price of a phone call to send the message, sending it takes a fraction of the time that speaking it would, which will lower your telephone bill. If you send the message over a network, the transmission is virtually free—you've already paid for the network.

Another cost benefit of e-mail is that electronic messages are just that—electronic—so after you're done reading them, you can just delete them. You don't have a piece of paper to throw away, you don't have 20 extra copies of the memo, and maybe you've saved a tree or two over the course of a year. Unfortunately, there are still those users who seem to be unable to read e-mail on a screen, and have to print every message out before reading it, but even these types can see the benefits of the paperless office—something that is still a rather long way off, in our opinion!

E-mail Will Change Your Workplace; We Guarantee It

Whether it's a positive change or not depends very much on your corporate culture and structure. On e-mail, communications are egalitarian: the janitor looks pretty much the same electronically as the CEO (though in our experience the janitor can probably spell better). Not only do people all look the same on-line, but now everyone has access to each other and communication becomes more lateral.

Most managers who have noted this phenomenon speak highly of its benefits, stressing that it has improved communications throughout the organization and helped them become more team oriented. Decision making can include more people when everyone has a voice, and employees who have a voice tend to feel better about their work and have more of a sense that their opinions matter. However, in an organization that has traditionally been highly hierarchical and autocratic, the transition to a very different communication style might be difficult.

Another important issue is privacy. Most corporations take the stance that since they own the computer equipment, they own everything employees do with it. It's not usually necessary to enforce rigidly this type of rule, but the policy exists in case of abuse. Employees, on the other hand, usually use e-mail for casual communications as well as business ones; in highly e-mail dependent organizations, e-mail is replacing the telephone as the preferred means of communication.

The safest strategy is to assume that your e-mail is not private. We've seen many instances of love notes, confidential information, or nasty remarks getting broadcast to the wrong people. Act as though everything you send via e-mail is public knowledge, and you should be able to protect yourself. At the scale of the corporation, we advise that you formulate a corporate e-mail policy that goes on-line at the same time as the e-mail system. The Electronic Mail Association has a kit to help you do just that; see the Vendor List in Appendix D for more information.

Smileys and Abbreviations: The Lighthearted Side of E-mail

It's impossible to discuss e-mail without mentioning smileys, since they show up everywhere on the e-mail landscape. Some people hate

;-)   :-(

Figure 3.2. *Winking smiley (left) and frowning smiley (right).*

them, insisting that one should be able to convey any emotion with words alone. Dissenters argue that not everyone is a brilliant writer and that misunderstandings are a common feature of human interaction. Just as someone might take offense at a remark that your best friends would recognize as your style of joke, smiley defenders maintain, so can the spirit of sarcasm or teasing get lost in the cold electronic world.

Smileys were invented to save the day. You can transmit a wink, a grin, an expression of dismay, and much more with just a few well-placed punctuation marks. Figure 3.2 shows two examples, one a wink and the other an unhappy face. You don't see them? Turn the page sideways to the right.

Some smiley enthusiasts have developed smileys into an elaborate art form. The O'Reilly Press book *Smileys* gives hundreds of examples, showing a wide range of emotions as well as celebrities such as Ronald Reagan and Santa Claus. Publishing information is in the Resource Guide in Appendix D if you're interested.

The use of abbreviations is another cultural feature of e-mail. We've all seen "ASAP" and "FYI" for a long time. Use the following list to decipher these and others.

- ASAP as soon as possible
- BTW by the way
- DWIM do what I mean (usually directed at a computer)
- FWIW for what it's worth
- FYI for your information
- IM(H)O in my (humble) opinion
- OTOH on the other hand
- ROTFL rolling on the floor laughing (sometimes spelled ROFL)

SUMMARY

In this chapter we examined e-mail as a part of groupware and as distinct from it. We looked at the features and capabilities of groupware and of e-mail, and discussed why the boundaries are fuzzy. We covered what your organization can gain from e-mail and the kinds of changes e-mail may cause. We wrapped up with a note about the lighter side of e-mail.

chapter 4

E-mail Design Fundamentals

Before You Begin Your Installation

The previous three chapters introduced you to the benefits of e-mail and the concepts you need to understand when working with e-mail. Now we go on to the practical issues and discuss the things you need to know to implement your own e-mail system. So this chapter covers what you need to think about before you start your e-mail installation, including what to look for when shopping for an e-mail system, how to design your e-mail flow, how to lay out your mail network, and how to name your users.

E-mail Shopping List

With e-mail, a number of things become possible that were not previously easy, and the previous chapter discussed some of them. Your users will require some of those features, while others might fall into the "bells and whistles" category. Certainly the ability to send and receive text messages is a minimum requirement for any e-mail system. What other features do your users need? You may wish to create two lists, one for features you must have, and another for features that would be nice to have but that you can live without for the time being.

When making your features lists, be sure to think ahead. A feature that seems like a frill today might become a necessity in the future. While it's impossible to predict the future accurately, you can probably perform some extrapolation based on your company's business plan. If you know you are going to need a more advanced system in the future but cannot afford it now, try to select one that allows a fairly easy upgrade path to your dream system, if at all possible.

If you think you will eventually need an e-mail system with advanced features and functions, we recommend that you purchase the sophisticated system at the outset if you can possibly afford it. You don't have to use all of the fancy features right away, but they'll be there when you do need them and you won't have to upgrade to new software.

Now that you have a list of every feature your users need, think about some features that can make your own life easier as e-mail system administrator. These might be features that you use all the time, or features that help you indirectly by helping your users. In the following sections we describe some of the most important e-mail administration features.

Importing User Names

Does the package allow you to import user names from the network? This won't matter to you if you have a fairly small user base, or if you install a LAN at the same time as you install the e-mail system. But if you have more than about 30 users, it will be a real pain to type in each user's name. In such a case, an import feature will be a great help.

This feature is nice when you first install the e-mail system, but you'll appreciate it even more if you ever split user groups across multiple servers, or combine multiple servers after a merger. These scenarios are quite likely for growing and successful companies, and an import feature can greatly reduce the headaches.

Repairing Corrupted Databases

Make sure the package you buy allows you to repair a corrupted message database with relative ease. These databases don't get corrupted often, but if they do it can really mess up your entire e-mail system, and you'll need a quick way to fix it. Some systems have a feature right on the administrator's menu that lets you rebuild the message database without losing any messages; you should look for this or a similar utility.

The e-mail system vendor might assure you that it's impossible to corrupt the database, but we advise that you test it thoroughly in your test lab anyway. (We discuss the test lab further in later chapters.) Try this: create a message within your multitasking environment (Windows, for instance, but any Macintosh program will work too), send it, and turn off the sending PC just as you send it. This is a fairly reliable way to crash the message database. Can other users send, read, or receive e-mail? If not, the database is probably corrupted. Can you repair the database with the provided utilities? If not, start looking for another e-mail package.

Encryption

Yes, the privacy issue does come up a lot in the world of electronic communications. E-mail, as you will soon discover, can take on a life of its own. It goes everywhere and lots of people see it, some of whom you did not expect to see it. An encryption feature can be very useful to protect sensitive data, whether you're sending the company payroll charts or romantic notes to a colleague.

If you're sending the latter, though, you should keep in mind another privacy matter. Most organizations are of the opinion that since they paid for the equipment they own everything you send using that equipment. This means that your mushy notes are company property, and company representatives have every right to read them. The U.S. courts generally side with the company on this matter, too—something every e-mail user should know. We're not familiar with the situation outside the United States, but we do advise that you inform yourself and your users.

Search Capabilities

You know you have the message somewhere, but you just can't seem to find it, and the prospect of viewing every message you've received in the last four years is just a bit overwhelming. You need a search function.

When evaluating e-mail packages for this feature, look at how many fields they let you search. Some only search for text within the message subject line, others search a special keyword field, and others let you search the entire message body. Many also have a feature that allows you to search by the name of the sender, but beware. Some of those that search for user names search both the sender and receiver fields with no means to select one or the other, which can be rather annoying.

Archiving

All those messages from four years ago are just sitting in the users' mailboxes, taking up space. It's time to archive them. Archiving messages gets them out of the message database, so archiving is a critical feature from the administrator's point of view.

Archive files usually reside on either the user's local hard disk or a network drive, depending on your e-mail package. Archived messages are usually stored using some sort of compression, which reduces space even further. In a good archiving system, users can still read, search, and delete messages, but not all packages offer all these features. An archive system from which messages cannot be deleted is not particularly useful, in our experience. The importance of messages expires over time, whether in a mailbox or an archive, and it's important to have deletion features to reflect that.

Another useful archiving feature is in the administrative realm. In some packages, it is possible for the e-mail administrator to archive messages as soon as they have been read. This certainly helps keep mail server disk usage under control, but be sure it doesn't restrict your users' ability to read or remove their messages.

Reporting Features

To stay on top of e-mail usage, you need to be able to get a statistical picture of your e-mail system. It's useful to see how many messages each user sends and receives, how much server disk space each user is consuming, and how much total e-mail traffic is flowing across your network. Keep an eye on these numbers so you can tell when it's time to ask someone to clean up—or time to install a new disk drive or even a new mail server.

Interoperability and Compatibility

Make sure the e-mail package you choose supports every single platform on your network. Now, this may seem obvious, but it might not be easy, depending on your network configuration. We know of an installation where the graphics people use Macintoshes, everyone else uses PCs with Windows, and the e-mail system only works on PCs. The graphics artists are needlessly isolated from the company culture in that environment, when they could be as equally empowered as the PC users if only the right e-mail package were in use.

Another interoperability consideration is for your remote users. If the remote access software does not have the same interface as the LAN version, any users who travel will have to learn two interfaces, which they will probably not appreciate.

Be sure to consider any language issues. If you will be communicating between regions that have different languages, such as French and English in Canada, look for a package that offers versions for all languages your organization uses.

The Server Question

Now that you've selected the e-mail package that will make everyone happy, you need to think about how to install it. You might want a single, dedicated server for all e-mail, or it might make more sense to share the burden among multiple servers.

The determining factors here are the numbers of users and servers you have. If you have only a small number of users, it's much easier to maintain the e-mail system if everything is in one place. In a very large installation, on the other hand, you'll probably benefit from dividing to conquer.

You're probably now wondering how many users constitute a large installation. Let's just say that the answer depends on your e-mail system. Check the specifications for the software. The manufacturer probably lists some ballpark numbers of users for each installation. If you have fewer than the maximum, you'll be fine on a single server. But watch those numbers—that's also how you'll know to add more servers later!

Keeping E-mail Flowing

The next step in designing your e-mail system is deciding how to connect all those servers and gateways. Your primary goal here is to make sure that if a link goes down anywhere in the network, the problem will have as little impact as possible on your e-mail traffic.

If you have only one e-mail server, you don't need to worry about these issues too much right now. The funny thing about networks, and e-mail, is that they are always growing, so it's a good idea to read through this now and get familiar with the strategy. You might be surprised at how soon it becomes relevant to you!

Map Reading

If you've read our previous book, *Network Design Essentials,* you know that we're big advocates of network maps. Your network map is your guide to everything that is happening on your network, and it's the first place you should go any time you want to change something on your network. Adding an e-mail system certainly qualifies!

A network map is based on a map of your building. At a minimum, it shows all the walls, elevators, electrical wiring, and telephone wiring. On top of those basics, it should indicate all the network wiring, major hubs, servers, workstations, and other network items. You need to note where these things are when you lay out your e-mail system, because e-mail will increase the traffic over your network, and you want to make sure you arrange things so that the increased traffic does not cause problems. It's also possible that during the layout phase you'll discover a need to add more bandwidth to certain sections of the network; you'll need to refer to your network map to see where you can do that and what it's going to require.

The Org Chart

Now take a look at your organizational chart. This is a table that shows everyone in your organization and the groups in which they work. In most organizations, people communicate most often with people in their own groups, and it's safe to assume that e-mail traffic will follow the same patterns. With your organization chart at hand, figure out which groups will be sending the most messages among themselves, and which distinct groups will need to communicate with each other most often. Figure 4.1 shows an example.

Now add in all the e-mail users who do not show up on your org chart. Are you planning to grant any external vendors access to your e-mail system, for instance? Many companies exchange invoices or documents this way. What about your remote users? Be sure you include everyone who will use the e-mail system, and try to predict where the message traffic will be heaviest.

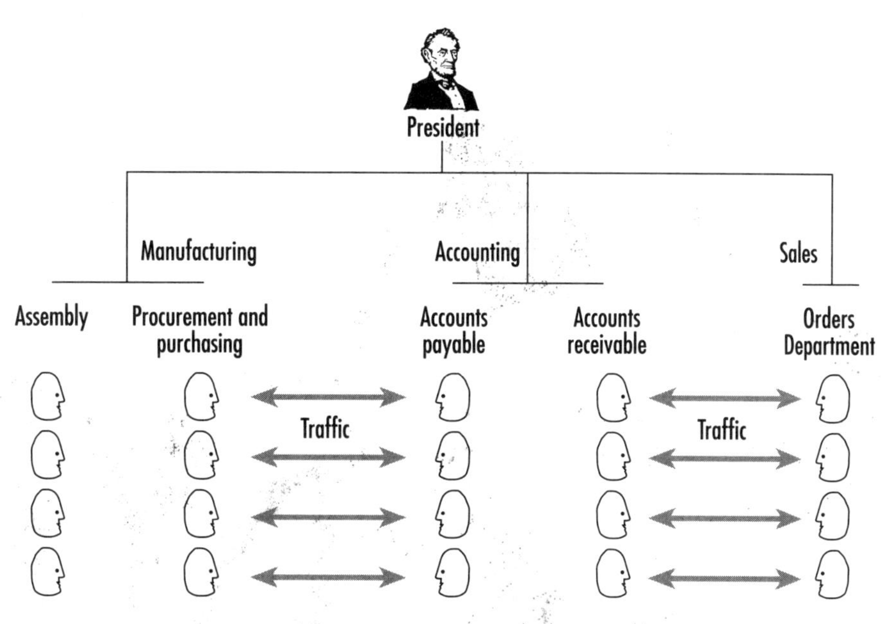

Figure 4.1. *Organization chart with e-mail traffic patterns added.*

Back to the Map

Now that you have some idea of who in the organization most often talks with whom, return to your network map to find out which servers these groups use. Your server arrangement probably reflects your company structure, at least to some extent, because that's the most natural way to arrange networks. You might have one server for each product the company produces, or one for accounting and one for everyone else. Whatever your arrangement, with a little luck it also reflects the patterns of your expected message traffic. If not, see whether you can make any adjustments to correct weak spots. If you need to move a group to a new server, or add a new backbone link, identify that need now. It will be much easier to make these changes before you implement the e-mail system than it will be afterwards.

At the end of all this analysis, your goal is to have the groups of people who communicate most often together on the same e-mail server, with high-speed links between servers of those groups. You can use lower speed links to connect the servers of groups that do not communicate as frequently.

Minimizing Problems

You need to consider two other factors before you finalize your e-mail server layout: performance and reliability. The way you arrange your e-mail servers can have a big impact on how quickly e-mail moves between servers, and on the amount of trouble a link problem can cause. Let's look at some examples.

Daisy-Chain Layout

A very straightforward layout, this type of arrangement just connects the servers together in a string, as Figure 4.2 shows. Notice, though, that if the link between Servers A and B fails, Server A is isolated from the rest of the system until the link comes back up. Furthermore, e-mail traveling from Server E to Server A passes through four links. In a typical store-and-forward e-mail system, the delay can be as much as 15 minutes between servers, so the same message that takes 15 minutes to get from Server E to Server D could take as much as an hour to get to Server A.

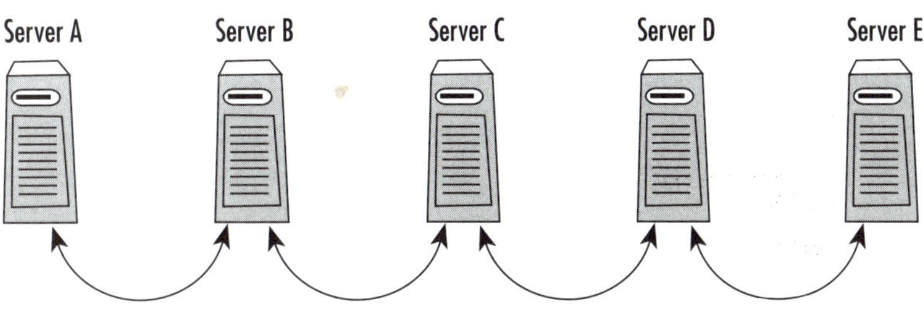

Figure 4.2. *Daisy-chain layout is easy to implement but error-prone.*

Web Layout

The next layout you might try is to link all the servers to each other, as in Figure 4.3, but if you have more than just a few servers, the number of links quickly becomes impossible to manage, if not prohibitively expensive. For small enterprises, though, this arrangement is quite feasible.

Hierarchical Layout

Another type of layout is a tree structure. The tree might reflect the organizational chart or may be arranged around workgroups within the organization. In such a layout, one or more e-mail servers act as central points for e-mail, distributing and processing mail from the attached servers. Figure 4.4 illustrates this type of layout.

This type of arrangement has weaknesses too, though. If the link between Server A and Server B goes down, for instance, Servers B, D, and E are isolated from the rest of the e-mail system. When we evaluate the speed of sending messages, we see that a message between Server D and Server F takes twice as long as one between D and E, and four times as long as one between D and B. To solve these issues, add extra links between those servers with high traffic, thereby creating a hybrid of a web and a tree layout. For medium-sized and larger organizations, this is the most common type of network and messaging layout.

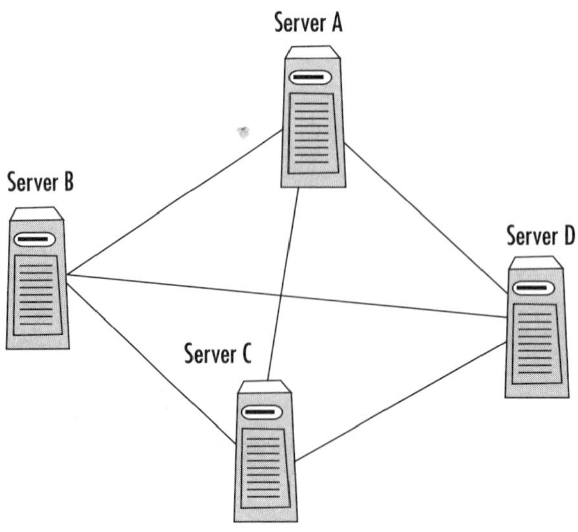

Figure 4.3. *A web of e-mail servers.*

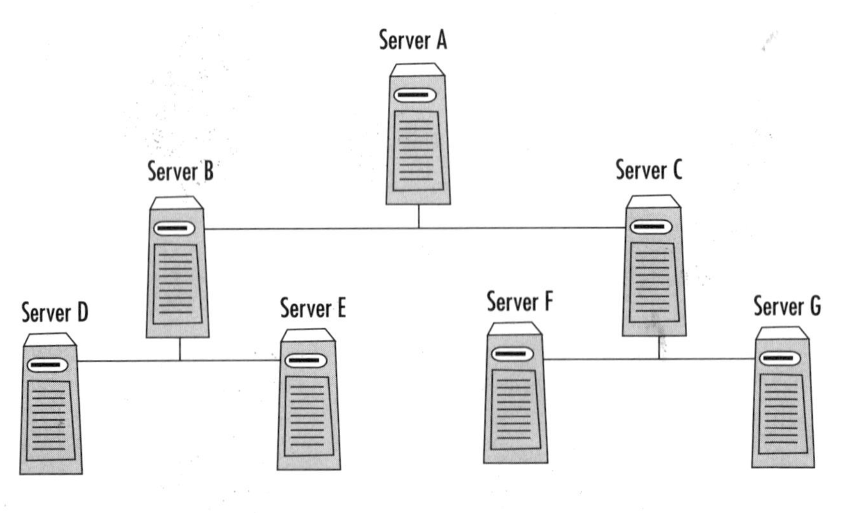

Figure 4.4. *A tree arrangement of e-mail servers.*

Making Maintenance Easy

Maintenance, as you might imagine, is an extremely important aspect of e-mail administration. Since it's a set of tasks that you have to perform often, do everything you can now to make it easier. The key elements here are server placement, ease of backups, and user names.

Server Placement

If the server sits in the broom closet, then whenever it's time to perform server maintenance, you sit in the broom closet too. Try to place your server where you can get to it easily, someplace that gives you room to work without compromising system security. The server location depends on other factors as well, of course, such as traffic, clean power, and air conditioning. See *Network Design Essentials* for more information on server placement that works for you, not against you.

Easy Backups

Server backups are a big part of the e-mail administrator's job, so make them as painless as possible. If you can automate the backup, you're halfway home. If you can go a step further and arrange for the e-mail backup to happen at the same time as the network file server backup, you're in great shape. Many e-mail systems make this fairly easy by storing their message databases and address databases on the LAN file server.

User Names

If at all possible, give your users e-mail names that are identical to their LAN user IDs. This will make life much easier for everyone—for your users, who only have to remember one login name, and for you, because less confused users are happier users. Furthermore, if the unthinkable ever happens and you have to rebuild the message database, you already have a pretty good list from which to work: the LAN user list.

Summary

You now have all the information you need to get started on your e-mail installation. You have a good idea of what features to look for in an e-mail package, you know how to lay out your e-mail system to maximize its reliability, and you have some useful pointers for making your life, and the lives of your users, easier.

chapter 5

Deploying Your E-mail System

Not So Fast!

In the previous chapter you selected an e-mail package and mapped out your e-mail system. You know which users go on which servers, where to locate those servers, and how to arrange things so that your e-mail system is as trouble-free as possible. So you're ready to go around to every workstation and load software, right? Well, we don't advise it quite yet. E-mail systems are rather complicated beasts, and you'll be much better protected from their oddities if you take a few more precautions first.

Into the Laboratory

Creating a test lab is the single nicest thing you can do for yourself as part of an e-mail installation. If you're the impatient type it might seem like a hassle, but believe us, it's worth every minute you spend on it.

Your test lab is the place where you can find all the incompatibilities and problems with the e-mail software before your users find them. You can test the e-mail software to see how it behaves in unusual situations, too, to prepare yourself for when that situation arises in the real deployment.

Setting Up Your Test Lab

The first thing you need to have in the test lab is a test server. Configure this machine as closely as possible to match the configuration of the computer that is slated to be the actual e-mail server. It's especially important that it have the same processor, the same amount of memory, the same display adapter, and the same communications hardware. The amount of disk space is less critical, but be sure it's not dramatically more or less in your test machine than the amount available on the planned production server. Most of all, be sure that the system software is identical to that on the real server.

Next, get at least one representative of every workstation in your installation. Make sure that you have these machines configured exactly the way your users have theirs, down to the amounts of memory and display adapters. Matching software versions is also extremely important. You don't want to get to the real e-mail installation and discover that the new e-mail software doesn't work with DOS 6.2, for instance, because you only tested it with DOS 3.31, 4.01, and 5.0 in the lab. Now connect these representative clients to the server, emulating as much as possible the connections of your real workstations.

At last you are ready to load the e-mail software on the test server. Take your time, making notes of any problems or questions, or of anything you'll want to remember when you get to the real installation. Note also how long the entire process takes, so you'll know how long to allow for the real thing.

Next, go to one or two workstations and load the client software. (If you don't have a LAN, skip this step and go straight to testing!) Again, go slowly, making careful notes. Test each workstation before going on to the next. If you discover a configuration problem, make the necessary change on all computers before going on to another. In this stately manner, install the e-mail software on each of the workstations, and test as you go. At this point you might want to consider roping in a few of your power users to bang on the e-mail system in your lab—they will probably think of things to use it for that you never would have dreamed of, and could therefore help you head off some unforeseen difficulties. We'll have more to say about power users in the next section, too.

When you have e-mail working flawlessly on every computer, be sure to test any gateways you plan to use. Once they're working reliably, you're ready to start scheduling the installation.

Planning Strategies for Installation

Installing e-mail is not normally an afternoon task, as your time in the test lab shows. It requires plenty of time and planning, and it's easiest if that time is free of interruption. That way you get peace and quiet, which can reduce the chances of your making a mistake. It's also a good idea to schedule your installation around your users; you don't want to alienate them before the system is even running. For these reasons, we strongly advise that you schedule your installation during times when your users are not around, such as evenings and weekends. Otherwise, the effort might well take twice as long and you'll find yourself staying into the evening or weekend anyway!

Since it's probably necessary to take a server off-line to install the e-mail server software, a weekend is your safest time slot for the initial deployment. That way, if something goes wrong Saturday morning when you begin, you have a day and a half to fix it, as opposed to the wee hours of the night. Once you have the server running and a few users on e-mail, you can add other users more quickly, so evenings will probably suffice.

This leads us to another point—stepwise installing. Go slowly, a few users at a time, just as you did in the test lab. The chances are very good that you will encounter some problems during installation, no matter how careful you were in the test lab. If you try to bring the entire user base up on e-mail in a single step, you could find yourself with 30 or 40 annoyed users glaring over your desk. If, on the other hand, you start with three or four users, you can contain the problems and address them before you expand the deployment to the rest of the world.

If you have power users willing to be guinea pigs, by all means take advantage of them! These are users who know more than average about e-mail, and perhaps even about your particular e-mail package. You want to get these folks up on e-mail as soon as possible, because they are much more likely to find problems than the users who never get beyond sending simple text messages. Power users can be invaluable at every stage of an e-mail installation; we advise that you find them and coddle them, and in return they can help you create the most robust, useful e-mail system possible.

Summary

On the basis of the information in this chapter, you should now be convinced that it is to your best advantage to create a test lab to try out your e-mail system before inflicting it on your users. You are also armed with some tips to guard against cranky users and to ensure a smooth installation.

chapter 6

Building for the Future

Grow? We Just Installed It!

Once your e-mail system is up and running you'll find that word of your success spreads quickly, and soon everyone in your organization will demand access to e-mail. Even if your initial deployment brings e-mail to the entire organization, the size of that group is likely to grow, and this growth can cause you all sorts of problems if you're not ready for it. By planning for growth at the outset, you can save yourself a lot of headaches later. In this chapter we discuss how to plan for growth and how to guarantee that your e-mail system's success is complete and enduring.

Give Yourself Growing Room

Growth problems can attack your mail system from a number of directions. In this section we talk about what you can do to protect yourself by making sure you have plenty of room for extra users, message traffic, storage, and mistakes.

Install the Fastest Link You Can Afford

The faster the connection, the less time your messages take to get from one machine to another, and the less time your e-mail server has to spend dealing with the error-prone area of transmissions. Speed is a virtue in computer environments, all the way around.

If you plan for any of your users to access the e-mail system remotely, be sure they have the fastest modems you can afford. Sure, you could upgrade later, but with 14.4-kbps modems available for under $150 in the United States and 28.8-kbps modems becoming commonplace, why wait? Do it now and win the benefits of reduced overhead, plus the gratitude of your users.

In a LAN environment, be sure the network interface cards (NICs) on the e-mail server are as fast as possible. NICs are the bottleneck in many systems; so don't let this happen to you.

If you install a new dedicated server for your e-mail system, attach it to the rest of the network with a fast link. Don't use coaxial ARCnet if you can possibly avoid it! If you upgrade your networking technology to a higher bandwidth, or incorporate some type of fast switching hub to accommodate the expected increase in network traffic due to the new messaging system, aim at the high end. When you estimate traffic volumes for your e-mail server, make sure you talk to other e-mail administrators using the same system (or at least, a similar one). Because the traffic estimations are supplied by e-mail vendors, they don't often match actual usage patterns. Talking to real users can help you establish realistic configurations.

The bottom line is: you don't want to have to reinstall things in six months. As a general rule, we recommend that you incorporate 30 to 40 percent excess capacity in your initial installation—it's amazing how fast an e-mail system can grow, and how quickly that excess becomes necessary.

Give Users Fixed-Size Storage Areas

Disk space, as everyone in the computer world knows, is like income. The more you get, the more you need. You typically need exactly as much as, or maybe a little more than, you already have. To extend the analogy: once you start using all the income you have, you have to start budgeting; the same is true with disk space. Some e-mail packages provide tools to help enforce space budgeting.

Most e-mail packages allow you to specify how much storage space each user receives, and we advise that you take advantage of this feature if it's available. Between 5 and 20 megabytes per user should be sufficient if people send each other large files such as graphics. If your organization uses e-mail only for short text messages, two or three megabytes per user should be enough. Keep in mind, however, that people quickly find other uses for e-mail once they get used to it, so the amount of space that's adequate now might not work in a year.

It is possible that your e-mail package does not allow you to stipulate how much space is reserved for each user. In that case, you may have to implement some sort of purging policy, whereby messages over a certain age are removed from the message database (six months is typical). It might even be useful to combine this feature with a fixed-space approach. Two points about purging, though: first, never delete files before you have backed them up, and second, be sure everyone understands the purge policy thoroughly. You do not want angry users in your office wondering where their old messages went. Even worse, you might have to tell them that you didn't back up the messages before the purge!

Your e-mail package might also offer some features that make purging easier, such as usage profiles for all files. Such a feature might give you the ability to search for all files not accessed for the past six months, for example. The underlying network operating system might also have features that can help, such as NetWare's ability to track the date each file was most recently accessed.

In our experience, it's much easier to impose limits on users at the outset rather than after the system is established. People are not likely to take kindly to restrictions brought in later, especially if the new rules mean they have to get rid of stored files! Prevention beats cure, no question about it.

Save Room for New Users

As soon as everyone outside your group sees your nifty new e-mail system, they'll be clamoring to get on, too. Are you ready? You can, and should, plan for this type of growth. Select an e-mail package that allows as much growth as you can possibly imagine you need plus a bit more.

If your company has seven employees and the business plan projects a 10 percent increase in size per year, you are probably safe with a package that allows a maximum of 100 users. Don't forget that outside vendors might want to access the system and that some customers might jump at the chance to deliver their orders via e-mail. What about that cooperative venture you've been talking about with another company? That's 50 more people. Better check that e-mail package again, and see if it lets you upgrade easily to another 100 or so users.

Another way new users can surprise you is with their need for client software. A new employee comes on board and you go to install the e-mail software on his computer—oops, you're out of copies of the software. Ordering new copies can take weeks; in the meantime, your new hire is isolated from the electronic life of the firm. Prevent this scenario by keeping communication lines open with the personnel department and planning ahead. If you can afford it, keeping extra copies of the software will give you room to be pleasantly surprised when a new hire comes your way, rather than being caught off guard.

Likewise, make sure you have enough disk space for new users, especially if you have allocated a certain amount of space per user. When you install an e-mail system, allow 30 to 40 percent extra space for growth, and when your utilization gets close to 80 percent of the total, it's time to start looking around for more space.

Planning on Mistakes

Planning to make mistakes might strike you as a pessimistic approach. But remember, when you make changes to your e-mail system you will be learning as you go, and so you will inevitably make mistakes—that's how we learn! The trick is not to deny that mistakes can occur, but to plan on them so you can minimize their impact on your users. If you plan for the unexpected, your only surprises should be pleasant ones!

KEEPING AN EYE ON GROWTH

After planning and installation comes the maintenance phase of your e-mail project. A big part of maintenance is taking a snapshot of the whole system at the time you first install it, and then periodically thereafter. The resulting data lets you track usage patterns and watch for signs that things are getting close to their limits. In particular, watch the disk space usage and network traffic patterns.

Watching Disk Space

If you have implemented space allotments, stay on top of how fast allocated blocks get filled. Users will probably complain when they start encountering their maximum limits, but you want to know what's happening before they hit the ceiling (both literally and figuratively). Check their consumption every month or two, and remind people to archive old messages before they reach their limits. If more than 60 percent of your users are close to 80 percent of their allotments, and you've also noticed that people are sending bigger or more elaborate messages, consider raising individual allotments to grant your users more space.

If you control disk usage by periodic purges, be sure to give everyone at least a week's notice before each purge. Also, it's a good idea to allow extra time for those users who may be traveling. Finally, don't forget to back up those messages before purging them from the mail server!

Watching Traffic

Back when we made a list of all the things you want to look for in an e-mail package, we mentioned good traffic reporting. Here's where that feature comes in handy. It's useful to know how many messages each user sends and receives, the total number of messages sent in any period of time, and the average amount of space consumed on a daily basis. Track these numbers every two weeks, or perhaps only monthly, and you may be able to anticipate problems before your users find them for you.

It's particularly important to track server and network utilization, both before and after you install e-mail services on your network. If you've added e-mail to a server that supports other services (like file, print, database, or other services), you'll want to make sure that e-mail is not the straw that breaks this particular server's back. This will call for more frequent monitoring during the first few months of use, as your users begin to incorporate e-mail into their everyday routines.

If you've established a dedicated server for e-mail, you'll want to pay special attention to the traffic loads on the cable segments to which that server is attached. The increase in traffic from e-mail might introduce a bottleneck, so it's important to sanity-check your initial installation. Under some circumstances, it makes sense to attach an e-mail server directly to the backbone to relieve congestion; under other circumstances, it may be necessary to resegment the network, or to upgrade networking technologies to provide extra networking capacity. In any case, keeping an eye on utilization is the key to detecting and curing any traffic-related problems that may arise.

What's in a Name?

In the world of e-mail, names do matter, because names are really addresses. Without a valid address, a message simply can't be delivered correctly.

E-mail names usually follow one set of rules or another, called a *naming convention*. If the rules make sense, your users will be better equipped to deal with e-mail, so it's important to design your naming convention carefully. Select a convention for user names that is easy to remember but not too bulky, and one that will grow with your e-mail system. In the following sections, we'll explore naming conventions in more detail and try to give you some points to keep in mind while designing one of your own.

The 14 Michaels Syndrome . . .

Small organizations tend to be informal and are seldom autocratic; often, everyone uses first names, from the president on down. It's quite tempting, then, to use everybody's first names everywhere, from the phone directory to the e-mail system. Sadly, we can't recommend this approach. You probably want your ten-person company to grow, and as soon as you have two Heathers, things get messy. You could start adding the first initial of the last name to the new user names, or maybe switch to using last names only, but pretty soon it's hard to send mail to anyone.

Your best bet is to choose a naming scheme that reflects how people do business. If no one knows each others' last names, they won't think much of an e-mail system based on surnames. The old standby "first-name last-name" system works fine in such a case. In a more formal environment, though, surnames might be quite appropriate. Another popular approach is to use the first initial and the last name as a single e-mail cognomen: under this regime Margaret Robbins becomes mrobbins, and Ed Tittel becomes etittel. Let the local custom guide you, especially if it's predictable.

. . . and the 47 Servers Called "Server"

Maybe it's an urban legend of the networking world, but we've heard from a couple of sources about an organization that named each of its servers "Server," a convention that worked fine as long as the servers were on separate networks. The trouble started when they began to connect all those machines in a large internetwork—changing the name of a server can be difficult in some networks.

Another company we've worked with (we'll call them the ABC Company) called their servers ABC-1, ABC-2, and so on, a logical convention, but then the company name changed. (Admittedly, that type of thing is pretty hard to predict.) Another company started with the same convention but later rearranged the network so that each project had its own server. The names were still unique but no longer reflected each server's purpose.

As these examples show, it's difficult to know how growth will proceed, so meaningful names can be tricky. A peek into the crystal ball, though, usually yields somewhat more meaningful names than "Mail Server." Novell, for instance, uses a three-letter prefix plus a descriptive name for its servers, so that the Austin e-mail server becomes AUS-EMAIL, as opposed to the Provo e-mail server, which is PRV-EMAIL. This has the benefit of grouping all servers from a single site together when searching a global server list for a particular one to access.

Standards and Naming

Recall our discussion in Chapter 2 of addressing and directory searching. Directory access is a complex issue and can only be solved at the global level, and this is the problem that the standards committees hope to solve with the X.500 protocol. You might want to register to be an X.500 organization in the future, but the early systems are only now in their testing stages. For the time being, all you need to know is that your e-mail user names must be unambiguous. In other words, you may very well have two e-mail users named Ann Jones, but they both can't use identical e-mail names (not to worry—your e-mail package probably prevents that anyway).

Summary

Now you're armed with the knowledge of what types of things can grow out of control in an e-mail system, and you know everything you need to keep this growth from being a problem to your e-mail system. Now that you've laid all the groundwork, let's get even more practical in the next chapter and deal with those two famous constraints: time and money.

chapter 7

Managing Budgets and Installation Plans

Time and Money

Before you can begin installing your e-mail system, you need to know some general concepts and watch out for some common pitfalls. The previous two chapters prepared you for these. In this chapter we get more specific and describe the budgeting process for an e-mail installation. Budgeting is simply allocating limited resources as efficiently as possible, and for most of us the two most limited resources are time and money. Here are some tips for maximizing both.

Managing Budgets

In an e-mail installation, three things cost money: equipment, software, and time. This section examines budgeting issues for each of these areas.

Equipment

An e-mail system requires you to spend money on equipment only if you need a dedicated mail server. If, on the other hand, you decide to install the e-mail system on an existing LAN server or spread it across several LAN servers, you don't have to buy a new computer to get e-mail running. Whether you need a dedicated server for e-mail depends on both the space available on your existing LAN server(s), and the e-mail package itself. Most small e-mail installations should be fine without a dedicated server.

If you do have to purchase equipment, be sure to allow for the costs of NICs and cabling, and get a system with plenty of RAM and disk space.

Another potential equipment expense is for computers for your test installation. If such funding is hard to come by, you could borrow systems from elsewhere in your organization for testing. You might need them for several weeks, so be sure that your equipment loans will last for a reasonable length of time—one afternoon will not be enough! The worst case scenario is when no borrowing is possible; should this occur, your best bet is to rent the equipment you need for the duration of the test (most rentals are by the week or the month). Rental expenses may seem high, but the cost of such rentals is small when compared to the lost productivity that can result from testing on a production network.

Software

You'll need to purchase one copy of the e-mail server software for each mail server. If you're running LAN e-mail, you'll also need a copy of the client software for every user. Most e-mail packages offer site licensing arrangements, whereby you purchase one actual copy but can install it on a specified number of workstations. Chapter 9 offers some tips on squeezing the most out of your software budget. Buying multiple e-mail licenses should be cheaper than full retail. So you can use the number of licenses times the retail cost of each end-user license, plus the retail costs of any server licenses you need, as an upper bound for software costs. Ordinarily, discounts should be at least 20 percent for multiple-copy purchases (over 10 users, over 2 servers).

Time Budgeting

You need to allow plenty of time for your e-mail system, especially at first. Besides the time devoted to installation, you'll also find yourself answering user questions, solving configuration problems, and adding new users. Additionally, people need training, and you're the most likely candidate for that job. The following checklist documents those e-mail tasks that will most likely require some of your time.

- Setting up test lab, installing test software, shaking out bugs
- Installing production e-mail system
- Training staff to perform backups, add users, and other administrative tasks
- Training users—see Chapter 20 for more details
- Performing system maintenance—allow at least an hour per week

How long should your installation take? This figure depends on the size of your installation, the complexity of your e-mail system software, and your experience at this type of task. Given these caveats, however, we asked some leading e-mail vendors for typical install times, and these are the figures they reported:

- Microsoft Mail: 1 weekend
- DaVinci Mail: 1 weekend
- cc:Mail: 1 day

Managing Installation Plans

Yet another aspect of time budgeting is planning how to spend budgeted time. This section discusses the types of things you need to plan for, from initial testing to the final installation.

Assembling the Test Lab

In Chapter 5 we introduced the concept of a test lab. This is one of those things that might seem like a hassle but is worth every bit of effort you put into it. We encourage you not to skip straight to the installation; a test environment gives you an opportunity to learn about your system without anyone breathing down your neck! It also lets you learn, and make mistakes without affecting your users directly.

To set up your test lab, you first need a computer configured identically to your e-mail server. If you have a dedicated server, great—you can use that machine as your test server prior to initial installation. Otherwise, get a computer that has the same amount of memory and disk space, the same NIC, and the same system software as the target e-mail server (you'll need to do this even for dedicated servers as soon as you go into production mode).

Next, collect computers that represent each type of client machine in your installation. These computers should also have similar hardware and software configurations to those they represent. Be sure not to skip any configurations; if you do, Murphy's Law guarantees that the configuration you ignore will be the one that breaks the e-mail system, and you won't know about it until it's very inconvenient to fix the problem.

The time involved in setting up the test lab will vary depending on your hardware and software, but you should probably allow at least a week of setting up and testing before you plan to unleash the system on your users. If your e-mail vendor or a third party offers e-mail administrator training, you may want to attend before you do anything else.

The Real Installation

During the test phase, make careful notes of the time you spend at every step along the way. This information will help you schedule the next phase: the actual installation of the e-mail system. If you have to take a server off-line to install the system software, you'll have a good idea of how long that takes based on your test installation time. You'll also be able to predict how long it should take to install the client software on each workstation, because you've already done it in the lab.

A Little at a Time

Plan to phase in the e-mail system rather than to install it on every machine at once. You'll find that your workload is much greater the first few days after installing the software on client machines. Users will have more questions at this time, and this is also when configuration problems are most likely to surface. Your life will be much easier if you're dealing with only 3 or 4 new users at a time rather than 30.

The discovery of new configuration issues or other problems will decrease with each batch of additional users as you apply what you've learned in previous installations. While this means that your workload will lessen over time, it also means that you should be extremely cautious during the earliest phases. Allow a few extra days between the first group or two in order to give yourself room to deal with the unexpected. And of course, test everything carefully in the test lab first!

The Installation Plan

The preceding discussion explains why you need to create a test lab and why it's always a good idea to install your e-mail system incrementally. The following list enumerates the items that your installation plan should address.

- Obtain equipment for the test lab.
- Install software in the test lab and test every aspect (see Chapter 12).
- Make sure you have enough disk space on each server (your tests will tell you how much is needed).
- Install e-mail server software on the production server.
- Make sure all users have e-mail names.
- Make sure workstations have enough free disk space (typically 1–5 MB).
- Install the client software on a few users' workstations (preferably power users), test thoroughly, and test again.
- Continue in this fashion until all users are on-line.

ONE MORE THING

In addition to time and money, there's one more thing you have to manage: expectations. Be conservative in your time estimates, and resist the temptation to tell people what they want to hear. If you think it will take two weeks to install the new e-mail system, or to add a new e-mail server, schedule for four weeks. That's right, double it. If you're early, no one will complain, but if you encounter an unexpected snag, you have room to cope without panic. We're sorry to say this, but you will encounter snags along the way. If you hit some really big bumps in the road, you may even have to call in some experts; the next chapter explains how.

SUMMARY

This chapter gave you some pointers on estimating the costs involved in deploying an e-mail system, from the equipment, to the software, to the time. Many of these costs are paid with your time, so we discussed the key features of an installation plan as well.

chapter 8

Getting Outside E-Mail Help

Where to Look

Electronic mail installations can be very complicated, especially if your network arrangement requires diverse systems to interoperate. Compatibility problems can be tricky to solve and are sometimes even harder to track down. If you need help with this kind of problem, the best place to start looking for help is from the vendor who makes your primary e-mail system. Its support people should have some experience with many types of interoperability issues and may be able to tell you just what you need to know.

Be warned: asking the vendor doesn't always work. In some cases vendors don't offer support, or the support they do offer isn't adequate. It's also possible that your e-mail package has no vendor to go with it—perhaps it's unsupported shareware or a package from a now-defunct company. At this point, many people head to the support forums on CompuServe or other electronic venues, and in the first half of this chapter we give you some tips on how to get information from these sources.

If a "hunt-and-peck" approach doesn't appeal to you, or you try it and you still have no answers, you may have to hire a consultant to help solve your problems. The second half of this chapter describes what you need to know to bring in expert assistance and to make sure it's a productive experience for all parties involved.

Getting Help on Your Own

A sure way to learn a lot about an e-mail system is to try to support it yourself. If you're the person responsible for keeping things running, you'll learn all about the e-mail package, the gateways, and the client software, and possibly a good deal about the underlying message protocol as well. Read all you can about the system, and talk to other people who have similar systems. You can find these people in user groups, or via electronic messaging systems like CompuServe, as we describe later in this chapter.

These electronic messaging systems are especially convenient since they can grant you access to hundreds of experts on thousands of topics all over the world, 24 hours per day. On these forums you can pose your questions to thousands of people, and you will probably get an answer—or maybe several answers—within a few days.

Consider some basic etiquette points before you dive in. These forums are read by hundreds of people every day. Many of them are experts in their fields, and all of them are busy, as are you. They form these groups in order to discuss topics of interest with other people of similar interest and expertise. Therefore, people tend to get a bit grouchy if you ask the same questions that dozens of people have asked and answered before.

To prevent being crushed by the burden of history, and to save yourself some time, look for a file containing a group's most frequently asked questions. On CompuServe, look through the forum libraries for answers to your questions before you post to that forum. You might find that your problem is one that many people have also had, and the solution might already be right there, just waiting for you!

If the information you need is not right at hand, don't get discouraged. Ask your question of the group that seems most related to the topic, and you'll probably get the help you need within a week or so. Even after you have your problem solved, you may well want to keep reading the forums you discovered—a wealth of information flows through them, and you may need to mine this vein again.

CompuServe

One of the largest bulletin board systems (BBSs) in the world, CompuServe is where many computer vendors maintain their electronic support centers. Name almost any computer equipment or software vendor, and chances are that it has a forum on CompuServe where you can ask questions about its products. Often a forum offers files that you can download as well. These files might include software upgrades, press releases, or announcements, or there may even be lists of questions and answers for people like yourself seeking information. The Resource Guide in Appendix D describes how you can access CompuServe. (In addition to the account information provided, you'll need a modem and some communications software to get on-line.)

As you might expect, many of the leading e-mail vendors and other computer vendors maintain forums on CompuServe. The list ahead names a few of them along with the CompuServe command that you need to enter to access each vendor's forum. If the information you need is not listed here, try using the CompuServe FIND command.

DaVinci eMAIL support	GO DAVINCI
Lotus support for Notes and cc:Mail	GO LOTUSB
WordPerfect Office support	GO WPUSERS
Microsoft Mail	GO MSAPP
Novell, Inc. (networking software)	GO NETWIRE
Novell networks and E-Mail information	GO NCONNECT
NetWare MHS messaging software	GO NCONNECT
Telecommunications information	GO TELECO

Usenet and Internet Resources

If you have access to the Internet, a whole host of information resources is at your disposal. One particularly useful source of problem-solving help is Usenet, which some people describe as a bulletin board system distributed over the Internet. Usenet newsgroups correspond to CompuServe forums, and newsgroups exist on every topic imaginable. For computing newsgroups we suggest the following, though there are many more:

comp.dcom.lans.ethernet	Discussions of Ethernet/IEEE 802.3 protocols
comp.dcom.lans.fddi	Discussions of the FDDI protocol suite

comp.dcom.lans.misc	Local area network hardware and software
comp.dcom.lans.token-ring	Installing and using token-ring networks
comp.dcom.modems	Data communications hardware and software
comp.mail.misc	General discussions about computer mail
comp.os.ms-windows.misc	General discussions about Windows issues
comp.os.msdos.apps	Discussion of applications that run under MS-DOS
comp.os.os2.apps	Discussions of applications under OS/2
comp.sys.dec	Discussions about DEC computer systems
comp.sys.hp.apps	Discussion of software and apps on all HP platforms
comp.sys.ibm.pc.hardware.networking	Network hardware and equipment for the PC
comp.sys.mac.comm	Discussion of Macintosh communications
comp.sys.mac.misc	General discussions about the Apple Macintosh
comp.sys.novell	Discussion of Novell NetWare products

If you do not have Internet access, these resources are not necessarily out of your reach. Our book on exploring the Internet, called *Internet Access Essentials,* will be available from AP PROFESSIONAL in the second half of 1994.

The act of sending a message to a newsgroup is called *posting.* Usenet honors a few etiquette rules about posting, and you should try to observe them if you want a useful answer to your question instead of a testy one. Usenet readers are very busy and dislike seeing the same questions several times per week. For this reason, many newsgroups have collections of their most frequently asked questions, or FAQs, and you should read these before you post to their respective groups. Doing so will assure you that your question has not already been answered and will also ensure that you are posting to the correct newsgroup for your topic. Not only that, but the FAQs are usually full of helpful information; you might learn answers to questions you didn't know you had!

User Groups

When enough people use a product and want to meet regularly to share ideas with each other, they form a user group. At their meetings they might discuss new techniques for using a feature of the product, or someone might reveal a good way to work around a missing feature or a bug. For these reasons, user groups can be wonderful sources of information when you're tracking down problems. They can also be good sources of experts if you decide you don't want to solve something yourself!

Finding user groups might not be easy. Ask around on CompuServe to see whether such a group exists for your product, or your e-mail vendor might be able to help you find one. In some cases vendors are very supportive of their user groups and have joint meetings with them, while in other cases the vendors and users rarely interact.

Another place to look is in the listing of weekly or monthly meeting in the business or technology section of your local newspaper. Some user groups announce their meetings in these places.

The Resource Guide provides contact information for a couple of e-mail system user groups to get you started.

Hiring Consultants

Your work doesn't end with the decision not to do the entire installation yourself. Your e-mail project will go much more smoothly if you can give your consultant a complete and detailed picture of what you need done and what you expect from the finished system. Otherwise, consultants cannot give you accurate bids, much less deliver complete work. Do your homework before you call them, and you'll greatly increase your chances of getting a useful and productive consultation.

Finding Consultants

When looking around for a consultant to help you with your e-mail system, ask other people for recommendations—word of mouth is a great source of information. Check with the vendors who sold you the software; they should also be familiar with the experts in your area. Finally, ask the providers of your networking equipment or software; they might have some good advice as well.

Checking References

No matter how you find a consultant or how highly recommended she comes, be sure to ask for at least three references. Make sure the consultant truly has experience in your system, not a system that "looks just like it" or any other inexact match. E-mail systems are complex and tricky beasts, and unless you are feeling very generous, you probably don't want to pay someone to learn a new system at your expense—you could do that yourself! When you call his or her references, ask the individuals if they had any problems with their systems after their initial installation, and whether they were satisfied with the follow-up support from the consultant.

Payment Arrangements

It's very much in your best interest to negotiate payment by the project, not by the hour. Structure the compensation according to the nature of the problem you need solved, and arrange the payment schedule to reflect the completion of the project. For example, if you are hiring a consultant to install two gateways, pay a certain portion when you sign the contract, a bit more after the first gateway is installed and tested, some more after the second gateway is in place, and the remainder of the total upon demonstration that the entire e-mail system is working reliably and flawlessly with the new gateways.

Any time you're paying someone by the project, the following rule holds: the more of your money consultants have, the less of their attention you'll get. You will have to pay them some of the total up front; 20 to 50 percent is typical, but the less you give them at first, the more leverage you'll have to make sure things are done to your satisfaction.

As the job progresses, pay meaningful increments of the total price, based on milestones that make sense for your particular project. Be sure all parties understand the milestones before the work begins.

The last installment should be the largest, perhaps 15 to 30 percent of the total, and you shouldn't deliver it until you are completely satisfied with the installation. Don't sign off on completion until you have tested everything and assured yourself that all of the system's features are working. Once a consultant has all your money for a project, the usual way to get him back is often to pay by the hour; as long as you haven't fully paid him, he will usually be willing to work to earn what's still outstanding.

Making Sure You're Satisfied

The only way to tell whether the consultant did his or her job is to test the system, so you need to make testing part of the contract. Stipulate that you will not accept the work until the entire installation has been tested to your satisfaction. In Chapter 12 we list some of the most important things to test; you are sure to think of others, depending on the unique properties of your system. It's good to make final payment contingent on successfully completing the test phase; it's even better to make it contingent on successful operation of the system for some period after testing is finished (from two to four weeks is not out of the ordinary).

Summary

Because electronic mail systems often involve so many different vendors' products, from the e-mail system itself, to hardware, network operating systems, and gateways, they are very complicated to install and maintain. You may find that you need to get outside help, and this chapter described some of the sources and how to find them, from electronic bulletin boards to electronic mail consultants. This chapter also discussed some caveats of each approach.

chapter 9

Smart E-mail Buying Techniques

An Introduction to Cost Cutting

When you buy any computer system, the two major expense categories are hardware and software. In the world of e-mail, the big hardware expense is for the mail server, but only if you opt for a dedicated server. If you piggyback your e-mail system onto an existing server or servers, you may incur no hardware expense at all, unless you need to upgrade your network or your server to handle the increase in traffic that always comes with e-mail.

Unless you need a lot of new hardware, though, you're not likely to be able to get much of a discount. Vendors are not nearly as likely to make deals with you over a single NIC or a few cables as they would be if you were buying in bulk (20 or more units of anything).

The software side of e-mail is a bit different. When you install an e-mail system you need at least two copies of the client software, or licensing for at least two users—e-mail is not much use if only one person uses it. You might be able to bargain for better prices based on your expected number of users, and in this chapter we discuss how to go about doing so.

Before you buy, analyze your needs carefully. If your current needs and expected needs are not elaborate, you might be able to use some of the excellent software that is available at no charge, as we discuss later in the chapter.

Finally, keep in mind that not every expense related to your e-mail system shows up on an invoice. The last part of this chapter discusses some other costs you need to be aware of, as well as how to keep them down.

Maximizing Your Software Budget

When you are about to make a significant purchase, it's always a good idea to shop around. This section gives you some shopping advice to consider before you go looking for e-mail software.

Planning Ahead

Before you do any shopping at all, make sure you have a clear idea of what you need. Go back to the features lists in Chapters 3 and 4, and also review the checklists in Chapter 26. Make lists of the features you must have, would like to have, and don't really need. Next, count the number of users you plan to have at the initial installation, and estimate how many you will have in one year, two years, and five years. Combining all of this information gives you a good idea of what you need.

Many first-time e-mail purchasers start their search by looking at packages and selecting a package based on the features it offers rather than on the features they need. They can end up frustrated, not only because they later find they lack necessary features, but also because e-mail systems are extremely difficult to change once they're in regular use. By planning ahead, though, you can avoid the problem altogether.

Negotiate for Site Licenses

Software is typically sold in one of two ways: single-use packages and site licenses. Single use means that only one user is licensed to use the books and disks that come with a package; installing it on or using it from another computer is a violation of the license agreement.

Site-licensed software, on the other hand, has a licensing structure that reflects the structure of the networks on which it runs. With this kind of license, you still get a single set of disks but the software is licensed for a specified number of users. You install it on the network, where its users will access it. Sometimes such software has a built-in checking mechanism, so that if you have a license for 20 users and 21 people try to use it, the twenty-first user is not allowed access until one of the others stops using it. Not all site software has this feature, though; sometimes you're on the honor system.

Site licenses can often provide a significant cost savings because the manufacturer wants to encourage you to buy more of the product. Therefore, when you're trying to compare prices of e-mail packages, be sure to compare them by first adding up the total base installation price (the cost of setting up the system on your server), then looking at the price per user. Comparing just the totals might give you a skewed perspective.

The price per user might also be useful when you go to negotiate your total package price. If you select a package that does not offer a site licensing structure, try offering to pay for it on that basis anyway. In some cases, the vendor might be willing to take a reduced margin on the total sale in favor of greater volume (and the expectation of more sales to you in the future).

Mail-order Sources

Mail-order software suppliers might be more able to give you better price reductions than local vendors because of their higher volume and lower overhead. The trade-off is that mail-order suppliers are less likely to be helpful if you need support.

You'll find advertisements for mail-order suppliers in any network magazine. Some of the common publications are *LAN Times*, *LAN Magazine*, and *Network Computing* (all listed in the Resource Guide), and you can probably also find periodicals on your particular network type.

Even if you ultimately decide to buy from a local source, shop the mail-order outlets before you go into a local outlet. The price information gleaned from these investigations gives you a good idea about what you should expect to pay for your system, or at least helps you establish a target for price negotiation.

Investigate Third-Party Alternatives

No e-mail package is complete in itself. Every package available lacks some features, but in many cases the slack is taken up by third-party vendors. cc:Mail from Lotus, for instance, has several add-on packages you can purchase for gateway software. Some of these gateways are not Lotus products, but are offered by third parties.

As you shop, find out what third-party offerings are available for the systems that interest you. You might find it saves money if you buy the bulk of your e-mail software from one major vendor, then augment it with add-ons from other developers. As always, however, there's a trade-off—any time you try to integrate systems from different vendors you run the risk of compatibility problems. To minimize these woes, find out if other people have already created your proposed combination of products. Be sure to avoid exotic arrangements. Also, make sure the vendors offer support for interoperability issues.

Noncommercial Options

If you're suffering from sticker shock after pricing commercial e-mail packages, you might be astounded to discover that many fine packages are available free of charge. Others have licensing arrangements whereby you can try out the software for a while before you commit your money—the amount of time varies, but during that time you have a full-featured system. This is distinct from the demo packs you can get from commercial vendors, which give you some features to experiment with but which may have many of their most useful capabilities disabled.

If these types of software are available, you might wonder why everyone isn't using them. There are many reasons. For one thing, these noncommercial systems are often written by just one or two people who do not have the time, means, or inclination to market the products to the huge markets that interest larger companies. Sometimes noncommercial software vendors abandon their products, meaning that users can no longer get support. Others market their software with the clear understanding that support is not part of the arrangement.

Nonetheless, such software is often of excellent quality and can be well supported. We describe two such packages below.

Pegasus Mail

This product runs over Novell NetWare networks and has client support for a number of platforms, including DOS, Macintosh, and Windows. Pegasus Mail supports both SMTP and MHS message formats. Novell ships a simplified version of Pegasus Mail with its NetWare 3.12, but that version does not have all of the features.

The creator of this package supports it vigorously and retains all rights to it, but does not charge for it. You can get more information about Pegasus Mail, or the package itself, from CompuServe (GO NOVUSER and search for keyword "Pegasus") or by snail mail to the address listed in the Resource Guide. That address is also where you can write to purchase manuals (which are not free but would probably be helpful).

Guide to Successful Bargaining

Now you've decided exactly what you need, and you've found a set of software that provides all your desired features, but the total price comes to a bit more than you wanted to pay. Before you go in to bargain with the vendor, here are a few tips.

Buy a Little Extra . . .

When you plan how much to buy, base your figures on your future needs. That is, be sure to allow some extra e-mail client software or user licenses for growth. In our experience, 20 to 40 percent extra is a good allowance on the initial purchase. Look at your two-year and five-year projections when calculating, but don't go overboard. Can you reasonably expect that you will still be using this package in five years? If you have planned well, the answer is probably yes.

. . . But Not Too Much

It's a good idea to buy a bit more than you need at the start, especially if it means you can get a good price from the vendor with the higher volume. But don't let yourself get carried away with the spirit of bargaining, either! We really can't recommend buying enough software for five years at the time of your first purchase—too many things could change during that time. Instead, your best bet is to buy enough to get you through to the manufacturer's next release. Remember, a sale is not saving you any money if you're buying something you don't need!

Most of All, Be Respectful

When you enter into a bargaining situation, treat the other person with respect. Some people take the approach that bargaining means getting everything they can while preventing the other person from taking advantage of them. This is almost never the case. The other person, like you, is trying to earn a living, and the only successful bargain is when both parties walk away satisfied. Begin by asking politely whether the company has any bulk discount pricing. Mention respectfully that you'll be buying more in the future, but don't lie. If they are not interested, that's fine, but if they are willing to work with you, negotiate patiently and fairly to find an agreement that pleases you both.

Costs That Don't Appear on Invoices

Some of the hidden costs for e-mail systems can't be measured in mere money, but they might become outrageously expensive over time if you're not ready for them. Before you buy an e-mail system, make sure you understand what type of support you can expect from the vendor and from any necessary third-party suppliers.

Specifically, make sure that the product works with everything you already have, from network operating system to workstation software. Find out what type of support is available should you run into difficulties. You might even want to try calling the vendor's support line once or twice to see what type of reception you get. You might get to speak to someone immediately, or you might end up waiting on hold for a very long time. It is possible that the only way the vendor offers support is by selling you a type of support package—if so, be sure to add that cost to your budget. Remember, too, that time costs money, if only to pay your salary, and that a system that requires an inordinate amount of your time may not be as cheap as its sales price makes it look.

Summary

This chapter gave you some pointers to help you make the most of your e-mail budget, including where to shop and how to bargain for discounts. We also listed in this chapter some sources of inexpensive or free e-mail software, and reminded you of some hidden costs so they don't surprise you later.

part

Making E-mail Happen

II

Overview

In Part I we mapped out everything you need to know before you install an e-mail system. In this second part of the book, we take the theory into practice. We start out by assembling our tools and designing the system, then we go on to the actual installation. We move from there into the maintenance and upgrade phases, and give you some tips on keeping the system running smoothly and making sure the users get the most possible use out of it. Finally, we wrap up with a peek at where e-mail is headed and what the future might bring you.

The Planning Stages

In the first three chapters of this section, we move from the classroom of the last section into the test lab. In Chapter 10, Tools and Techniques for Building E-mail Systems, we describe the tools you need to gather and their uses, from the network map to the company organizational chart. Chapter 11, E-mail Addresses and Naming Schemes, walks you through the details of naming schemes, explaining why you need to consider them and what to watch out for.

Finally, in Chapter 12, Ensuring Proper E-mail Delivery, we set up the test lab. This is where you pull together all the things you've learned so far and create your first e-mail system. A large part of this task is testing, and in this chapter we give you some suggestions and tips on ensuring successful testing.

The Installation Itself

Once the test lab installation is running smoothly, you're finally ready to "go public." In Chapter 13, Planning for Installation, Chapter 14, Living through Installation, and Chapter 15, Maintenance Begins at Installation, we walk you through the process, from creating a test plan, to getting through the actual installation, to performing the first few maintenance tasks after everything's installed. Congratulations—you now have a live e-mail system!

Growing and Changing

The best thing about e-mail, or any successful system, is that it tends to take on a life of its own. After the system's been running for awhile, you'll notice it trying to expand beyond its confines. This is a good sign—it means people are using the system and that all the work you've done to this point has been useful. It also means you have more work to do! Chapter 16, Managing Upgrades and Replacement, Chapter 17, Growth Can Be Painless, and Chapter 18, Rules for Keeping Things Running, offer some advice on how to manage the inevitable growth gracefully and maintain the system in good working order. If, despite your best efforts, trouble does befall your system, Chapter 19, Dealing with Disaster, offers some tips on minimizing the effects.

Finally, Chapter 20, Training Users, covers the wide topic of training. This is must reading to find out what topics to include in training, where to get training materials, and how to set up training classes.

Thinking Ahead

The e-mail world is changing fast, and features that seem like frills today might become necessities tomorrow. In Chapter 21, Planning for the Future, we take a look into the future and discuss what's coming in terms of messaging software and what you need to prepare now to make sure you're ready for the future when it arrives.

Tools and Techniques for Building E-mail Systems

Dandy Designs Come from Perfect Plans and Expert Execution

In Part I of the book we laid the groundwork for understanding e-mail systems, from what they do to how to do it. We also covered the concepts you need to know to design your own e-mail system, to budget for it, and to get the most for your money. In this second section of the book, we give you all the information you need to design your system. We start in this chapter by discussing the two tools you'll need the most—your network map and your organization chart.

Using a Network Map

We've mentioned the network map a few times already, but you might still be unsure what this really represents. You're probably picturing a conventional type of map—a bird's-eye view of a building or a group of buildings—and you probably would not be surprised to see indications of network cables and even servers on the map.

The network map is all of these things and much more. True, it does show the building floor plan—in fact, it should show the floor plan for every building and every floor that your network covers. Yes, the map shows all network cables and where they run, as well as any telephone and electrical wiring. It even shows heating and air conditioning ducts and any large motors (such as for elevators). All of these things could affect your network, so they need to be on the map!

The map also shows what types of cable your network uses, and where these types change. It shows the lengths of all cables, the types of connections between them, and the types and locations of any routers, hubs, concentrators, or repeaters. It shows the networked machines and where they're located; you should be able to check your map and locate every server, workstation, and printer on the network.

The map tells you all about those servers and workstations, too, including their software versions, memory amounts, disk sizes, NIC types, and processor speeds. The map includes a record of each computer's configuration files, as well as the types of drivers, monitors, and display cards attached to each one.

In addition to all this, the network map records live data about the network—data traffic, error rates, and usage profiles. It contains records of historical information and plans, such as every change you've made to the network, changes that users have requested, and things you need to do in the future.

In short, every possible fact about anything that could affect your network goes into the map. You might be wondering how to get all of this information onto a blueprint of the building, but you don't have to. As you've probably gathered, we're using the word "map" rather loosely, because the net map is much more than a picture from above: it's a picture plus an extensive database. Some software vendors market programs to help you collect all this information; you can buy one of these or create your own network database. Brightwork and dtech are two such vendors; you'll find contact information for them in the Resource Guide in Appendix D.

What to Look for on the Map

Your network map is a wonderful resource when planning an e-mail system, because it gives you just one place to look for anything you want to know about your network. Once you've selected an e-mail system, you need to determine whether your current network will support it, and your network map is the best place to look for the answer.

Start with the servers. You probably already have a good idea whether you want to install your e-mail system on a dedicated mail server or on an existing server (or servers). If you plan to have a dedicated server, your map will give you clues about where to put it. Consider not only where you have space, but also where the network backbone lies, if applicable.

On the other hand, if you plan to add your e-mail system to another server, use your network map to decide which one. Consider not only which server has disk space, but also what server hosts which users and what type of connections service that machine.

Your network map should tell you a lot about the connections. It should, for instance, indicate which sections of the network are wired with twisted-pair and which sections with fiber-optic cable. Depending on expected traffic loads, you might not want to attach a new dedicated mail server to the rest of the network via the slowest link on the network. This traffic information is another reason to keep the map close at hand during planning. Compare current traffic loads to the amount of traffic you expect with the new system in the picture, and use these two data sets to help you decide where to install the e-mail system so that it stresses the network as little as possible.

You might decide, based on this analysis, that your current network cannot bear the increase in traffic an e-mail server could add. In this case, study your map to decide where to add more bandwidth, such as between two servers that did not previously need to communicate much at all but that will now be sending e-mail back and forth all day.

Before you put away the map, study the capabilities of all the computers in the network and compare them to the requirements given by your e-mail software manufacturer. Make sure your servers have enough disk space, that your workstations have enough memory, and that all systems have appropriate software revision levels. Your network map and database can help you check all of this at a glance.

Now Catalog the Required Changes

Having scrutinized your network map, you now have a much clearer idea of your network's strengths and weaknesses. The next step is to make a list of all the necessary changes and upgrades that the network needs before you can install e-mail. A list of changes you should consider follows:

- *Server and workstation hardware upgrades*—more disk space or memory, upgrades to faster network interface cards

- *Software upgrades for servers and workstations*—all computers must be running the software revision levels that the manufacturer recommends
- *Network infrastructure*—new cabling, higher bandwidth cabling, new routers or hubs
- *Network software*—drivers, network operating system changes or additions that the e-mail package might require

Start shopping for these items well in advance of your desired installation date because you may have to order some things from the vendors, and because installing the upgrades alone could be a time-consuming effort above and beyond the effort of installing the e-mail system.

Building with Your Network—Not against It

The network map gives you a picture of your network's current traffic patterns, and so you can use it to help you fit the new e-mail system into the network in the best possible way. If you have one overloaded and one underloaded server, for instance, that will show on your network map through usage patterns and traffic data. In such a case, using the latter as the mail server would be best. On the other hand, if the server you've been planning to use as a mail server has a weak link to the network, you know that you need to add more bandwidth to that server to allow it to do the extra work.

Use your network map to help you find the most efficient placement for your e-mail system, rather than starting a fight with your network architecture that you can't win!

Using the Organization Chart

Another important tool in designing your e-mail system is a description of how the company is organized, how the people divide themselves into groups, and which groups work most often together. In most companies, the document that contains much of this information is called the *organization chart*, or simply the *org chart*.

The Basic Org Chart

An org chart describes relationships between members of an organization, and in most cases it represents a hierarchical structure. Figure 10.1 shows an example.

Using the Org Chart for E-Mail Design

You'll find it very useful to structure your e-mail system based on how your users are organized, especially for creating mailing lists. In most small to moderately sized organizations, it's a good idea to have a mailing list that reaches everyone (for company-wide announcements, news, etc.), but that single list is insufficient, so you'll also need to create some more specialized groups. Let's walk through some examples using the sample org chart in Figure 10.1.

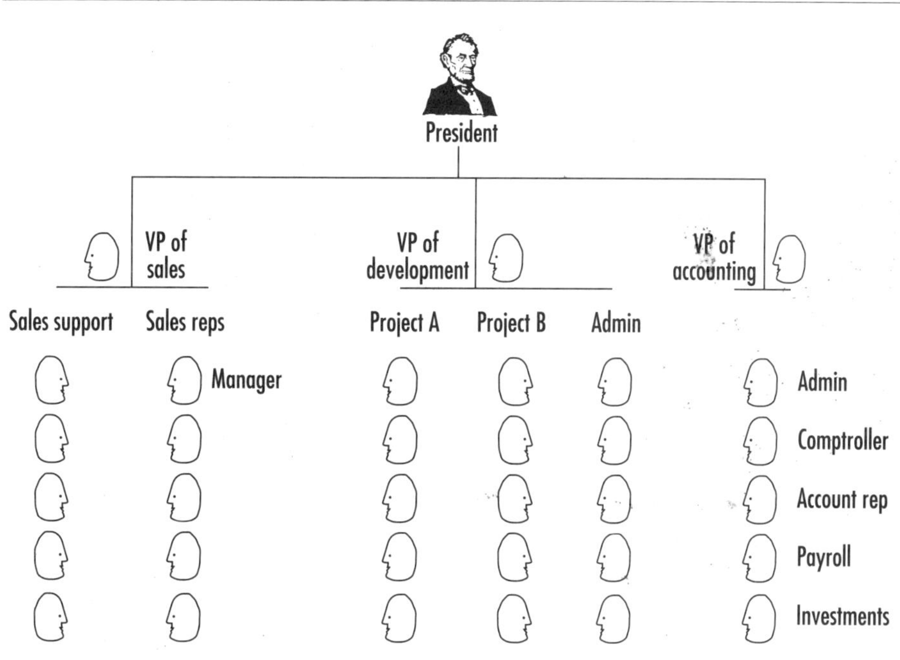

Figure 10.1. *An example of an org chart.*

The most obvious candidates for their own mailing lists are the groups that you see as you scan down the chart. The sales department, for instance, should have a mailing list, as should the sales support team. Similarly, the development department, including the vice president, should have its own mailing list, as should the people working on projects A and B.

Now look at the org chart horizontally. It's probably a good idea to have a mailing list for senior staff, for instance, so that the president can easily send mail to all the vice presidents, and so that other people can send mail to all of them. The sales manager, for instance, might want to send sales reports to the entire senior team every week or so. A couple of other groups emerge when we scan the chart horizontally; consider creating a mailing list for all the developers, for instance, and all of the administrative personnel.

Many groupings probably exist in the company that do not show up on the org chart. The people communicating are the ones who know about these groups, so make sure they know that you can create groups on request, or that they can create their own—your job is to do whatever you can to make the system useful for everyone.

Finally, look at your org chart when dividing users among post offices. If you have to use more than one post office (because your installation has reached the limits of your e-mail software, for instance), it makes sense to divide the users into groups based on group membership, or possibly on physical proximity (especially when wide area links are involved).

Combining Your Tools

The network map and the org chart are valuable tools, but even more so when you use them together. If everyone on a particular project, as shown on the org chart, works primarily on one network server (according to the network map), consider making that machine their mail server as well.

Similarly, if the org chart shows a single department but the network map shows that the department has two servers which are located in different buildings and between which little traffic flows, these are hints that you can split that department across two mail servers without too much trouble.

When mapping out your e-mail system, think past the initial installation. If the company business plan projects that the accounting department will grow to 110 employees in the coming year, don't load the entire department onto a mail server with a 100-person limit. Split them apart now (or plan to upgrade the e-mail software) to save yourself headaches later.

Summary

Any time you build something, having the right tools spells the difference between a successful experience and a miserable one. This holds true in e-mail system design, too, so in this chapter we discussed the two principal e-mail tools, the network map and the organization chart.

chapter 11

E-MAIL ADDRESSES AND NAMING SCHEMES

WHAT'S SO IMPORTANT ABOUT ADDRESSING, ANYWAY?

For networking in general, and e-mail in particular, names and addresses are the keys to system access. Simply put, without a valid address, there is no network or e-mail access for a user. Likewise, without a valid address for a network resource—like a server, a printer, or another user—that resource is completely unreachable. Without an address, the resource might as well not exist.

Even more than with the postal service, there is a strong and profound relationship between names and addresses for computer networks and, by extension, for electronic mail systems. To understand this relationship, though, we have to take you on a detour to understand the difference between logical names and physical addresses.

Let's Get Physical!

At the crudest level, a physical address is a bit pattern, or a sequence of bytes, that uniquely identifies a particular device on a network. In most cases, the address must also identify a particular program or process on the device, because network access is seldom a solitary thing, but rather an extension for all different kinds of capabilities.

For instance, your e-mail program will typically have its own special physical address, in addition to the word processing program you may be running, which is reading and writing information from a networked file server. When a message to you arrives at the e-mail server, it's common for your e-mail software to interrupt your word processing program to flash a message on the screen that says something like:

```
Message received from user TBENNET
Enter CTRL-ESC to return to program
```

This is possible because your e-mail program has a special physical address of its very own, consisting of the physical address of your computer, plus a special extension that identifies the e-mail program, to which the server directs its incoming mail message and which then provokes an on-screen notification. This is necessary because multiple types of network connections are common from a single user, or a single machine, and the network has to know how to deliver the right information to exactly the right consumer (in this case, the e-mail program).

This capability is what lets you use multiple network or e-mail connections from a single computer and is also what makes sure that requests of the network, and the attendant replies, get properly delivered. Think how confused you'd get if your word processing program were suddenly inundated with mail messages!

Hardware Is Physical; Humans Are Logical?

Computers are very good at manipulating strings of ones and zeros—to some extent, that's all they do—but humans don't do well with digital information. Therefore, most networking and electronic mail packages create a linkage between physical addresses and strings of alphabetic letters that humans can understand and, hopefully, remember. These strings of characters are the names that we use to interact with our systems; they may be the login name we use to access the network or an e-mail name that identifies us to the e-mail system we're using.

Under the hood, the software maintains a relationship between the name and the underlying physical address. This lets humans identify themselves to the software they're using. It also lets humans, even network or e-mail administrators, largely ignore the details of physical addressing.

In fact, many networked software packages, including e-mail, maintain a database of names with address relationships that may not even require a constant relationship between logical names and physical addresses. This explains why you can sometimes log into e-mail, or the network operating system, from a workstation other than the one on your desktop. The software makes sure that your name is valid—and checks any applicable passwords to verify your identity—but it provides a degree of flexibility between names and addresses that permits users to move around, as security considerations dictate.

Then, too, names can have meanings, which allows them to be organized: they can be built around a specific kind of hierarchy, such as an organizational chart (org chart) for a company. They can be selected from a collection of related terms, such as the names for different kinds of rocks or flowers (these are all real examples, by the way) or from the names of characters in Tolkien's *Lord of the Rings* trilogy. They can even reflect the functions of various departments within an organization, for example, marketing, engineering, operations, and accounting. Within the bounds of what's legal for a name (and this varies from system to system), there's no limit to the combinations that people can—and do—select for use as names.

E-mail Names

From an e-mail perspective, what's important about your name is:

- Your e-mail account and identification or authentication information
- The server where your e-mail files and profiles are stored
- Your current physical location (the machine you're using), and the software you're currently using

The account information identifies you to the system and lets you access your mail. The server acts as your e-mail "post office": it's where your incoming mail resides, where you deposit outgoing mail for delivery, and is typically also home to the database that stores your account information. Your current physical location and program determine exactly where messages must be picked up and delivered, and also govern how you interact with your e-mail package (from Windows on one machine, perhaps, and from DOS on another). All of these aspects of a name are essential to e-mail access.

Components of a Naming Scheme

Looking at an e-mail name is a lot like examining an address on a snail mail message: there's information that identifies the user, but there's also information that locates the user in terms of both a specific post office (through the ZIP or other postal code) and a specific location.

The combination of all this information uniquely identifies both sender and recipient, which helps explain why Bob Jones of 121 Main Street in Muncie, Indiana, can send a letter to his cousin Bob Jones on 121 Main Street in Des Moines, Iowa, without introducing too much confusion. Even though the names and addresses are nearly identical, they're different enough to be told apart, and that's the key to successful delivery. The same is true for e-mail, as we'll explore further in the sections that follow.

Addresses Have Parts

From a physical perspective, addresses have three important components:

1. The address or location of the network on which the addressed physical device resides
2. The address of the physical device itself
3. The address of the program or process on the device to which the information must be delivered

From a delivery perspective, parts 1 and 2 supply the routing information needed to get from sender to receiver and are analogous to the street address and city, state, and ZIP (and country) information in a snail mail address. Part 3 provides the designated recipient (or sender) and corresponds to the sender's or receiver's actual name in snail mail.

Addressing and Routing

In this context, it's important to remember that routing and addressing are two different but related activities, both for networking in general and e-mail in particular. This is where the difference between snail mail and e-mail is most pronounced.

For e-mail, addressing is a labeling or naming system defined by a set of rules used to create addresses that follow a particular format or syntax rigidly defined and interpreted by computer software. For snail mail, addressing consists of supplying sufficient information to identify sender and recipient unambiguously but with lots of latitude regarding format, abbreviations, and spelling.

For e-mail, routing consists of identifying the endpoints of a transmission from origin to destination, with a varying number of intermediate transfer point addresses coming into play during the movement of the message from sender to receiver. Stated differently, network routing is a set of rules that define how to interpret addresses and how to act on those interpretations. For snail mail, routing consists of delivery to a receiving post office, transfer to a central distribution point, followed by delivery to a delivering post office, and delivery to the specified address. From a formal perspective, snail mail uses much less dynamic or sophisticated (not to mention slower) address interpretations than do network-based systems.

The Mother of All Naming Schemes

Ultimately, the parts of an e-mail address provide the information necessary to identify a particular network, a particular set of e-mail servers or "post offices," and a unique sender and recipient for a message. Locating precisely the right elements depends on knowing how to interpret names and construct usable routes from sender to receiver, so that messages may be correctly delivered. The need to construct broad but precise naming systems has been a concern for computer science for some time and has led to a variety of naming approaches and schemes.

Given the convergence of all kinds of communications and digital technologies worldwide, it's widely recognized that an addressing domain with a global scope is needed to bring every possible network community together. An addressing domain derives from the mathematical concept of a domain, which is a space that contains all related elements from a particular set of objects, as defined by a rigorous set of rules. In plain English, the concept of a global addressing domain boils down to the set of all possible addresses in the world, organized by a particular set of rules for how addresses can be created and organized. It's an abstract concept, and one that leaves plenty of room for human creativity and perversity alike.

X.400 Addresses

The International Standards Organization's (ISO) Open Systems Interconnection (OSI) body has obligingly created a special form of notation for specifying addresses, which comprises a completely open-ended syntax for creating and organizing names within a well-defined framework. The objective of this standard is to support the cooperation of application processes in open systems. Therefore, this notation, while completely applicable to e-mail, especially to the OSI's X.400 e-mail standard, also applies to how systems, networks, and processes may be addressed in general.

In communication systems a name is a unique designation for an object. In the context of electronic mail, names exist primarily to identify users. An address also identifies an object, but with respect to a given set of rules and a specific model or organization for how objects are related to one another. An address is a name because it uniquely identifies an object, but a name is not an address, because it must be translated into an address in order to be appropriately used.

X.400 refers to user names as originator/recipient names (O/R names) and specifies various forms for such addresses, all of which follow the same basic model covered in Table 11.1. The basic idea is that O/R names are sets of attributes, where each attribute consists of a named type to identify the information it contains, and a value, which identifies a definite assignment for the attribute, for the name in question. It's quite abstract, so we'll lay out the table and then follow up with an example that should make this gobbledygook clear. Attribute types (in the left column) in brackets are optional, but at least one bracketed value must be supplied; those not in brackets are required in order to qualify as valid X.400 addresses.

Attribute Type	Description of Attribute and Possible Values
Country name	Two-letter country code as defined by ISO 3166
Administration domain name	Name of the administrative domain to which the originator or recipient belongs, or to which the private management domain of the O/R belongs
[Private domain name]	Name of the private management domain to which the O/R belongs
[Organization name]	Name of the organization to which the O/R belongs (company, university, agency name, etc.)
[Organizational unit name]	Name of a department, branch, division, or subdivision of a particular organization (for example, a department name like "marketing," a location like "Austin," or a division like "DPD")
[Personal name]	Name of the originator or recipient
[Domain-defined attributes]	An open-ended address component, suitable for mapping non-X.400 systems into standard X.400 attributes (for example, a DECnet, SNA, or cc:Mail user's system-specific information could be accommodated here; as we'll see in the real-world examples that follow, this can add interesting capabilities to some e-mail systems)

Table 11.1 *X.400 O/R address attributes explained.*

Table 11.2 provides the meaning for each attribute type/value combination of an example address. An actual address consists of the concatenation of the names of the attributes referenced, along with the actual values. The address that corresponds to the example in Table 11.2 would read as follows:

```
Country name = 'us'.Administration domain name = 'sprint'.Private
domain name = 'ge'.Organization name = 'ae'. Organization unit name =
'cin'.Organization unit name ='engr'.Personal name ='Jean A. Garza'
```

Because the explicit syntax is so long-winded, this would typically be abbreviated as follows:

```
C = 'us'.A = 'sprint'.Pdn = 'ge'.O = 'ae'. OU = 'cin'.OU ='engr'.P =
'Jean A. Garza'
```

Since even that is a pretty long and detailed string to create, most e-mail systems support aliases or provide address books—including

Attribute Type	Value	Meaning
Country name	'us'	United States
Administration domain name	'sprint'	Name of the administrative X.400 domain provided by US Sprint
Private domain name	'ge'	Name of a centralized private domain administered company-wide by General Electric
Organization name	'ae'	Abbreviation for GE's Aircraft Engine subsidiary
Organizational unit name	'cin'	Abbreviation for Cincinnati plant
Organizational unit name	'engr'	Abbreviation for engineering department
Personal name	'Jean A. Garza'	user name, structured explicitly as surname, first name, initial, with optional field for modifiers like 'Jr.' or 'Sr.'

Table 11.2 *Example of an actual X.400 address.*

both X.400-compliant and non compliant ones—to let users pick from menu selections or use short, specific names to supply all the necessary information.

As we've already indicated, X.400 e-mail systems are still fairly atypical today. However, the name and addressing model supplied by X.400 has had a profound impact on e-mail technology in general. It also provides a good model for understanding how addresses can be specified and created, which is why we took you through what might otherwise be a sterile exercise in arcane terminology.

Naming Schemes in the Real World

As we've already indicated, X.400 e-mail systems are still fairly atypical today. However, the name and addressing model supplied by X.400 has had a profound impact on e-mail technology in general. It also provides a good model for understanding how addresses can be specified and created, which is why we took you through what might otherwise be a sterile exercise in arcane terminology.

In this section, we'll examine the naming schemes from more broadly used e-mail systems, including those for NetWare's Message Handling System (MHS), Banyan's VINES Network Mail, Internet mail (also known as SMTP—Simple Mail Transfer Protocol), and Microsoft Mail. While we'll see a lot of common elements among these schemes, it's important to remember that each of these systems is sufficiently distinct to require gateways to bridge any two of them.

X.500's role is to define a standard for interlinking directory systems—and by extension, naming and addressing—into a unified networking environment. As all of these vendors and environments move to support X.500, interoperability will hopefully get easier, and gateways more ubiquitous and less expensive or difficult to use. In the meantime, the following sections are just a small subset of all of the many different approaches to managing e-mail addresses available today. Indeed, taken as a whole, the e-mail landscape is a messaging Tower of Babel.

NetWare MHS

Novell's NetWare Message Handling System (MHS) is governed by a specific set of rules called the Standard Message Format, abbreviated as SMF. At the time of this writing, the current version of SMF is version 71, abbreviated as SMF v71.

SMF v71 provides for a rich naming scheme, largely based on X.400 syntax and requirements. SMF distinguishes among multiple classes of message delivery, including local delivery (between users on a single messaging server), remote delivery (between users on multiple message servers) and gateway delivery (between a NetWare MHS user and a user on a different messaging system, reachable through a known gateway). Consequently, SMF also accommodates two address formats: basic, for transferring messages between applications that use the SMF interface, and extended, for transferring messages between an SMF and a non-SMF environment through a gateway. It's important to note that SMF compliance is all that's required from NetWare MHS; over 100 vendors offer MHS-based e-mail packages today, and all of them are capable of freely interchanging messages.

SMF Address Syntax

The syntax for basic and extended SMF addresses looks like this:

```
username@workgroup
username@workgroup (comments) {extension} [server]
```

Table 11.3 identifies the elements of these two formats.

Address Component	Description
username	Specifies message recipient within a workgroup, which can be an alias or a distribution list name. The username field is ignored until it is processed by the routing messaging server for the named workgroup, where it is mapped to the directory where the incoming message is stored.
@	Delimiter (punctuation) that separates *username* from *workgroup* name.
workgroup	Specifies the message destination; a *workgroup* can be any of the following: *server-name:* specifies the name of the receiving messaging server. The receiving messaging server specified is always the final server on the path to the message's ultimate destination. *workgroup:* specifies the name of a *workgroup,* or a collection of messaging servers, with which *username* is associated. *Workgroup* is a logical name, and messaging servers use routing tables to deliver a message within a *workgroup*. The user may not be aware of the physical server that supplies incoming or accepts outgoing messages for delivery. *gateway:* specifies the named *gateway* through which the message will be routed. This, too, can be a logical name if appropriate routing definitions exist.
(comments)	This is an optional element, containing up to 64 printable ASCII characters, and is meant to supply a full-blown username for the recipient. For instance, a user's SMF name might be jhowell, but the comments field could indicate "(James E. Howell)" to provide a more accurate rendition of *username's* given name. Comments must be enclosed by right and left parentheses, "( )".
{extension}	Supplies the recipient's non-SMF address, if applicable. The contents of extension are carried with the message and any system notifications, but are otherwise ignored by NetWare MHS. The format of this field requires a type identifier, followed by a colon, followed by the contents of the extension field. The type identifier must be one of X400, X121, TELEX, FAX, PDS, SMTP, or some other value defined for a specific SMF v71-based application. This helps identify the type of gateway or service required for the message and lets e-mail be telexed or faxed to some recipients, as well as delivered through a gateway or more conventional means. Extensions must be enclosed by right and left curly braces "{ }".
[server]	Supplies the name of the destination server used to route messages when available messaging routing servers support no definitions for the workgroup specified in the recipient address. This information is used internally while the message is in transit; applications and gateways strip this element from the address before forwarding the message. The name of the server must be enclosed in square brackets if the global naming server does not know about the workgroup contained in the address.

Table 11.3 *NetWare MHS address components (SMF v71).*

Name type	Example
Long name	Evelyn Nesbit@Sales.San Jose.Aptos Corp.com
Short name	evelyn@sj-sales
Workgroup	Sales.San Jose.Aptos Corp.com
Server	sj-sales
Default workgroup	Sales.San Jose.Aptos Corp.com

Table 11.4 *SMF v71—A set of name definitions.*

Name	Comment
Evelyn Nesbit@sales.san jose.aptos corp.com	capitalization not required
evelyn@sales.san jose.aptos corp.com	short name plus workgroup
Evelyn Nesbit@sales.san jose	long name with abbreviated workgroup
evelyn@sales.san jose	short name with abbreviated workgroup
Evelyn Nesbit	long name with default workgroup
evelyn	short name with default workgroup

Table 11.5 *Legal names derived from Table 11.4.*

SMF Address Formats

NetWare MHS supports both long and short name address formats, to supply pre-SMF v71 backward compatibility and to support full hierarchical names in keeping with X.400 requirements. Table 11.4 defines a set of SMF v71 names for the same user. Table 11.5 provides examples of legal addresses that can be derived from those names, illustrating how parts of the name hierarchy can be omitted from within shared messaging domains. Because the combinations of what's legal and what's not can be a subject to themselves, we'll leave this discussion a bit short of exhausting all the possibilities. Suffice it to say that MHS, like many other e-mail systems, offers a sufficiently flexible naming scheme to support a broad range of possible applications. For a single e-mail server, the entire community can function well by using only short names; for a large, multisite organization, the naming system provides a way to completely identify every user in the whole community, even when there may be several "Jim Smiths" to distinguish among!

Banyan VINES: StreetTalk and Network Mail

Banyan's networking environment, VINES, uses an explicit, distributed directory service called StreetTalk. StreetTalk maintains the names and attributes of all network resources and enables other network services, including e-mail, to enforce user access control to those resources. StreetTalk also keeps names consistent across multiple systems and servers—that's what makes it distributed.

StreetTalk Name Syntax

Under StreetTalk, all objects on the network are identified with a three-part name that takes the following form:

```
item@group@organization
```

The first part of a name identifies a particular network *item*, such as a user, a device, or a network service. The second part identifies the name of the *group* to which that item belongs. An organization name, the third part, exists as a logical mechanism to associate multiple groups together.

For each item, StreetTalk maintains a set of attribute information as a part of the directory database that it manages. This set includes the following:

- Class: Each item is a unique member of one of these classes: user, nickname, service, list, or group.
- Category: Within a given class, items are broken into categories to further distinguish them. For instance, within the class service, there are different categories for type of service, including file, print, database, and other services.
- Associated records: Each item can have up to 999 specific attribute records associated with it, to completely describe its contents. For a user record, this would commonly include typical location, address, telephone, and some personnel record information (job grade, title, etc.).

Based on user names, system managers can control access to users, groups, or organizations to restrict and apportion the use of shared network resources. The associated records for items are important because they contain the real information that describes a particular item. StreetTalk can use this information to search its directory database and can perform all kinds of searches based on pattern matching.

Network Mail Address Formats

Banyan's Network Mail is a distributed electronic mail service that works with StreetTalk and that supports interconnection with other mail systems via gateways. The mail service supports store-and-forward transmission across both permanent network links and temporary serial links, including explicit routing through remote servers.

Mail is organized into mail messages, which consist of text and addresses that are delivered to a user or a list of users. Like MHS, the user name or list name ultimately maps to a named directory on a server, which becomes the ultimate repository for incoming mail messages.

Because StreetTalk provides address lookup, users can query the StreetTalk database to obtain e-mail addresses, and they can build up personal address books over time. Valid addresses include user names, list names, nicknames, patterns (including wildcards), or remote addresses. All of these items, except remote addresses, can be obtained from the StreetTalk database. Remote addresses include the names of one or more services and are used either to route messages to a mail gateway that connects a VINES system to another mail system, or to route messages to VINES services that are physically separated from one another and only intermittently connected by temporary (typically, dial-up) links.

Each VINES server can contain only a single Network Mail service, and every server has a special access list, called an internet access list, that controls whether it sends and accepts mail from remote servers. If an address is a StreetTalk name, Network Mail communicates with StreetTalk to verify that the recipient exists and can accept a message. For remote addresses, Network Mail attempts to locate and communicate with the gateway named in that address. Network Mail is especially good at monitoring message delivery status, and it collects useful information on both successful and failed delivery attempts. The combination of a directory service—StreetTalk—and integrated e-mail—Network Mail—has proved very attractive to Banyan's customers.

As this chapter is in process, Banyan has announced its acquisition of Beyond, Inc., developers of a sophisticated messaged product called

Beyond Mail. It offers interesting mail filtering and control capabilities—including automated message sorting and deletion of electronic junk mail—and promises to extend Banyan's e-mail offering in the future. At this point, we can only guess what will emerge, but this technology is clearly worth watching!

Internet E-mail (SMTP)

The common form of e-mail in use on the Internet—but certainly not the only form—is the somewhat misnamed Simple Mail Transfer Protocol. We think it's misnamed because it's not really that simple (our tongue is planted firmly in cheek here) and it's not entirely a protocol, but rather an application that uses an eponymous protocol to ship messages around the Internet. Since this is in keeping with other shibboleths in the TCP/IP community, namely, FTP or File Transfer Protocol, it's obviously customary at this point.

Internet Address Syntax

SMTP uses the well-known Internet addressing scheme, which can be represented in one of the following ways (and others as well, which we omit in the interest of brevity):

```
username@organization.extension
username@country-code.organization.extension
username@organizational-unit.organization.extension
username@server.country-code.organization.extension
```

where the terminology should be understood as follows (here, square brackets indicate optional address elements):

- username is the e-mail name of either the sender or the recipient of the message. As the format section that follows indicates, this is seldom the same as the full name of either party.
- [server] is the optional name of the messaging server (SMTP host) from which the message originated. This information can be handy for larger organizations that typically have multiple sites and a multitude of messaging servers.
- [country-code] is only optional in the United States, where the older form of internet address shown in the first of the three repre-

sentations above is still the most common form used. The country codes are formally called international domain names and are documented in Appendix B of this book.

- organization is the name of the organization to which the sender or recipient belongs.
- [organizational-unit] is the optional name of an organizational unit to which the sender or recipient belongs. Like the server field (also optional) it can help to locate a user more precisely in an organization with multiple e-mail servers.
- [extension] indicates the type of organization named in the address. Extension names are formally called old-style U.S. domain names and are documented in Appendix B of this book.

With over two million Internet e-mail users on-line, and more joining the party daily, the breadth and scope of SMTP's naming scheme are obvious (the availability of TCP/IP addresses for all these users is another matter entirely, but will hopefully be resolved before all the addresses are taken!).

Internet E-Mail Address Formats

SMTP optionally allows users to specify a comments field to include a complete username, along with their e-mail address. This takes the form

```
"John Q. Public" <username@organization.extension>
```

where the e-mail name is surrounded by angle brackets ("<username...>") and the full name is enclosed in quote marks (""). SMTP also allows gateways to be referenced for remote e-mail delivery, which can take many forms, but always references an Internet address for the gateway to be used (for example, compuserve.com to send a message from SMTP to CompuServe), along with an appropriate user address for the other side of the gateway to ensure proper delivery.

The large number of gateways and address formats available to SMTP are too numerous to document exhaustively, but a fair sampling occurs in Appendix C of this book. It illustrates gateway syntax for a large number of addresses entering and leaving the Internet e-mail world.

Microsoft Mail

With a copy of Mail in every box of Windows for Workgroups, and an administrative license in every NT Advanced Server, Microsoft is staking out a major presence in the e-mail marketplace. Microsoft is increasingly viewing electronic mail as a pivotal technology and is upping its commitment and involvement in building enterprise e-mail system.

As we write this chapter, Microsoft has just announced the planned introduction of its Enterprise Messaging Server for the second half of 1994. Its current code name is "Touchdown," which we think underscores the company's view of e-mail's importance to its future success. This new architecture will augment existing Microsoft Mail capabilities by adding management tools, rules-based messaging, and message-driven workgroup application support. While the details are still hazy, we think this means that applications will be able to use e-mail to share information over the network, and that forms and database capabilities will become easier to use in the Microsoft Mail environment.

Microsoft Mail Address Syntax

As befits a GUI-based e-mail system, Microsoft Mail does an outstanding job of shielding its users from the underlying complexities of addressing. Consequently, the syntax of addresses is also largely invisible. For convenience, we isolate the elements of a Microsoft Mail address as follows, based on investigation of its administrative utilities and its programming interfaces:

```
mailboxname@network.postoffice
groupname@network.postoffice
```

Each of the elements can be further described as follows:

- *mailboxname* is an abbreviated form of its associated user's name but is part of an extended database record that also includes the user's initials, surname, employee number, title, organizational division, department, mailing address, and voice and fax telephone numbers. Mailboxes themselves have an associated mailbox name, an access password, a user type that indicates the level of e-mail system access allowed, user privileges regarding messages, and their file and directory usage profiles.

- *group* permits arbitrary distribution lists selected from the Postoffice Address List (Microsoft's name for its e-mail address book) to be created, named, and maintained. A group is a valid e-mail recipient, which acts as a distribution point for delivering copies of a single message to multiple recipients.
- *network* identifies the address of the network number or identifier where the sender's or recipient's postoffice resides.
- *postoffice* is the name of the e-mail server where the sender's or recipient's e-mail folders reside; it acts as the repository for incoming and outgoing messages for that user.

From the user's perspective, this information is seldom obvious. Their interaction with the e-mail user directory occurs through a windowed pick list of mailbox and group names, which they can select as recipients for any e-mail message. Gateway access is equally straightforward, in that gateways are presented to users as "external postoffices" that can also be addressed through a pick list. Syntax and format will be an issue in entering the targeted recipient's name and e-mail address, but that's a limitation of the e-mail system on the other side of the gateway.

All in all, Microsoft Mail offers a simple and straightforward way to handle e-mail addressing. So simple in fact, we do not devote a section to address formats as we have with the other e-mail systems discussed in this section!

Other Naming Schemes

We'd like to foreshadow the end of this chapter by stating explicitly that there are many more naming schemes, and addressing techniques, used in e-mail packages around the world than any book devoted entirely to the subject could cover. For one thing, there are too many different e-mail packages out there to cover completely. For another, by the time anyone had covered all of them, the majority would have changed (as Banyan's acquisition of Beyond, Inc., will no doubt change what we've written about their Network Mail service and possibly even StreetTalk as well).

However, the basic principles that have emerged are the needs to identify users with some kind of e-mail name (and often, with a pointer to a full name) and to locate users both by organization (and often with one or more levels of organizational units) and by the e-mail server that handles their e-mail or the workgroup to which they belong. The ever-present need for gateways to access other kinds of mail systems also makes the need for remote address references equally acute.

No matter what the actual form or syntax for an addressing scheme, or the rules that govern the construction of valid names, we can count on these basic elements no matter where we look or what kind of e-mail package we encounter. With a clear understanding of these elements, the intricacies of e-mail names and the addresses that go with them should make more sense.

Summary

Any time you want to send an e-mail message, the most important ingredient for successful delivery is a properly formed address. In this chapter we've looked at the naming schemes and addressing techniques that make successful e-mail delivery possible. Even though many of the e-mail systems we investigated—most notably Banyan Network Mail and Microsoft Mail's Enterprise Mail Architecture—are "under construction" and will probably change, the mail must still go through.

While there's been a mass of details to digest along the way, the basic elements involved have remained consistent. Where names and addresses are concerned, e-mail is still e-mail, no matter what brand, protocol, or network may be involved!

chapter 12

Ensuring Proper E-mail Delivery

Seeing Is Believing

This chapter discusses the techniques to ensure that e-mail gets delivered properly. Since the only way to really assure that messages are getting through is by testing them, this chapter describes how to set up your test lab, how to test your installation, and how to track down problems. Later, when you install the system in the actual production environment, you can perform the same tests and troubleshooting techniques to make sure your installation is successful and complete.

Setting up a test lab has several advantages. Most obvious, you can discover and solve problems in a low-pressure environment. Because you have access to equipment that has no other use in the test lab, no one will be leaning over your shoulder or unable to work while you track down problems. Instead you can find and solve them in relative peace and quiet. Furthermore, if there are any severe difficulties with your system (for example, your e-mail system may not work with your users' current workstation configurations), you can find and fix them early, before anybody becomes dependent on the system.

Admittedly, a test lab has a cost. It takes time to do it right, and it might be difficult for you to collect the necessary hardware for uninterrupted use. Nonetheless, we strongly suggest that you do whatever it takes to give your e-mail installation a thorough testing before you unleash it. Take our word for it—you really don't want to find these sorts of problems in a production environment, because some of them can bring production to a grinding halt!

SETTING UP THE TEST LAB

This section walks you through the test lab, describing each component and pointing out the most important features. Try to find a dedicated space where you can try everything out, someplace with a minimum of traffic.

Server or Host

The most important computer in your test installation is the test server or, if you're working with host-based e-mail, a test host (or at least an emulator). This computer should be configured identically to the actual server or host machine, to the greatest extent possible. In particular, make sure it has the same NIC, the same amount of memory, and the same display hardware. Most importantly, make sure it has exactly the same software—the same versions of everything that the actual mail server is running. Matching disk space is not as critical; just make sure that the amount of disk space on the test machine is not radically greater than or less than that on the actual server.

Workstations

Collect one representative of every possible client configuration, down to the specific graphics cards, software versions, disk sizes, and memory amounts. Try every different combination you can think of, even down to the brands of workstations. You do not want to get to the live installation and find that the Rakete graphics cards in the Dell computers don't work with the new e-mail system although they work fine in all the Compaq computers, because you only tested the Compaqs in the lab.

Making Connections

The final step in setting up your test lab is to connect all the clients to the server, or the workstations to the host. Again, configure the connections in exactly the same way as the real-world systems are configured.

Installing the Software

Before you install any software, check your disk space. The manufacturer probably recommends a certain amount based on the number of users you plan to have, so compare that number to the amount your server has available. If you don't have enough space, remove or archive files until you have enough room. Some packages simply won't run without adequate disk space, and others might give unexpected errors. When calculating space, be sure to allow at least 20 percent extra for growth.

The next step is to prepare a list of e-mail user names. If you can pull the list from a list of network users (or their account name), great. Otherwise, create the list by hand. It's important to be thorough here—make sure every e-mail user has a user name.

Once you have all that information at hand, follow the manufacturer's instructions for installing the software. Take your time, and make notes of every step as you go. In particular, note any configuration parameters you have to enter during installation—you'll want these later when you get to the real deployment. Also, make a note of what time it is when you begin, so that you have an idea of how much time to allow for the live installation.

Next, go around to each client in your test network and install the front-end software. Again, take your time and make careful notes. Especially important here is to note any changes you have to make to the client configuration in order to get the software working. If you have to change any configuration files, environment variables, system defaults, or other parameters, write the changes down. You need to be able to reproduce these changes exactly when you release your e-mail system to the world, so make it easier on yourself by making careful notes now.

Test, Test, Test

Getting everything running on the test network usually takes some fiddling with configuration parameters, naming, or other system settings. Be patient, and call in help if you need it. Once you get to the point where you can transmit simple messages, though, you're halfway there! The next step is to test the system features, one by one, as we describe ahead. After you've tested all of these features, you have a reasonable basis to expect that your system is ready to install.

This is a great time to call in some of your power users. These are the folks who know all about the e-mail system because they may have used this system or one like it before. Typically, power users are people who just have to know every detail about a system—they enjoy nothing more than exploring every aspect of a software package. These people are great allies to have, because they can think of things to test that you never would. They may also be able to help track down problems should they arise.

What follows in the next section is our list of features that should be part of your test plan. You don't have to run your tests in this order, but since we've organized it from the simplest to the most complex operation, you'll probably find it convenient to do so.

Basic Features

The first step is to make sure every type of workstation can access the e-mail system. Next, test whether all users can send messages to everyone else in your test network, and make sure these messages arrive in the recipients' mailboxes exactly as they were sent. Another basic feature you should test is whether every user can send messages to a group of people by using a mailing list.

If your system has bulletin boards or other global access mechanisms, make sure everyone can post to them and read the postings—both their own and others'.

Enclosures and Attachments

Now you're ready to try some more complex operations. Send some test messages with enclosures or attachments (your system might call them something else). Make sure the messages arrive intact by opening the attached file; how you do this depends on how the file was created. This might require that you save the file to the local hard drive, then try to open it with the same application software that the sender used to create it. In a simpler situation, you can just select the file—some systems are smart enough to know what program to call up for each file. Either way, make sure that the relevant program can recognize the file and that the file has the same format and content as it did on the sending machine.

Check graphics carefully, too. If your package has a feature that allows users to create and send graphics within the e-mail program, test it and make sure it works with every type of workstation, especially if the display hardware is different between systems.

Forms

If your system offers support of forms, make sure you can create them, fill them out, send them, and retrieve them. Further, if your organization is going to use custom forms, make sure every user who needs to can get to them—and if access is to be restricted, make sure that the lockouts work for the correct sets of people as well.

Make a list of every possible use of custom forms in the real installation, and test each situation. For instance, if you'll have a custom form for users to report their work hours, make sure everyone can fill out the form and that the accounting department can import the forms into the payroll program. Also check exports if you have any programs that need to create forms for other programs to use.

Test the Gateways

At this point, everything is working within the local network, so it's time to test connections to the wider world. You might find that it's trickier to set up these tests, especially because it's so much harder to simulate the environment. You can't very well set up a prototype Internet, for instance, to test your Internet gateway!

For this reason, proceed especially cautiously at this phase of the testing. You probably won't crash the remote e-mail system, but a lot of test messages could annoy the users of that system. Work with the administrators at all of the remote sites—they can set up test users for your experimenting.

Start your testing the same way you did with the local system: send some simple text messages. Don't forget to test in both directions! Once you have those working reliably, you can move on to testing enclosures, attachments, and graphics files.

Note the difference between plain text files (probably ASCII if you're using PCs) and binary files, such as program executable files or graphics files. The former type of file uses only seven bits of every byte, while the latter group needs all eight bits. This is a great place for incompatibilities to crop up, since some systems routinely strip that "extra" eighth bit from every byte they send. Your gateway software should handle this, but you might need to make some tuning adjustments. If you get text files through the gateway with no problems, but graphics or program files are corrupted, you should suspect that some tuning will be required for character encodings or communications settings.

Try sending some really large files—over a megabyte in size—to see how the system behaves. Do such files take a long time to send? Are they exactly the same size when they arrive? Again, test in both directions.

Some operating systems allow you to embed objects in messages, that is, you send a pointer to an object that actually still resides on the sending system. Gateway problems frequently appear when sending this type of file. To test, send a document with an embedded object such as a drawing and make sure it arrives correctly. Now make a change to the object on the sending machine. Is it correctly updated on the receiver? Be sure your system supports this feature, though, before you suspect a problem!

Bad Stuff

The best time to find out how the system behaves when bad things happen is during the test phase. Try composing a message on one of your workstations and turning off the workstation just as you send it, to simulate a power failure. When you turn the workstation back on, is it still possible for that user to access the message database? How about other users? If the message database is corrupted, you have an opportunity to test the repair tools as well.

Troubleshooting

You are going to run into problems in your test installation. Rather than being bad news, it's actually good, because every problem you find in the test lab is one fewer that you find in the live installation. However, finding a problem is a lot different from finding a solution. In this section, we offer some suggestions to make it easier to figure out what's gone wrong.

Check the Manuals

Sometimes it's a long shot, but you just might have a problem that the software manufacturers are familiar with. Look in the system manuals for a section called "Troubleshooting" and see if any of the descriptions match what you're seeing. Maybe you'll be lucky and find an easy answer! If not, approach the problem with the following strategies.

Write It Down

This is the cardinal rule of computer configuration. Every time you make a change, write down exactly what you did so that if it breaks something, you can undo the change and get back to your previous state. This is one of those things that seems like an annoyance until you need it!

Never Change More Than One Thing at a Time

Computer systems are amazingly interdependent—you change one little thing and ten things stop working. If you change two things, the number of components affected multiplies. The two changes together might have fixed your problem, but you have no way of knowing which change fixed it, and you therefore have no reference point if the problem crops up again. This is why you need to take a very systematic approach to problem solving. Make a single change, and test it. Make another change, and test it. Write each one down as you go, and note the results (see previous rule).

Break the Problem in Half

No, it doesn't mean you split it into two problems! This is a very useful technique in troubleshooting known as binary problem solving. The word *binary* contains the prefix "bi-," which means two, and when you solve problems with this method, you divide the system into halves and isolate which half the problem is in. Then divide that half in half and do it again, and so on, until you isolate the problem.

For instance, if e-mail messages are not getting through to one of your computers, divide the network in half. Are they getting halfway?

If so, the problem is in the other half of the network, away from the sender—divide that portion in half and determine whether messages are getting that far. Continue until you find the point at which the message is getting lost.

Skillful problem solving with this approach is a bit of an art and requires practice, but the concept can be very useful any time you're trying to track down a problem.

Question Everything

We can't think of how many times users have called us in to help with a problem. We ask what has changed since the system was last working, and they say nothing. "Oh," someone might add, "we did install a new driver, but that couldn't have had any effect."

This is fatal logic. In the world of computers, everything could have an effect! It's difficult to train yourself to make no assumptions, but it's the most important thinking habit you can have when you're trying to track down problems. Every change, no matter how insignificant it seems, has the potential to affect your system.

Summary

Probably the most important feature of your e-mail system is reliability. People will only use it if they can be sure the messages will arrive correctly. Therefore, test every aspect you can think of in a test lab before you install the system. Power users can be a great help in this testing, so try to pull some of them in to help you.

chapter 13

Planning for Installation

The Payoffs of Careful Planning

From what you've read so far, you've learned how to design your e-mail system and lay it out to best serve your organization. You've also created a test environment and tested the entire system thoroughly, so you're just about ready to start the production installation.

In this chapter we go over the last few matters that need your attention before you start installing. We list all the things you need to check before you begin, and we offer some suggestions on things you might want to consider scheduling. Finally, we give you some useful hints on how to ensure a smooth installation, from minimizing the impact on your users to minimizing the chaos for yourself.

Make a List, Check It Twice

Before you begin installing your e-mail system, it's a good idea to make sure that you have all the software and equipment you need. By assembling everything now, you can save yourself a lot of trouble and grief when you sit down to start installing the system. We've discussed some of these items before, but we pull them all together here so that you can glance down the list and make sure you haven't forgotten anything. You might want to get a piece of paper to make a list of your own as you read through this section.

Equipment Upgrades or Updates

If you need to add a new NIC to the mail server, note that now. Also make a note if you need to upgrade your server processor to a faster revision, add extra RAM to the server, or increase the server disk space.

The next thing to examine is your network capacity. Back in Chapter 10 we sat down with the network map and the traffic expectations and determined where in the network you will need to increase bandwidth, if at all. Find these spots again, and make notes about any new media, routers, or hubs that you will need.

Finally, don't forget those workstations. If the test lab experiment revealed that a certain type of display board is incompatible with the e-mail system, for instance, make a list of all the workstations that have that type of board so that you know where you need to replace display hardware. Other such upgrades might include adding more RAM or disk space to workstations, or installing faster NICs.

Your time in the test lab should have revealed most of these needs, but be sure also to check the e-mail system installation requirements. Since e-mail manufacturers naturally want you to think their package is a very light user of system resources, their recommendations typically represent the minimum necessary for acceptable performance. Nonetheless, such recommendations are the best starting place for finding weak spots in your current system, though nothing beats careful testing in the test lab.

Software Upgrades or Additions

The next thing to check is the set of software that the manufacturer requires to ensure that the system runs correctly. Make sure you have all the necessary drivers and support packages by comparing your list of server software to the list of manufacturer-recommended software. Once you've confirmed that your server has all the necessary software, make the same checks on all the workstation software, and note any missing pieces on your installation list.

It's important to check not only that you have the correct software, but also that the software is adequately updated. You might have the necessary communications drivers, for instance, but they might all be a year old or more. If the e-mail system relies on a feature only available in the newer drivers, it won't work for you until you update your drivers to the latest version.

If your mail system has a feature that allows you to export forms for use in other programs, make sure that those programs are also up-to-date. This means checking the version numbers of all spreadsheets, word processors, or other software that should interoperate with your e-mail system. Thoroughness now will really pay off when you get to the final installation.

Patches and Fixes

Finally, make a quick call to the manufacturer of your e-mail system and find out whether it has issued any recent patches, fixes, or updates to the package. If you bought the e-mail software off the shelf from a software supply shop, it might have been sitting there for a few months. Between the time the manufacturer sent it to the shop and the time you bought it, the manufacturer might have found and fixed several bugs, but these fixes won't be in your version of the software. It's much better to call the company now and make sure than to install the software and try to debug the problems yourself.

Most of the time you can rely on version numbers to tell you whether you have the latest release of a package, but not always. Some software vendors ship software with certain version numbers but release intermediate versions that they don't announce. For instance, a vendor might be currently shipping version 3.5 of its product, but if you read the label carefully you find that the diskettes are labeled with version number 3.5h. When you call the vendor you find that it's up to 3.5m. In the vendor's opinion, the changes are not great enough to warrant changing the version number, but they could be great enough to cause you headaches if you don't know about them.

SCHEDULING TACTICS

Now that you have a list of all the things you need to install, the next task in creating the installation plan is mapping out the schedule. In this section we list and discuss the major time-consuming areas of the installation, from training to testing.

Pre-Installation Training

You might be lucky enough to find a training class offered by your vendor on installing and managing your e-mail system. If you can find such a class, it's often a good investment to have at least one person from your organization attend. Allow a bit of time afterwards for the attendee to report back to the rest of the installation team.

Installing the Server or Host Software

Once everyone is trained you'll be able to start installing the new software on the server or host machine. Your test lab experiments should give you a good idea about how long you need to allow for this phase of the installation. It's especially important to schedule this phase carefully, because it typically has to be done at a time when no one is logged on to the machine.

This step involves not only the installation of the actual e-mail system, but also the installation of any server hardware upgrades, new server software, or other enhancements that the server requires to run the e-mail system. Be sure to allow enough time for all aspects of the server installation.

To minimize the impact on your users, we recommend that you perform this phase of the installation at a time when people would not be using the system anyway, such as an evening or weekend. If you want to make things really easy on them (and yourself), schedule the whole installation for a three-day weekend. If it goes smoothly, you have a day or two of the weekend to congratulate yourself. If you run into problems, at least you have time to solve them without disrupting anyone's normal working schedule.

Installing the Workstation Software

The next item on your installation schedule is installing the software on each workstation. This can be a time-consuming step, so allow plenty of time. Allow time not only for installing the e-mail client software, but also for making any configuration changes to the workstations. These changes could include hardware enhancements like extra RAM or disk space, or software changes such as new drivers or more recent versions of operating systems or support software. Refer to your test installation notes for exact lists of what you need to add to each workstation.

Since this is a step that must be performed over and over on many different machines in pretty much the same way, consider enlisting help from other people in your organization. Doing so not only can cut down on the total installation time, but also helps to build trust and interest in the e-mail project. Good candidates for helpers are the folks you've identified as power users; their familiarity with e-mail makes them ideal assistants at installation time. If you opt for this approach, be sure to allow time to train them!

Post-Installation Testing

Once the e-mail software is installed everywhere, give yourself plenty of time for thorough testing. Again, your experience from the test lab is the best indicator of how much time is enough. We recommend that you run through the entire suite of tests at this point, from sending simple text messages between users to sending binary files through the gateways. Refer to Chapter 12 to review the elements of thorough testing.

In practice you'll probably do some of the testing as you install the software on each workstation, but the cumulative time for installation and testing will probably be the same as if you'd performed the two tasks in discrete steps.

User Training

No matter how easy your e-mail package is to use, most users will benefit from some type of training. Even if they don't need much training on how to use the package, a training class is a good opportunity for you to inform everyone about the unique features of your local e-mail setup and your corporate e-mail policy. By scheduling such classes now, you can help ensure that the space and equipment are ready when you begin the training. Chapter 20 offers some suggestions on training topics.

Real-Life Installation Times

For your reference, we asked all of our case study sites how long it took them to install their entire systems, from opening the package to getting the last user on-line. Every installation has different features, of course, but these figures may help you estimate the installation time for your system:

Ozz Research Computing, Inc. (Microsoft Mail, 5–8 users)—4 days' planning, 1 day installation

Vtel Corporation (cc:Mail, 97 users) —2 days' planning, 1 day installation

MD Anderson (Various Mail, 5400 users)—4 weeks planning, 2 days' (weekend) installation (see Case Study, Chapter 32, for details)

Work around People, Not over Them

The two aspects of scheduling are figuring out "how long," then deciding "when." We're not going to tell you the most auspicious day to begin your installation, but we can offer some advice about what should be going on that day.

Briefly put, nothing should be scheduled on that day. The best installations are those that your users know nothing about. They leave on Friday for a long weekend, for instance, and when they get back on Tuesday they have full e-mail capabilities, like magic. Users love it—they don't have to wait while the server or host is unavailable during the installation, or while you are fussing with their workstations trying to install the client software. Installing when they're not there is great for you too, because you don't have to wait for anyone to finish a task before you can use their workstation, and you don't have impatient users asking you every 15 minutes, "Is the server back up yet?"

So, for reasons of both consideration and convenience, we advise you to schedule the installation for a weekend. We especially like long weekends, because that extra day gives you some nice breathing room. If you finish early, you have that much more time to relax!

The Wonders of Incremental Deployment

We have one final piece of advice on the topic of scheduling. When you install your e-mail system, bring the users on-line a few at a time. Start off with a small group of your most literate e-mail users, those who have used e-mail packages before and who know how to use a large number of the features. Encourage these folks to use as many of the features as possible, as early as possible, so you can find any bugs or subtle incompatibilities before they are affecting the entire group of users.

Once these five or so power users report that the system is solid and reliable, add a few more. Again, wait a few days, keep testing, then add the next batch. New problems are likely to crop up at each stage, but they will probably appear less frequently as the installation grows. By continuing in this stepwise fashion, you limit the number of problems you have to handle at any one time and thus stand a better chance of retaining your sanity throughout the entire process.

Summary

For best results during installation, nothing beats careful planning. In this chapter we discussed the elements of an installation plan, listing everything from the tasks that need to be performed during the installation to the areas that require scheduling. We offered several tips and reminders to help ensure that your installation is as hassle-free as possible.

chapter 14

Living Through Installation

The Big Day

Finally, all the plans are in place, you've run all the necessary tests, and you're ready to install the e-mail system. This chapter walks you through the steps, from loading the software onto the server to sending out your very first messages.

Installing the System on the Server

The first phase of installation is loading software onto the server. To make sure everything goes as smoothly as possible, check and double-check every aspect of the system every step of the way. Proceed slow-ly—it saves time in the long run!

Find Out What's New

Before you begin, check with your vendor's technical support department to see whether it has released any patches or fixes to the e-mail software. You need to know about these before you begin so that you don't end up trying to debug something that was fixed months ago. If your software package has been sitting on the shelf of a software shop for a few months, there could easily be lots of fixes you haven't heard about yet. Call now and you could save yourself a lot of frustration later on.

While you're talking to them, double-check the configuration of your server to make sure you meet the requirements for its recommended hardware setup. Tell them what software is currently on your server, and ask whether they know of any incompatibilities between their system and your configuration. If this conversation yields any affirmative answers, take careful notes—you need to address these issues before you install the system.

Install Upgrades and Patches

The next step is to make any necessary changes to the server. This could include adding more memory, more disk space, a different NIC, or different software drivers. If the e-mail vendor supplies you with any fixes or patches, install them exactly as directed—such fixes often have rather arcane installation instructions! This is no time to break from the beaten path and do things your own way.

Loading the Software

You're just about there, but first, check over everything one more time. Compare the list of hardware and software requirements on the e-mail package to the configuration of your server. Make sure your system matches at least the minimum requirements for disk space, memory, user ports, and processor speed. If the package recommends compatible software versions, ensure that your software is not older than the recommendations.

For future reference, write down the whole configuration, including software version numbers. If you have to call the vendor with any problems, this information helps them tremendously.

Okay, go ahead! Follow the manufacturer's directions carefully. If the installation process prompts you for any configuration data, be sure to make a note of your answers for future reference. You already did all this for the test installation, though, so you probably won't encounter any surprises here.

Making E-mail Available to Users

Once the e-mail software is installed on the server, you're ready to configure your users' environments to access it. This might mean installing client software on each user's workstation, activating some ports on a host, or changing user configuration files to reflect the addition of e-mail. The exact steps required are different for every installation. You figured out everything necessary for this in your test lab (see Chapter 12 for a refresher), so this step is simply a matter of applying your discoveries to the real world. This is where that time in the test lab really pays off!

Depending on your installation, you might need to change a number of parameters or files. The following list enumerates some of the most common ones:

- *Initialization files (ending with .INI).* All Windows configuration information, for instance, resides in .INI files.
- *Operating system configuration files.* In DOS, these files are called CONFIG.SYS and AUTOEXEC.BAT.
- *Environment variables.* Some packages require them to be present or set.
- *Conflicts.* Some Macintosh file extensions, for instance, do not coexist gracefully with others. If your e-mail package generates files with an extension that is already used by other software in your system, be sure to change the default extension before you install.

Success! Sending Your First Message

Congratulations! The e-mail package is installed on the server and on the first set of user workstations. To make sure it works, it's a good idea to send a couple of test messages to the users and make sure each of them can reply.

Once you're sure that every system is working, send a message notifying all users of the e-mail policies, if any, and the training class schedule, so that everyone has the same information on these matters. You might also want to send a user survey at this time, asking people what they think of the system and how they plan to use it. Coupled with the results from a similar survey in a few months, this information might be useful in justifying the system to your supervisor, or maybe even justifying the cost of an expansion!

Ubiquitous E-mail

Once your first round of users is up and running with e-mail, wait at least a few days before extending the user base. The first group is very likely to find some problems that you'll want to fix before bringing more users on board.

Continue in this manner, adding a few users at a time, until the entire target user population has full e-mail capability. This stepwise deployment is a great way to please your users and keep your sanity during the installation process. When it's all over, pat yourself on the back for an installation well done!

Summary

This chapter covered the actual installation of the e-mail system, from loading the software onto the server to configuring user workstations and sending that first message. This is a good time to sit back and assess the configuration, and the next chapter offers some tips on doing so.

Maintenance Begins at Installation

No Rest for the Weary

Your electronic mail system is now installed—congratulations! But wait, don't pop open that champagne just yet. You have a few more things to do before you can take a well-deserved break.

OK, we're exaggerating a little bit. You don't have to perform all of these tasks the minute you finish installing the system, but don't let more than a few days pass before you do them. The point of maintenance is to minimize the impact of problems, and the key ingredient to maintenance is regularity. Get in the habit now of performing these tasks regularly, and you'll go a long way toward assuring a reliable system.

"What tasks?" you're probably wondering. The two key aspects of maintaining your e-mail system are making regular backups and keeping careful records. Make a backup of the entire e-mail system right away—Chapter 18 gives you more detail on doing this. In this chapter, we discuss what records to keep, where to keep them, and how often you need to update them.

Reintroducing the Network Map

It's called a map, but it's much more than a map. Recall Chapter 10's discussion of the network map, a map of the building with every component of the network indicated and labeled. It goes hand in hand with the network database; in fact, they're so closely tied that we usually refer to them as a unit. The database portion of the network map is where you record every single detail about your network, no matter how insignificant it might seem. It's only insignificant until you need it!

As soon as your e-mail system is running, add a section to your network database in which you can record information about e-mail. If you use a commercial network database package, there might already be space for this information.

What to Record

Make a note of everything you or someone else might ever want to know about your e-mail system. This includes your naming scheme, configuration, routes, and addresses. If your installation has several IP (Internet Protocol) addresses, for instance, make a note of each one of them, along with the domain name of each associated computer. Record the names of all the users and the mailboxes to which they are attached. If you have gateways, describe them and the connections to them in as much detail as possible. You kept careful notes during the testing and installation phases—this is the place to store those records.

Your goal here is to make accurate enough records so that if your entire e-mail system—and you—were to vanish overnight, someone could come in and recreate this system with just the information in the network database. Don't forget, you won't be able to keep all of this information in your head forever, the someone who has to rebuild the system from just these records might just be you! Make it easy on yourself by recording everything you can think of now.

Now and Forever

Recording the initial snapshot is part of the job, keeping it up-to-date is the rest. Be sure to update this information every time you make a change to your e-mail system, whether adding a user or an entire mail server. Get in the habit of making a note of changes when they happen; it may seem like a hassle, but someday you'll be glad you did!

The message traffic when you first install the system is probably close to non-existent, so we are not going to insist that you record these numbers right now. Do, however, make a point of recording traffic data two to four weeks from installation, and every two to four weeks thereafter. Eventually usage patterns will declare themselves, and this information will be your clue to deciding when to add more disk space, or possibly even more servers. Chapter 16 discusses this topic in more detail.

Possibly you don't have a network map yet. Don't let that stop you from recording all of the details of your e-mail system, though! Start now to get in the record-keeping habit, and make a note to yourself to build a network map sometime soon.

Summary

Before you become too complacent about getting your e-mail system running, take a few minutes to record the configuration details of the system. Careful record keeping is critical to keeping things running smoothly, so record every detail about your e-mail system as soon after installation as possible. Update this information every time you make a change, too.

Managing Upgrades and Replacement

E-mail Never Sits Still

Great work! You've designed and installed the entire e-mail system. Everyone is using it happily, you're performing the regular maintenance tasks, and everything is going fine. You may be able to relax for as long as a couple of months.

Sooner or later, you'll notice that the e-mail server's disk space is filling up fast. You've asked people to clean up their files and honestly believe that they've done their best to comply. Or maybe the company has grown so much that you have room for only one or two more new users on the current mail server. Maybe the signs are not so dire—perhaps you run across a notice in a computer journal announcing that your e-mail vendor has just released a new version of the product.

No matter what direction the sign comes from, the meaning is the same: it's time to upgrade. Installing upgrades can be a lot of work, but you have a big advantage because you've laid a lot of the groundwork already. You have a network map and a detailed record of the installation of your e-mail system, so adding to the system is fairly straightforward. In this chapter we discuss the issues that affect upgrades, and we give you the foreknowledge to make sure the process goes smoothly.

So You Say You Want to Upgrade Your Software

The first question to ask yourself is whether you really need to do this upgrade. This applies particularly in the case where the vendor has announced a new version of the software. We don't recommend upgrading simply because it's possible. There's no need to subject yourself and the users to the hassles of upgrading unless everyone can really benefit from doing so.

Reasons to Upgrade

If your installation has been plagued by software bugs that have bothered you or your users, and the new release purports to fix them, by all means, try it. These bugs could be as trivial as failing to automatically spell-check a message or as disruptive as occasional random database crashes. The only rule we offer here is that if the bug bothers a large percentage of your users, take your chances on the upgrade (keeping in mind the upcoming caveats). If, on the other hand, the release promises to fix bugs you hadn't even noticed, there's no need to rush into installing it.

The other big reason companies release new software versions is to add new features to their packages. Again, we recommend temperance. If the new enhancements are features for which everyone has been clamoring, then this is your chance to be a hero (again!), and you should go ahead with the installation. But if the enhancement list generates reactions along the lines of "why would anyone want to do that?" you're safe in holding off the upgrade until later.

Note, however, that today's fancy feature becomes tomorrow's essential. Users might be quite blasé about a feature when you first ask them about it, but a few months later they might be pounding on your door demanding it.

Some Cautions about Software Upgrades

Before you install that software, consider these cautions. First of all, do your homework, and second, watch out for any version with a zero in the number.

Software version numbering might seem fairly random, but most software houses do attach some meaning to the numbers. The number to the left of the decimal point is usually called the major release number, and the one to the right is called the minor release number.

Preliminary releases of new products typically have major release numbers of zero, and minor release numbers indicating the number of versions of the pre-release that have been created. For instance, a version number of 0.14 would indicate that this is the fourteenth iteration of the pre-release software.

These pre-releases are also called *beta* releases, and you might see one if you have volunteered to test a piece of software before it is actually available. Note, therefore, that this is software that the company does not yet consider to be production quality—use at your own risk!

New major release numbers generally indicate that the company has significantly enhanced the product. They sometimes also mean that the files created with the new release are not compatible with previous release levels. For instance, a word processor version 3.4 might not be able to read the files created by version 4.0, but 4.0 probably has a number of helpful features and capabilities that 3.4 lacks.

The minor version number indicates the number of small changes the company has released since the major release. At some companies, the minor release number indicates only bug fixes, not enhancements, but at other companies it indicates small enhancements as well. Check the release data that the company issues to see what types of changes are included.

From this discussion, you can see that a major release number of zero means that the release is test-level software, and a minor release number of zero indicates that the release has new features but possibly no bug fixes.

For this reason, some software advisors tell you to stay completely away from any release that has a zero in the number—wait until the company has had a chance to firm up the software. We won't go quite that far, but we do include the information as a word to the would-be wise.

To protect yourself from unstable first releases, check around before you install. Read what the trade press has to say about the release, check with your contacts on CompuServe or with your local consultant, and ask your dealer what he or she has heard from anyone else who has installed it. Ask your user group, too. If a release has problems, word of mouth usually gets the message out fairly quickly.

Other Types of Upgrades

The preceding discussion applies only to the "new release fever" type of upgrade. All other types are spurred by need; some pressing lack of resources is the only reason you would consider doing all the work upgrades require. In these cases, you've already done the "do we really need this" evaluation and have come up with a resounding YES for an answer. All that remains, then, is implementing the upgrade.

Whether you are adding another disk drive or more RAM to the mail server, installing a whole new mail server, replacing the existing server, or making any other change to the mail system, you can apply the same principles as outlined in the rest of the book. We review them next, with some notes about what's unique to performing upgrades to a running system.

Designing the Upgrade

Chances are that the upgrade requirements are pretty obvious. If your e-mail software allows one post office per server, for instance, and 100 users per post office, and you have 97 users, it's time to add a new server and install a second post office there.

Possibly your upgrade needs are not so clear-cut. Perhaps overall e-mail performance has been slowly declining, or certain parts of the system don't seem to behave as well as others. This is a good time to get out that network map. Spread it out next to your e-mail system and network traffic data, and see if you can figure out where the bottlenecks lie.

Recall from Chapter 10 the description of the network map. Much more than just a layout chart, it details every aspect of the network. You also learned in that chapter how to store network data with the layout information, so that you have only one place to look for the answers to any network questions.

Once again, consider the layout of your network and analyze your traffic patterns against it. After a bit of study, you should easily be able to see the overtaxed parts of the system. This is when you'll really thank yourself for all the careful traffic record keeping you've been doing!

Back to the Test Lab

Okay, you've decided what needs to be done, so you can just sit right down and install the new feature, right? Well, unless the change is extremely small, we don't recommend it. Before you unleash the changes on your hapless users, we suggest you create a test lab again and make sure the new feature works with everything in your system—all servers, workstations, and gateways. You might not find it practical to test every combination in your test lab, but the more testing you do away from the real world, the easier your installation will be.

Remember, there's a tremendous amount of software available today. While your manufacturer has probably tested its software pretty thoroughly, it can't possibly have tested all the different combinations of hardware and software that are likely to occur in the real world. Actually, the chances are extremely good that you will be trying some combination that no one has ever tested before. For these reasons, test every change carefully and approach every new feature with a problem-solving attitude. By planning for trouble you can actually minimize it.

Deployment

Once you're satisfied that the new feature works as you wish, you're ready to bestow it upon your user population. Follow the same steps as before, creating a careful installation plan first. Again, unless the change is quite small, it's really worth the trouble to make a list of everything you need to do and create a schedule for yourself. It seems that it's always the little things that cause problems, and careful planning can keep these from biting you.

Find out when most of your users will not be around, and plan your installation for that time. If this means working another weekend, try to give yourself a day off during the next week. You deserve it!

SUMMARY

A measure of success of your e-mail installation is how fast it grows. As more people start using it and finding more things they can do, your system resources become more and more strained. Finally you can ignore it no longer—you have to expand the system, and this chapter described how to do that in the most efficient and considerate way.

chapter 17

Growth Can Be Painless

Graceful Expansion

We've talked in previous chapters about the tasks required to keep your e-mail system running optimally, from maintenance tasks to replacing and upgrading equipment. These sorts of tasks are part of e-mail administration even if your system never grows at all. It's much more likely that the system will grow, however, and by preparing for that growth you can ensure that it finds you calm and relaxed rather than in a panic.

The possible sources of growth are numerous. For instance, as the company grows, new users will start using the e-mail system. If your early e-mail system serves only a small group within your total organization, you can expect growth to come from other groups in the organization who see the benefits of e-mail and want to join in the fun. Sometimes companies merge, and they must then merge their e-mail systems to ensure good communication throughout the new organization. A more invisible, but significant, source of growth comes with increasing expertise from your current users. As they get more familiar and comfortable with e-mail, they use it more often and for more different purposes, and for that reason alone you might soon need to increase the system capacity.

No matter why you're growing, everything will be easier for you if you anticipate and plan for growth. Throughout the book we've advised you to build growing room into all of your plans. In this chapter we address the matter more directly and offer strategies for coping with various types of growth.

Watching Those Numbers

The first thing you need to know is whether you're growing. Seems obvious, doesn't it? Of course, if you're talking about the number of users, that type of growth is easy to see because you can count them. But other aspects of e-mail system growth are not so obvious, and this is where system monitoring tools will be useful. They can help you track message traffic and disk space consumption, as we discussed in Chapter 15.

We urge you again to take such measurements right after you first install the e-mail system and regularly every month thereafter, so you can see trends as they emerge. After all, it's pretty hard to see when something about your system becomes abnormal if you don't know what normal looks like!

Whether your tracking tools come from the e-mail system itself or you find some third-party solutions to help you make these measurements, it's helpful to know what information you should record. To that end, we suggest that you get in the habit of tracking the following items:

- number of users enabled for e-mail
- number of active users (believe it or not, some users will never touch e-mail!)
- number of messages each user sends per day and week
- number of messages each user receives
- number of messages each user is storing
- number of messages of a particular age, and how much space they consume
- amount of disk space allocated to each user
- amount of disk space each user consumes
- amount of disk space allocated to entire e-mail system

- amount of disk space the entire e-mail system consumes
- total number of messages sent and received, by day and week

Once you gather these numbers, you'll find that charting them with a spreadsheet or graphics package will let your eyes pick out trend lines almost instantly. We also recommend taking averages of individual user statistics for number of messages sent, received, and stored, and for individual storage space consumption as a quick way to determine trending for your e-mail system.

Controlling Disk Usage

The first place you are likely to notice growth is on the mail server's hard disk. As they get used to e-mail, users send more and more messages, but some of these people won't keep their mailboxes tidy despite all your exhortations. If left unchecked, e-mail storage space eventually fills up with old, outdated messages that can choke out the important, timely messages that should be legitimately stored on the server. Your problem is how to tell the difference between these two types of messages, or more generally, how to keep the mail server from getting instantly overrun by its own success.

The Aging Method

We suggest that you use anything that your e-mail package offers to simplify this management task. Many e-mail systems allow you automatically to purge all messages that have specified characteristics. For instance, creation dates can tell the system automatically to delete all messages that are more than three months old. The cut-off period will vary according to your users' needs, but two to three months allows users a reasonable amount of time to process their messages and save any important ones. Some e-mail administrators advise that this period be no longer than one month, as our case studies reveal.

If you do choose this method, keep these suggestions in mind: add a discussion of the purging policy to your training classes, and make sure everyone in the organization knows about them. Nevertheless, don't expect users to remember! Before every purge, send a notice to everyone to inform them that a purge is scheduled, and instruct them to save any messages older than the expiration date that they want to keep. Give at least a couple of days' lead time for everyone to read this notice, and don't forget that traveling employees might need extra time before they can read it.

Finally, always, always, make a backup before purging old messages. We can't emphasize this enough. If you don't have a complete, up-to-date backup of the entire message database when it's time to purge, delay the purge process until you do. Otherwise you risk losing potentially important information forever.

A Storage Area of One's Own

One limitation of the expiration method for controlling disk usage is that users can cheat by simply forwarding messages to themselves indefinitely. Forwarding changes the creation dates of the messages but doesn't reduce server disk consumption. Therefore, another key approach is to limit the amount of space each user's mailbox can occupy. Not all e-mail systems offer this feature, but it can simplify your maintenance life so much that it's worth demanding from any e-mail package you might consider buying. Users generally like this method of space control better, too, because it gives them the power to determine which messages are important to them, rather than forcing them to save important messages before some arbitrary time has elapsed.

Public Storage and Private Storage

Another key concept for all users is the difference between public and private storage space. On a host-based system, for instance, you might already have disk allocations for each user, in addition to any space limitations you choose to impose on e-mail space. Similarly, for a LAN-based e-mail system, the e-mail public storage is on the mail server, and users typically also have private storage on their local PC hard drives. Many e-mail packages allow users to store messages in folders and archives on their local drives or in their private storage areas, thereby easing the burden on the server.

Include in your training classes some time to discuss the distinction between these types of storage, and encourage users to store messages in their private disk space as much as possible. This might be slightly confusing to some users, especially if your package has been designed to be so easy to use that different types of folders and storage mechanisms behave exactly the same, whether on the server or a user's local drive. Nevertheless, it's an important distinction, especially if disk allocations are tight or if you also use a timed purge approach for older messages.

Some Cultural Notes

No matter what type of storage control mechanism you decide to implement, it will be easier for you in the long run if you introduce those controls at the same time you introduce the e-mail system. People will be more resistant to constraints placed on them after they become familiar with their e-mail system; if those constraints are present—and well explained—from the beginning, users might not notice them at all. Several e-mail administrators agree that this is a key factor to success, adding rather ruefully that they wish they'd done so when their systems were first installed.

If you do have to change your message storage rules after introducing an e-mail system, we strongly recommend that you do some prechange training and consensus building. You should also explain as clearly and bluntly as possible why the changes are necessary. This may cause heated discussion in the short run, but will result in better-informed and better-behaved users in the long run. Above all, changes in system policy must not appear inconsiderate or totally arbitrary, lest users reject the system entirely.

Adding New Users

Next to disk space, the most likely cause for growth in your e-mail system will come from adding new users. Several strategies can help this process go smoothly.

First of all, make sure you always have enough copies of the client software for all anticipated new users. This means you need to keep communications open with your personnel department so that you're prepared when any new hire reports for work. Especially if e-mail is important within your organization, any employees who are unable to use it will be isolated from a significant portion of their daily activities while you—and they—wait for the software to arrive.

Since adding users is such a common task, you'll find it helpful to standardize the process as early as possible. You might create a checklist, for instance, to make sure that you don't overlook any steps. As a starting point, every new user needs:

- a network login name
- an e-mail name
- documentation for the network and e-mail system
- training in using the system

New user documentation and training should include not only general points about network and e-mail software, but also any local policies and procedures unique to your installation or organization (purging schedules, or personal communications policies, for instance).

Knowing When to Expand

After reading these warnings about limiting usage, it may seem tempting always to economize on e-mail services and features. Parsimony is usually well-advised, but be sure you know how to recognize false economies.

If your usage data indicates that people are using the e-mail system more not only at peak times (often first thing in the morning and right after lunch) but at non-peak times as well, for instance, or if server space both overall and per user gets crowded, take these as signs that you should consider expanding the e-mail system. Similarly, when you approach the limits of the e-mail package for numbers of users per server or post office, it's time to start thinking about splitting to more post offices.

If you stay on top of usage patterns, you should be able to notice when it's time to expand before your users do. Don't wait until things get unbearably slow to take action! Chapter 26 gives you some more suggestions on how to know when it's time to grow, when you just can't effectively economize any more.

Summary

If you're not ready for it, growth becomes something you have to fight, rather than something you can control and even embrace. It's a tribute to the success of your e-mail system that it grows, and with the tips and techniques in this chapter it will continue to grow smoothly and gracefully. The old Boy Scout motto of "be prepared" applies to e-mail system management, just as it does to so much else in life!

chapter 18

Rules for Keeping Things Running

Small Efforts That Yield Big Rewards

Maintenance is a simple thing that's easy to overlook and even easier to delay. When a system is running flawlessly, it's easy to rationalize that nothing bad will happen if you skip the boring maintenance tasks for another day.

Unfortunately, you're probably right—most likely, nothing bad will happen. We don't call this unfortunate because we want bad things to happen, though! It's unfortunate because every time you skip a maintenance task and the sky doesn't fall, it reinforces skipping maintenance. Take it from those of us who have lived through disk crashes without adequate backups—backups are extremely important, and once you've experienced such a crash you'll never again blow off a backup. Enough people out there have already made this mistake, so we urge you to learn from the failure of others rather than failing to back up yourself!

Maintenance is one good habit to keep your e-mail system in good working order, but it's not the only one. Another dimension of keeping things running is testing, as we explain throughout the book. Every time you make a change to your e-mail system, test it out thoroughly first, just as you did when you first installed the system.

Another good habit is careful user training. Keeping users informed and well trained not only ensures that they are happy with the system but reduces your workload as well, since they're not constantly running to you with questions.

In this chapter we discuss all these aspects of maintaining a happily running system, with some tips on how to make these tasks a little easier on yourself.

SERVER MAINTENANCE

Most e-mail maintenance tasks involve keeping your mail server tidy and efficient, and making sure that if anything happens to it that you can recover with a minimum of trouble. All of these tasks must be performed habitually; otherwise they're useless. Therefore, it's really worth the effort to automate them, either by writing shell scripts or by finding software that can do them all for you or at least remind you when these tasks have to be performed.

Message Purging

If you choose to implement periodic message purges, it's wise to make sure that they happen regularly. That way, your users get in the habit of expecting their messages to disappear after a certain length of time. If you skip message purges sometimes, or do them at varying intervals, users are not going to be as ready for them and something important will probably get deleted. If this happens, of course, their losses will not be a major problem, because you have already learned to back up the entire message database before starting the purge. Haven't you?

Database Compression

Suppose someone sends three messages, each two kilobytes (Kb) long. Then suppose your e-mail system stores them all on the server disk, right next to each other. Now, imagine what happens when the receiver of the second message deletes it. A 2-Kb empty spot is now available on the server, and so that's where the e-mail system places the next message that fits. Suppose this next message happens to be only 1.9-Kb long. The extra 0.1 Kb of space is now unused, and it's unlikely that another message can use such a small space. So that bit of space is wasted. Over time, your e-mail disk space becomes littered with such unusable empty spaces, at which time we say the disk is *fragmented.*

It's not nearly as dire as it sounds, because most e-mail systems have utilities to correct for fragmentation. These tools scan the server disk and move messages around so that they all make the most efficient use of the available space. After defragmenting a badly fragmented disk, you might find you have close to twice as much space available as you did before.

A crowded disk is not only full, it's slow, so defragmenting gives you more room and faster access times. It's easy to see why this is an important maintenance task, and we recommend that you perform it about once a month. If it takes a very long time to run the defragmenter every month (several hours or more), consider running it more often; if it only takes a few minutes, you can probably increase the interval.

Backups

The two most important parts of your e-mail system are the message database and the address list. After all, you can always reinstall the server software if your mail server crashes (though in some cases you have to contact the vendor for permission), but if you have to recreate the message database, things could get sticky.

We can't possibly overemphasize the importance of regular backups. If disaster befalls your server, having a good, recent backup could save the company from huge losses of productivity and will certainly save you a lot of headaches. We'll talk a bit more about backups in the next chapter, when we discuss disasters and recovery.

Record Keeping

Another item to add to your list of regular duties is keeping careful tabs on all aspects of the e-mail system. This means monitoring disk space, message traffic, number of users, and other parameters. See Chapter 23 for a complete list of all the data you should collect.

User Training

It might seem odd to think of training as a maintenance task, but consider what would happen if you didn't train users at all. Everyone would store all their messages on the public storage space, they would store messages on local space only if they stumbled across the method, and worst of all, they'd probably all come to you every time they had a question. You would quickly tire of hearing the same five questions over and over, and might find yourself tearing your hair out over how to control disk consumption.

These users aren't malicious or trying to annoy you, they just need information. We strongly suggest that your training be regular and systematic. Build a set of agendas, one for each level of training, and create summaries that you can hand out both in class and afterwards. At the very least, make sure everyone understands how to make local copies of messages they want to keep, and explain the purge guidelines to them if applicable. Chapter 20 covers all aspects of training, from creating resources to suggested topics.

Address Book Updates

If you have multiple post offices, you instantly run the risk of your address books becoming mismatched. This happens when you add a user to one post office but neglect to add the same user to the other post offices.

Adding users to all post offices at once, every time you add a user anywhere, probably sounds pretty tedious. E-mail system manufacturers realize this, and many offer a utility that automates the process, so that when you add a user to his or her new home post office, that user's address is propagated automatically to all other post offices that you specify.

Another method is to wait until your system has undergone a significant number of changes, then propagate the set of changes to all remote post offices. This works best in cases where the remote users don't log in terribly often, or where the remote users access only a small portion of the address list. Many e-mail systems have tools to facilitate this function.

Test Those Changes

We'll go ahead and take the opportunity to emphasize this one more time: whenever you make a change, test everything it could possibly affect. It's much harder to fix a system that people are trying to use!

When trying to predict what a change might affect, be creative. In fact, it doesn't hurt to try to go to some extremes of what might seem absurd. The annoying thing about incompatibilities and surprise interactions is that whatever doesn't work is probably something you didn't expect and therefore didn't test for. Makes sense—you probably already took care of the things you did expect! The subtle moral of this story is, "Check everything you can think of, but be prepared for the occasional surprise."

Summary

In this chapter we discussed the various tasks required to maintain a happily running system. In the next chapter we examine the consequences of ignoring our advice, or of being surprised by circumstances or lack of foresight, and offer suggestions for dealing with e-mail crises.

chapter 19

Dealing with Disaster

Ready for Anything

Up to this point we've been concentrating on getting your e-mail system running and keeping it running, and we haven't given much thought to catastrophic failures. But planning for disaster is just as much a part of your e-mail administration job as dealing with system's installation and operation details. In a sense, once e-mail is running, a major part of your job is devoted to disaster preparation. After all, that's what backups are for.

If a disaster of some type does befall your e-mail system, the only thing that can ensure its recovery is some foresight on your part. If you haven't made recent backups, and stored them offsite, your only alternative is to rebuild the entire e-mail system by hand, from user messages to the address list to the routing database. Doing so is extremely tedious, time consuming, and nearly impossible to complete, since you'll be working from memory.

A quick definition here: we're defining a disaster as anything that renders your e-mail system unusable. It could be fire, flood or earthquake, or something less dire but just as fatal to the e-mail system, like a crashed disk drive or an irretrievably corrupted message database. (This last one shouldn't ever happen—if it does, consider changing e-mail software after you recover your messages!)

Since we've shown that backups are the only way to ensure that you can recover from such disasters, a big part of this chapter is devoted to the topic of backups, including how to make them and what to do with them. While there is a certain cost inherent in any maintenance task such as backups, the costs associated with trying to recreate an e-mail system by hand are even greater and will always occur under the most difficult circumstances imaginable.

Prevention First

When planning your backup strategy, the first question to ask yourself is this: if you lost your hard drive to some disaster, what information would you need to have on hand in order to rebuild the entire message, routing, and address databases? Think about the information your e-mail servers use to communicate with each other, as well as the users' message storage and the address lists. Remember the information stored on different servers, and any routing databases that your gateway software requires.

Don't forget your network map! We describe this creature in depth in Chapter 10, as one of the primary tools for e-mail system design (and in our book, *Network Design Essentials*, as a major tool for building networks in general). If some dire event destroyed your entire e-mail system, your network map—both layout and database—would be indispensable to recreating the system.

The Art of Backups

The most important feature of any backup plan is regularity. Since people are prone to forgetfulness or even laziness, it's a very good idea to automate backups of the e-mail system as much as possible. By installing some type of scheduled backup automation software on your e-mail server, or even writing a backup script if your system is a simple one, you can use the fundamental truth that computers are much better at boring, regularly occurring tasks than people are to your best possible advantage.

How Often Should You Back Up?

At least once a week back up everything in your list of critical files, including the entire message database, the address list, and the routing databases on every mail server in your e-mail system. If yours is a very active mail system with lots of crucial information on it, you'll want to back up more often, perhaps even daily.

When trying to decide what backup frequency is right for your needs, just imagine the worst scenario possible and calculate the trade-off costs to your organization. That is, compare how much effort and time it takes to perform each backup against how much data and time you can afford to lose. If the loss of a single day's messages would not cost your company a lot of productivity—or cost you your job—then go ahead and only do the backups every other day. Just make sure you know the potential costs!

It's not always necessary to perform full backups every time you back up your e-mail system. Most backup software allows you to perform partial backups, which means that you back up only those files that have changed since the last full backup. Partial backups are handy because they complete much more quickly than full backups, but you need both for total coverage. A common compromise is to perform full backups once a week, supplemented by daily partial backups.

Reusing Backup Media

Another important backup trick is knowing how to rotate backup media. For this discussion we'll assume you're using tapes for backups, but the same discussion applies to sets of diskettes, removable hard drives, or rewritable optical disks. At first thought, it might seem reasonable to use the same tape over and over for every backup, constantly writing over the previous backup. After all, the only important backup is the most recent one, right? Well, yes, but consider the worst case again: what if lightning strikes the building during the backup, the drive head scrapes across the drive, and the system becomes unable to reboot? Not only have you lost your disk drive, you've lost your only backup.

For this reason (and reasons less catastrophic, of course), we recommend rotating tapes. Avoid reusing a tape until you are certain that you have at least one good backup on another tape. Many installations rotate more than one tape at a time, and some have as many as ten sets of media so that they always have at least nine usable backups in storage.

Many folks also make a habit of creating one backup every month or so that they never reuse, which enables them to store periodic snapshots of the e-mail system. This strategy can be very useful if you ever need to go back and find a message or address list that has long since been deleted from the mail server. On the other hand, evaluate whether the costs of doing this make it worthwhile for your organization. If users have data that they think they will need to access in the future but that does not need to remain on the server at present, they should arrange to store that data in separate backups from the maintenance backup set.

Get Those Backups Out of Here!

Consider what happens if a fire or some other catastrophe destroys not only your e-mail server but your building as well. Maybe you've been making perfectly regular backups every day, but if you store them in the same building along with the e-mail system, they might as well not exist at all.

This is why many organizations store their backup media somewhere off their premises. Your organization should already be doing this for its LAN backup media, so you may be able to take advantage of an arrangement that is already in place. Most cities have services that allow you to rent space in fireproof vaults for your business records, and some even have courier services. They'll figure out which tape is next in your rotation, deliver it to your building, and take the previous day's backup away with them.

If you work with an outside service, you'll always have at least one backup off the premises. Meeting that service's pickup schedule for tapes can help keep you honest on your backup schedule, too! Look in the telephone directory under "Office Records Stored" for such services in your city, inquire at a users' group, or ask your colleagues at other organizations in your area. If you can't afford a courier service or the rental of offsite storage, at least get in the habit of taking home a full set of backup tapes once a week.

Test Those Backups

Testing is always easy to ignore, but before you ignore our injunction to test your backup system, let us tell you a story: an administrator we know had a simple change to make to the network server. Since the change was so simple, he didn't bother making a backup before shutting down the server (thereby breaking the first cardinal rule of network backups!). He made the change and booted the server back up—but it didn't boot. Something had happened to the server hard drive and nothing he did could repair it.

Even at this point he wasn't too worried, because he had recent backups, a full backup from a few days before and partial backups from each day since. So he set about restoring the network server from the backups, something he had never done before. By this time it was very late at night and he was tired and probably a little nervous, as you might imagine. We assume he was reading the restoration instructions, but all the same, something went wrong. Not only was he unable to restore the server drive, but he ended up destroying the backups as well.

Of course, this is an extreme case. But wouldn't you feel a lot better knowing that if a disaster ever did strike, you'd have some idea of what to do? By testing your backups in a low-pressure setting you give yourself the advantage of knowing that one more thing is within your control. That extra confidence can be worth a lot when you're under the stress of recovering from a crashed system!

If Disaster Does Strike

Should some catastrophe befall your e-mail server, your plan of attack will depend largely on the type of trouble involved. If the hard drive on your system crashes, you'll need to replace the drive before you can do anything else, and perhaps work with MIS or the LAN administrator to reinstall the base system software, if yours is not a dedicated mail server. In the case of a fire or other destructive event, you may have to rebuild the entire network completely (and you'll be really glad that you stored a copy of the network map offsite with your backups!).

Once the server is back up and running, use your backups to restore the message, address, and routing databases from your most recent full backup. Add on any incremental backups, according to the instructions for your backup software. If you're lucky, that's all you'll have to do!

In some cases, a server's name or network address after recovery could be different from the old server's. If so, you'll have to complete a few more tasks, and your foresight will really pay off here. First off, you'll have to make sure your on-site users' client software reflects this new information, or they won't be able to use e-mail at all. Some e-mail systems let you broadcast such changes, but some will require you to distribute this new information forcibly to each user. Whatever it takes to get e-mail running is what you'll have to do.

Also, all your external users—employees with laptops and remote access, or third-party vendors or contractors with dial-in or internetwork access to your e-mail—and all remote systems will need to recognize the new server name or address. For internetworks, e-mail service advertisements are most often handled electronically, and you should be able to get the new server incorporated without too much fuss by simply updating the post office list or lists.

But for external users, it's not good form to update other organizations' configurations or even their software. Therefore, you'll need to send them an e-mail message or a paper form letter that explains any changes so they, too, can get back into their mail. If you have to send an actual letter, use the diskette you have offsite which contains all external addresses.

Summary

The only sure way to be ready for disaster is to plan for it by considering everything you would need to recover your e-mail system if disaster did strike. This chapter discussed what types of things you should consider during disaster planning and offered some tips for recovery if something really bad does happen.

chapter 20

Training Users

Spreading the Word

Your new e-mail system won't get much use if your users don't know what they can do with it, or if they're intimidated by how little they know about it. Once it's installed, your next big challenge is to start teaching everyone how to use it. In this chapter we tell you how to go about meeting and besting that challenge!

Training Resources

With a little luck and a moderately well known e-mail package, you can probably obtain training materials from a number of different sources. The place to start, of course, is with the vendor manuals, or whatever documentation comes with your system. You might have to distill this information into a format suitable for training, but in some cases the vendor might even offer a line of training documents—it doesn't hurt to ask.

Another source of information can come from third-party books and documentation. Every major computer bookstore has a selection of books specifically geared to each of the most popular e-mail packages; you may be able to find something about your package in that collection. Some are even organized in tutorial format, which is ideal for training.

This is a good time to find your local e-mail user group and introduce yourself. These people are organized to help each other, and they're there to help you, too. Ask around to see how they handled training for their own users; you might get some good tips. (We don't want to suggest that you can get something for nothing from them. Many user groups charge a small membership fee to cover operating expenses, and they're usually worth it.)

The next step is to identify which training topics are unique to your installation and to create training materials about them. This could include forms for internal use, an unusual gateway mechanism, or anything else that only you and the people at your site would know. You'll have to create these materials yourself; but if you've followed our earlier recommendations and documented everything, you'll have a great base of information to draw from!

The Ideal Training Environment

People learn best by doing, so give everyone an opportunity to try out the features of the e-mail system if at all possible. Remember that test lab you set up before you installed the system? Perhaps you can scavenge those computers now so that users can get some hands-on experience during training.

One advantage of using your test network for training is that it need not be connected to the rest of the network, thus users won't have to worry about making mistakes. The very first thing every new user seems to do is reply to a message by sending the response to everyone in the company instead of replying only to the sender. If you can help your users get this out of their systems in an isolated environment, you'll probably reduce the amount of junk e-mail on your network significantly!

Depending on the size of your user base, you might find it helpful to group users according to experience. Creating two classes should do the trick, one for users who are familiar with e-mail but new to this package, and one for users who are completely new to e-mail. A third class might make sense, too, for users who have used your package before—you just need to inform them of the aspects unique to your local installation and the company policies governing e-mail. You might even be able to cover this in a short written document, without having to give this group a formal class at all.

Suggested Training Topics

The remainder of this chapter lists the key topics that every e-mail user should know and every e-mail class should include. Besides the basics of sending and receiving e-mail and dealing with e-mail messages, classes should also cover e-mail etiquette, privacy issues, and efficiency tips. If you have created some features unique to your system, the user class is the time to discuss those as well.

This list is not exhaustive, of course; you'll want to let your own e-mail system and local usage habits guide the content of your classes. Furthermore, the content of the class will probably evolve as you learn what features people use most often and what issues are most difficult to grasp.

If you have access to a user group for your e-mail system, or if you know someone else who is already using it, ask which features people use most often. Software users typically use only a small percentage of the total number of features in a product, so you can save yourself and your users a lot of time by finding out what these features are and training only on them.

Start with the Basics

Every user needs to know the elementary operations on the e-mail system: how to send a simple text message, how to read a message someone has sent, how to delete a message, and how to forward a message.

More advanced topics include copying messages, sending attachments (such as word processing documents or spreadsheets), and receiving and using these attached files.

At this level you might also include a discussion of the notification feature if your package has it. Note that such a feature can use a significant amount of system resources (both memory and computation power, especially in less powerful systems), so your users should know how to turn off the feature if they wish.

Advanced Topics

Once users are comfortable with sending and receiving messages, they're ready to start learning the more sophisticated features of the package. If your e-mail system offers scheduling capabilities or has built-in support for electronic forms, consider setting up an advanced class or two for interested users. If your company relies heavily on these features, you need to train everyone how to use them eventually, but we don't recommend that you try to teach it all in one class. Just as you did when installing the system, approach training in steps.

Local Specialties

Some e-mail packages offer a bulletin board feature, enabling users to post messages for everyone to see. In some cases these bulletin boards are visible to all users; in other packages, users can select which ones they want to see and ignore the rest. We've seen them used for everything from an electronic secondhand shop to announcing new users or network maintenance times. They can be very useful. If your package offers such a feature and you plan to use it, take some time before training begins to consider how you want to organize such message boards and what policies you need to govern their use.

If you are using a forms-based messaging system, have a list of all the internal forms for the organization. Be ready to discuss each one in the training class, and offer users tips to help them fill out and deliver the forms properly.

Maintenance

Users need to understand the importance of keeping mailboxes tidy. It doesn't sound important until the e-mail system has been in place for a few months and users have hundreds of old messages in their mailboxes. A little prevention is definitely worth the trouble.

If applicable, make sure users understand the difference between storing messages on the mail server and storing them on their local hard drives or in their local file storage areas. In some packages, it's possible to create lots of well-organized folders on the mail server, which keeps user mailboxes tidy but does nothing to help keep server disk use down.

You may choose to impose disk quotas on users. If you do so, be sure they know what the limits are and how to keep usage within those limits. If you choose to limit space by periodically purging old messages to tape, make sure everyone understands when messages expire and how to access purged messages if necessary. Assure them that you back up everything regularly (and make sure that you do!).

Etiquette and Advice

Electronic mail is a new medium with its own set of risks and peculiarities. If everyone observes a few simple guidelines, the introduction and use of e-mail will be much more pleasant and productive. Ahead are our recommendations to help your users skirt some of the most common e-mail pitfalls.

Don't Shout, We Can Hear You

Avoid writing in all capital letters—it's the electronic equivalent of SHOUTING and is also harder to read than mixed case.

It's Possible to Be Too Creative with Color

Here's another point in the ease-of-reading department. Some packages allow you to change the foreground and background colors of your messages. If you take advantage of this feature, select colors that are easy on the eyes—blue and white or yellow and black instead of fuchsia and green. If you opt for exotic color combinations, your message could get lost in the glare, and people with certain types of color blindness might not be able to read it at all.

Avoid Flaming

In the electronic world, it's sometimes easy to forget that there's another human being on the other end of the message. When you write a message in the heat of annoyance or anger, the message is called a *flame,* and such a message can be a lot more cutting than the same words spoken aloud. Think very carefully before you send a message; once it's sent, it can haunt its sender forever.

Urgency Overload

Some packages have a feature that allows you to designate priorities to messages, from Low (which nobody ever uses) to Urgent, which gets used a lot. Use this feature sparingly, and remember that everything is urgent when you're the sender. Think about it—if it's really urgent, shouldn't you phone, rather than risking that the recipient won't see the message for an hour or more?

Limit Receiver Lists

It's tempting to send copies of every memo to everyone who might be remotely interested, especially if you've ever annoyed someone by inadvertently omitting him or her from a list. Try to balance this tendency; if you just clutter up everybody's mailboxes, you are not advancing the cause of better communications.

Big Files and Remote Users Don't Mix

You have just completed the new brochure design, so you mail an electronic copy to everyone on the project team. One of the team members is traveling this week, and she dials in from her hotel room to the home system to get her e-mail. Presently your 1.2-Mb file appears, and you have just increased the company's long-distance telephone bill by quite a bit.

Some e-mail systems let remote users select which files to retrieve, but many don't. Make sure that all your recipients of large files are local, or really need the file. Alternatively, instead of sending the graphics or other large file to everyone, send a short note indicating where they can retrieve it, or offer to send it by request.

Double-Check that Reply List

As we observed previously, the first thing many new users do is reply to a message by sending the response to everyone in the company instead of just the sender. This is at best annoying to the receivers who have to delete messages that do not interest them, and is at worst very embarrassing to the sender, depending on the reply's contents.

This is particularly likely to happen in response to broadcast messages. For instance, the department manager might send a message to the whole department saying, "Everyone who wants to attend the luncheon please reply to me." The department members dutifully reply,

"Yes, I'll be there." The problem is that many e-mail systems automatically send replies to everyone on the original list—the users have to limit the list by hand.

Unfortunately, this mistake is not the sole domain of new users—even seasoned users slip up sometimes. Encourage everyone to double-check their response lists before sending replies, to minimize junk mail and embarrassment.

Don't Get Personal!

Because it's so easy to copy and send, e-mail moves fast and goes everywhere. We heard about a meeting where some people harshly criticized an absent colleague. The notes about the meeting went from one party to another, were copied all over the region, and within a day ended up by accident in that person's mailbox.

Believe us, this is not uncommon. Our advice: don't send anything you wouldn't want your best friend, your boss, or your mother to see. Assume that the message will go instantly to the worst possible recipient, and act accordingly. You could save yourself a lot of grief.

Save a Copy

E-mail makes it supremely easy to document your correspondence. Most e-mail systems allow you to save copies of everything you send, sometimes automatically and this can be a very useful feature. We also recommend that you save copies of important notes you receive. Believe us, all of this record keeping could come in handy someday.

The Company Line

The training class is also the place to discuss the company's e-mail policy. Inform users of the company's stance on personal messages and e-mail privacy. If the company routinely monitors e-mail traffic, the courts (in the United States, at least) require that the company inform employees of the practice beforehand.

The Electronic Messaging Association offers a kit to help companies formulate e-mail policies. It discusses privacy issues and gives some sample policy statements, and is available for $45 in the United States. For information on contacting this association, see the Resource Guide in Appendix D.

Summary

Training is a crucial part of your e-mail installation, and in this chapter we analyzed the factors that can make it a success. We discussed where to get training materials, how to organize your training environment most effectively, and what to teach the users. Your e-mail system is a unique combination of features in your e-mail package and local customization, and good training courses cover them all.

PLANNING FOR THE FUTURE

THINKING EVEN FURTHER AHEAD

Throughout this part of the book, and indeed throughout the whole book, we keep harping on planning. We do this to get you in the habit of thinking not only about what's happening on your network at present, but about how today's tasks can benefit you—and your users—tomorrow and in the years to come. By learning to think this way you can make the most of your e-mail resources, and with every change build your system toward a goal, rather than always fighting fires. It's always more efficient to solve two problems with one solution, but of course you can't make choices that satisfy both current needs and future plans if you don't have any future plans!

Only by thoroughly informing yourself can you know what types of plans to make. You need to know as much as possible about the industry's planned solutions, although that software may be pure vapor at the moment. Even if the software you're looking at exists only in the minds of its marketing executives, knowing what's behind the industry's promises and vaporware is useful. The set of all such planned products shows you trends in the industry, which can give you ideas about the types of solutions your organization might want to implement in the future.

Whenever you're making plans for the future of your e-mail system, remember that the most important consideration is your user base. No matter how popular, fashionable, or even useful a new product is to others, it's useless if your users don't need it. For this reason, you need to know not only what the industry is up to but also the details of what your users are up to. The more you know about your organization's business and work styles, the better you'll be able to select and implement helpful new messaging software.

Read, Read, Read

The easiest way to stay on top of what's going on the industry is to subscribe to one or two industry periodicals. You might want to select one that addresses general computing issues, and another that is specifically targeted to your particular installation type. The general-purpose publications include *LAN Times*, *ComputerWorld*, and *NetworkWorld*, to name only a few. Note that these types of periodicals are dense sources of information and that many of them appear weekly. You may find that you have to develop some new skimming skills to keep this research task from devouring large chunks of your time!

A visit to any big computer bookstore will show you that the number of computing-related magazines is too great for us to mention them all here. You'll also very likely find that there is a periodical devoted just to your network type, or to the type of operating system running on your workstations. Either of these types of magazines offer clues to future trends, as well as tips on current matters.

For another point of view, talk to other e-mail users. Go to your user group meetings—these are great places to meet people who have implemented unusual combinations of messaging software, and often such groups invite speakers who have special knowledge about new or emerging technologies.

What to Watch For

We talked a bit about groupware in Chapter 3 when we described the larger world of which e-mail is just a part. You can expect that the distinction between types of groupware will blur as we see the merger of message-based applications, forms capabilities, scheduling programs, and conferencing software. All of these types of applications mean increased message traffic in your e-mail system and may even mean that you have to change the current e-mail system in order to support them.

Another emerging area is the long-promised paperless office. Most of us have noticed that there's a lot more paper in most offices with the increased use of computers, but moving in the other direction remains a goal for many software companies. To that end, manufacturers are developing image-based forms systems in which forms simply travel between workstations over the network, and paper versions of the forms need never exist at all. If a form does not yet have an electronic version, a user can convert it using a device called a scanner. Some such systems propose that even signatures be electronic—using a stylus—you could sign a contract without ever picking up a pen. Acceptance of documents signed this way is likely to be slow, though, since the ease of making electronic copies raises some authenticity issues.

Image-reliant applications could really tax your system resources because they could lead not only to increased message traffic but also to much larger messages. Graphical representations of documents take up a lot more room than text versions, so if you want to implement a system like this you might have to increase network bandwidth as well as disk space on the mail server and workstations.

From electronic inventory and order forms to catalogs on CD-ROM, e-mail and messaging are also changing the nature of intercompany communications. You might find yourself sending a message to one vendor requesting a shipment of office supplies, then responding to another message by issuing an order to deliver product literature to a customer, all electronically. Some companies already have such systems in place, and more are following suit every day.

How to Get Ready

Only you can predict what your organization will need in the future, because no one else knows how your company does business or the specific data it needs to manipulate. With this information, coupled with your detailed understanding of your current e-mail capabilities and an idea about what the industry is planning, you can start laying the groundwork for a messaging system that will grow with your company's expanding operations.

If you think it's likely that your organization will have significantly increased message traffic within the first two years after installation, it behooves you to lay the foundation for that future system at the beginning. It's more likely, though, that your e-mail system will grow more slowly, so your best bets are to install expandable bandwidth and an expandable e-mail system.

To get some ideas about which e-mail systems are likely to be expandable, watch which vendors form alliances. You might find that it's a good idea to make your migration choices based on which vendors seem to be working closely with those whose products you plan eventually to adopt, but keep in mind that the world of messaging software, and especially that thing loosely called groupware, is very new and constantly changing. If a decision comes down to a choice between a vendor who appears to be headed in the same direction as your company and one that definitely suits your organization's needs today, opting for the latter is your safest short- and long-term solution.

Summary

When planning for e-mail's future in your organization, your best bet is to get as much information as possible and to keep yourself informed. By studying the way your organization works and the plans it has for the future, you can retain some focus as you try to work your way through the haze of the industry's promised and planned products. One thing's absolutely certain: the tools, the technology, the software, and the users will all keep changing!

part

III

Rules of Thumb

By now, you should be familiar with the procedures and practices for running an e-mail system, as well as with the underlying concepts and components involved in using e-mail. We sincerely hope that you've acquired an appreciation for the ordinary activities involved in feeding and caring for an e-mail system and its users and that you've also learned how very extraordinary the job of a network administrator can occasionally be, especially when it comes to managing e-mail.

This book has tried to acquaint you with the value of e-mail technology, but in the context of how to make it work to the benefit of your users and your organization. At this point, you should have some idea about how to design an e-mail system, how to ensure that one can be put in place, and what to do with it when you've got one.

You should also have an idea about how to document what's out there on your network (or at least what's planned to be out there), including e-mail. Armed with this information, you've also learned about how to plan for growth, about how to budget for installation or growth, and how to spend money and hire talent to help you do what needs to be done with your e-mail system. You've also learned to anticipate the new products and technologies that e-mail will inevitably bring, but to look with a jaundiced eye at vendors who promise you the world.

If any of this material sounds unfamiliar or strange, dig back into the chapters in Parts I and II and refresh your memory. At this point in the book, we've covered all of the material that we feel is needed for a general book on designing and running an e-mail system. This section is devoted to a collection of rules of thumb and includes checklists, how-tos, gotchas, and other information, organized around specific topics or activities that you will encounter as you confront your e-mail system. Use it as a reference tool before you go out to tackle the system, or as a guide back into Parts I and II. We hope you find it informative and useful!

Principles of Effective E-mail

Mastering Naming Conventions

Establishing and using a workable convention for e-mail names are among the best things you can do for yourself as an e-mail administrator. Building such a convention can be time consuming. At first, it might even seem like a waste of effort, especially if your organization is small and informal.

However, the naming scheme that you adopt, even if it's only a common default (the most common example for small groups is to use first names only), will set the standard for how well your e-mail system can change and grow over time. Even though it may seem like massive overkill, we strongly suggest starting from (or even building) an organizational chart, and deriving your naming scheme from a combination of that chart, plus an understanding of how X.400 naming actually works. For a quick refresher on this topic, please consult Chapter 11.

While a three- or four-part (or perhaps even longer) e-mail name may seem daunting, remember that you can define short name equivalents, called *aliases*, for your users' convenience. It may be that only you as the e-mail administrator will ever know that underneath the apparent naming convention lies a full-blown X.400 skeleton, but it may be that your company decides to go global at some point, or merges with or is acquired by a larger, more complex organization. At that time, your planning will pay off, and you'll be able to move your users into the new regime with aplomb and éclat.

Some Common Naming Conventions

Okay, so you may or may not buy off on the need to go through the org chart to X.400 naming exercise we recommend. Even so, you still won't be able to avoid the naming game altogether, no matter what type of e-mail system you adopt or use. To that end, we'd like to review a handful of common naming schemes in regular use, to give you some realistic choices for naming that have stood the test of large numbers of reluctant users around the country and around the world. We'll also try to point out strengths and weaknesses of each approach, along with potential gotchas.

- First name, last initial
  Description: user's first name plus initial from last name.
  Examples: "edt" for Ed Tittel, "margaretr" for Margaret Robbins.
  Pros: simple, easy, informal, fairly short.
  Cons: frequent name conflicts, "nickname" versus real name issues, length variability, best for small user communities.
  Gotchas: growth will require this scheme to be completely abandoned and replaced with another. This can be disconcerting for users. Also, resolving name conflicts will force some users to use unnatural names for themselves.

- First initial, last name
  Description: user's first initial plus last name.
  Examples: "etittel" for Ed Tittel, "mrobbins" for Margaret Robbins.
  Pros: simple, easy, usually short, works for large and small organizations.
  Cons: requires access to users' full names, some name conflicts (for common names like "Bob Jones" and "Jim Smith"), some length problems for long surnames (e.g., "Wickramanayake" or hyphenated names like "Worthington-Jones").
  Gotchas: growth will require this scheme to be altered, usually with multiple initials for common names (e.g., "jrsmith" and "jssmith"), and abbreviations for long surnames. This can be disconcerting for both senders and recipients.

- Initials plus department code
  Description: user's initials (usually 2 or 3) plus a short department code (2–3 characters).
  Examples: "etmkt" for Ed Tittel (in marketing), "mreng" for Margaret Robbins (in engineering).
  Pros: simple, short, logical, very limited name conflicts, works best for large organizations.
  Cons: requires access to users' full names, nonintuitive, requires establishing and maintaining a list of broadly available department codes.
  Gotchas: this scheme is easy for users' own assigned names, but hard for others' names. It demands a directory database, or a printed directory, to let users find e-mail names for intended recipients.

- Location code plus username
  Description: any of the naming schemes above, with the addition of a location code, usually at the head of the e-mail name.
  Examples: "a-etittel" for Ed Tittel (in Austin), "a-mrobbins" for Margaret Robbins (in Austin).
  Pros: simple, logical, limited name conflicts, works best for large multisite organizations.
  Cons: requires access to users' full names and locations, nonintuitive, requires establishing and maintaining a list of broadly available location codes, in addition to understanding the underlying naming convention.
  Gotchas: this scheme is easy for users' own assigned names, but hard for others' names. It demands a directory database, or a printed directory, to let users find e-mail names for intended recipients.

The criteria you'll use to select a naming convention will depend on several factors. These will include the size and composition of your organization, expectations regarding growth and expansion, and finally, the amount of time you can devote to maintaining the naming infrastructure.

Of the four schemes just listed, we recommend you try the "first initial, last name" scheme first—it's the most commonly used by far and should work for most organizations. Limitations on e-mail name lengths in some systems may force truncation of e-mail names because of surname lengths, but these truncated names still work in most cases. For convenience, we recommend that you consider limiting e-mail name lengths to six or eight characters anyway, or that you buy an e-mail package that supports aliases (which will invariably be short and sweet).

Do the "Directory Thing"

A common rhetorical question is "What's in a name?" For e-mail, the answer is "everything." At least everything that's typically needed for correct delivery of e-mail messages, that is.

That means your users need some way to ferret out the e-mail names for everybody in your organization (and most likely for the contractors, consultants, vendors, and whoever else from outside the company that may also be using your e-mail system). If you can handle the ongoing commitment this will entail, there's no better solution than an e-mail name database, because it will let users look up names through a variety of search techniques—last name, first name, organizational unit, telephone number, etc.—to get the addresses of the individuals they need.

Such a database works very much like a telephone directory, except it must provide e-mail names as well. Many companies that publish internal directories are starting to include e-mail names along with all the other information they list for each entry. If your organization already offers an internal directory, find out who maintains and publishes it, and ask if you can provide e-mail names to add to each entry.

Better still, an on-line database with search capabilities will let users interact with the same information in a much more accessible and up-to-date form. It's a sad truism that a directory is obsolete the day after it's published in many organizations; an on-line database can be updated on demand, ensuring that only the most current information is provided to your users.

When considering a database management system (DBMS) for e-mail directory use, it's wise to consider the following issues:

- The DBMS needs to be accessible from all of the platforms in use in your organization (the more platforms you use, the lower the number of options and, typically, the greater the expense involved).
- The DBMS needs to be readily accessible to the whole user community and provide speedy response to search requests. It will probably become one of the most heavily used programs in your organization, no matter what its size or complexity.

- The e-mail directory database should be available in a standalone, static form as well as interactively available. This will let remote users download copies and use them on the road or out of the office, when a dial-up interactive connection might not be feasible or too expensive.
- The DBMS should be able to support the definition, maintenance, and use of distribution lists as well as individual user's e-mail names. Managing such lists can otherwise become a major time drain (see the case studies in Chapters 30 and 31 for some examples). Database systems usually offer programming and scripting tools that can help to automate and speed up list handling.

Today, only a small number of e-mail packages come with built-in directory database or, better still, directory service access capabilities. We predict that this number will grow and that this practice will become the norm, especially as full-blown directory services become more commonplace in the networking world.

Spreading the Word: Advertising E-mail's Capabilities

Most users have no trouble grasping the basic capabilities of e-mail for sending and receiving text messages. They also quickly realize the benefits of using mail message attachments to send files, either individually or in groups, to one another. But they may not immediately grasp some of the other useful applications for e-mail in general, and for message-based applications in particular.

What's the solution? In a phrase, "It pays to advertise," that is, you must be prepared to supply examples and demonstrations of the other things that e-mail can do in order to get users ready to take advantage of them. We cover the related activity of user training, which can also address this topic, in Chapters 20 and 29, but you'll want to make sure to reach even that audience that doesn't make it to your brown-bag seminars or other training sessions.

For example, many companies are turning to e-mail for document and news delivery services. With the right e-mail server on the network, all a user has to do to get an electronic copy of any document you might care to distribute is to send a message to a particular address, whose subject field contains the name of the document to be sent in reply. By regularly distributing an e-mail message that includes the following information, you can successfully advertise this service and, hopefully, improve the delivery of information to your colleagues and co-workers:

- the e-mail name of the news/document server
- an annotated list of document names, with accompanying descriptions
- a sample message, with the subject field filled in, just to make things clear

If you can send the advertisement from the news/document server itself, users wishing to obtain news or documents need only use the e-mail Reply option with the subject field properly filled out to get the information they need.

Other possible uses of basic e-mail include text-based database forms. These can be set up to correspond to common paperwork items for your organization. By addressing them to a front-end program that knows how to interpret the message formats and convert them into database records, even terminal and DOS users can supply the equivalent of all kinds of electronic forms via e-mail. GUI-based users on Windows, Macintosh, or UNIX will probably be able to interact with visual representations of those forms on-screen, making the process even easier for them (for more discussion of this topic, read the case study in Chapter 32 on MD Anderson).

Whatever leverage your e-mail system might be able to supply, it won't be able to do so unless you advertise its capabilities to your users. Thus, the bottom line is to make sure you send them e-mail that explains whatever features and functions you want them to use. These topics should also be covered in training sessions, just to make sure your audience knows how to get the best from your e-mail environment.

The Electronic "Paper Trail"

Once e-mail comes into common, widespread use it will also become the medium for the exchange of all kinds of important information, ranging from funds transfers to personnel actions to all kinds of other important and sensitive information. For many users, the temptation to commit this information to paper is nearly irresistible. For others, the temptation to use the e-mail system as a form of "electronic records warehouse" is equally tempting.

Each approach, however, is fraught with potential problems: those who commit their important information to paper will have to accommodate it in a physical filing system of some kind, while those who leave it in the e-mail archives risk losing access to that information as files age their way off your on-line storage systems. For both cases, the solution is to encourage users to save copies of important messages electronically, but outside the e-mail system. That way, they can continue to access the information on-line without having to consume precious e-mail space allocations.

As messages age beyond usefulness (which ranges from one to three years, or beyond, depending on governmental or organizational retention criteria) they can be archived electronically on a backup medium of some kind. If you can work with your users to identify information that might have to be resuscitated someday, you can provide records of which archived information lives where. This will keep the chances of bringing old files and documents back to life good for a long time without having to keep all that information on-line for the foreseeable future.

One thing we learned in our case studies was that space consumption for e-mail messages is a chronic problem. We recommend that you work with your management and user community to devise an archiving and retrieval scheme that is usable, and that you keep on-line holdings to the barest acceptable minimum. Otherwise, you, your users, and your e-mail servers, may shortly find yourselves drowning in outdated e-mail messages.

Privacy and Control: Is E-mail Personal or Not?

Another thing we learned in our case studies of e-mail usage and from our surveys of common industry practice regarding e-mail is that e-mail in the workplace is hardly ever considered to be completely personal. Nor can it be regarded as completely confidential, either. Most organizations regard their e-mail systems as fundamental business tools, and the contents and use of that system as a business matter. This means your users must understand that e-mail messages are a matter of potentially public record.

According to the Electronic Messaging Association (EMA), the following parties have a stake in establishing responsible policies regarding access to and disclosure of company electronic mail:

- the employer
- the employees
- third parties (who use the e-mail system)
- law enforcement authorities (to investigate crimes, civil matters, or other legal issues for which e-mail may provide evidence)
- electronic communications service providers (where they supply some or all of the e-mail services in use)

Surprisingly, there is no legal right to privacy for communications in the workplace, except in some states, such as California, where some limited privacy rights have been established, or where collective bargaining or employment practices provide such rights. Then, too, there are potentially adverse legal liability issues and tax consequences that pertain to allowing employees to use e-mail systems for personal purposes.

The bottom line is that a clear policy on e-mail access, contents, and usage can protect both employers and employees. The safest assumption is that the contents of any e-mail message are neither personal nor private but a form of public business communication that belongs to the employer. Typically, employees are prohibited from using e-mail for personal uses, or at least must waive privacy protection for such use.

If it sounds like this is a tricky area, that's definitely the case. The EMA has published a white paper entitled "Access to and Use and Disclosure of Electronic Mail on Company Computer Systems: A Tool Kit for Formulating Your Company's Policy." We strongly recommend that you obtain a copy, if only to educate yourself about the potential issues involved. You can request a copy from the EMA by sending a request using one of the following contact points:

- By Telephone: 703-524-5550
- By Fax: 703-524-5558
- By Snail Mail:
  Electronic Messaging Association
  1655 North Fort Meyer Drive, Suite 850
  Arlington, VA 22209

- Via E-mail:
  EasyLink, Envoy 100, GEnie, MCI Mail, Pacific Bell, SprintMail: EMA
  AT&TMail: !EMA
  CompuServe: 70007,2377
  Dialcom: 52:PRD003
  IBM Mail Exchange: USEMA001 at IBMMAIL
  For information on X.400 or Internet addresses, contact EMA by phone.

As you'd expect, EMA offers a wide range of e-mail contacts (and obviously has lots of e-mail gateways in place).

Summary

Effective use of e-mail depends on broad availability, easy access, and guaranteed delivery of messages to recipients. If you work to provide access to the e-mail system, and make it easy for users to send and receive e-mail, the system will be used and perhaps even appreciated. The keys to success lie in making users available to each other, as well as providing the kinds of e-mail services they need. In this chapter we established some broad guidelines for naming schemes, advertising services, and e-mail usage that should help you realize these goals.

chapter 23

E-MAIL ESSENTIALS

SELECTING E-MAIL FEATURES AND FUNCTIONS

Today's e-mail packages come with more features and functions than you can shake a stick at. What we try to do in this section is to review as complete a set as possible, while sticking to the only two groups we think are worth considering:

- Essential, must-have features: no e-mail system should be without these.
- Nice to have but not essential features: they're not absolutely necessary, but they can be handy to have around.

If you run into other features, unless they have some immediate appeal, or meet a specific need we might have overlooked, they probably belong to a third category that we don't cover here—"interesting" bells and whistles—these are neither necessary, nor especially handy, but they may be touted by vendors nonetheless. Don't let these sway you either way, unless they have real value for your organization.

Each of the following subsections is a checklist that names a feature or function and describes its capabilities, and rates its usefulness. For clarity, we also separate end-user features from administrative features for each of the two categories.

Checklist: The Essentials

End-User Features/Functions

- **Distribution list handling**: It just isn't productive to resend identical messages to remind the same group of recipients about regularly scheduled activities. Making a "group" or distribution list is the way to do it. You can create a named address list to receive these messages, and then use that name to refer to the group.
- **Search**: If you really need to find a message, a search capability can be a real lifesaver. Make sure the search capability lets you query the message database by sender or recipient name, subject, and words in the message text. Anything less will lead to trial-and-error message reading.
- **News and notification**: Each e-mail package should notify recipients when a message is waiting to be read. Some notifications pop up a box in DOS or Windows applications; others, like NetWare's SEND utility, use the display's twenty-fifth line. An audible tone accompanies most of them.
- **Message filing**: Most e-mail packages let you save mail into folders that contain related message threads. For example, in marketing you may have folders for trade shows, brochures, customer demos, marketing research, and competitive research.
- **Message/status listing**: Most packages let you review your unopened mail as well as saved mail that you've already read. This list typically shows who the mail is from, its date and time, and what kind of message it is. Some packages will mark incoming mail you have read but not deleted; others will show urgent mail.
- **Mail forwarding**: Mail forwarding is the ability to redirect an e-mail message to another recipient electronically. In other words, this feature lets users send copies of mail messages on to other users.
- **Attachment handling:** To attach files—text or binary—and use wildcards or choose from pick lists. Be sure that the e-mail package you buy enables you to attach files to messages.
- **Print services**: Printing e-mail messages is a personal preference. To some, printing from e-mail represents a paradox: e-mail saves

paper, yet printing messages is sometimes required. Others view it as saving disk space on the file server: by printing messages you add to the clutter on your desk, but you help conserve common space. No matter what your viewpoint, some users will want or need to print messages; we think it's a must-have for that reason.

Administrative Features/Functions

- **Message protection**: To avoid losing mail, each e-mail package should have some way of backing up the message database. This database contains, among other things, the users on the LAN and the contents of all their mailboxes. Many mail packages store their messages in a default mailbox created automatically when you add users to the network. That way, when you back up your e-mail server you'll automatically back up the message database, too.
- **Repair corrupt mail database**: This feature seems useless until something goes wrong with your e-mail system. For instance, Windows might lock up when you're sending a message, and end up corrupting your e-mail database. No e-mail package is worth anything if its mail database is corrupted. Each package should contain a utility that enables you to rebuild or repair the database if this occurs. If not, keep looking for one that does.
- **Message storage management:** Most e-mail packages supply housekeeping features to make it easy for you to cull messages that are no longer needed, or to simply tell you how much traffic is too much. Keeping a lid on the volume is the biggest challenge, and you'll want to get as much help from the software as you can get. This is probably the most frequently used administrative e-mail utility, so consider it carefully.
- **Traffic monitoring and management**: Your e-mail package should be able to tell you the number of messages each user sends and receives, the total traffic e-mail generates, and the names of people who don't read their mail. In addition, you should have a way to delete messages that have been read and to age existing messages for archiving or deletion.
- **User profile handling**: You should be able to create profiles for each user, to specify where their e-mail gets stored (whether in an e-mail server directory or on users' local drives), how much mes-

sage space each user is allotted, and how many messages each user can store at one time.

- **Support for required platforms**: The package you choose should have DOS, Windows, and Macintosh versions if the users on your LAN use both DOS and Windows or Macintoshes. Put another way: if e-mail can't service all the platforms you use, nobody will end up using it, either!
- **Gateway support**: If you can specify the external e-mail environments your users will need to access, it's essential that gateways to those environments be available for your chosen package. Alternatively, if the package supports a strong X.400 or NetWare SMF71 MHS gateway, you may be able to inject a third-party e-mail server to act as a fan-out mail hub for those external systems. Either way, if you can't get to the systems you need to reach from the system you're looking at, you'll probably want to keep looking.

Checklist: Nice to Have

End-User Features/Functions:

- **Privacy protection**: By now, you should be aware that e-mail is for business purposes, and that the company that buys the software has the right to read the personal mail we generate every day on the job. Protect your messages with a password or, better yet, encrypt them, so prying eyes can't see anything. Actually, whether e-mail messages contain salary information, a vindictive slam against one of your co-workers, or the company budget, it's a good idea to protect that message. Too much sensitive information is left open for people who don't deserve to see it. Pick a mail package that enables you to encrypt stuff on demand, or don't store sensitive messages within the mail database.
- **Junk e-mail handling**: The electronic equivalent of junk mail is e-mail addressed to "all" or "world" or "everybody?" Some e-mail packages will let you filter unwanted messages, or save only messages with certain keywords in the subject field for your perusal.
- **Delivery confirmation**: If you've ever wondered whether someone actually reads the mail you send them, some e-mail packages

offer confirmation of delivery. Like a certified letter, you'll be notified when the user reads the message.

- **Import message text**: Some packages will let you bring messages in from a text file, which you can edit, add to, and then later send as an e-mail message.
- **Outbound message handling**: Most packages let you save an "outbox" of messages you've sent. Some delete these messages after a user-specified period of time. Others delete them after the recipient has read them.
- **Change addresses while composing**: Did you ever start writing a memo and then wish you could send it to somebody else, too? This feature enables you to add readers to your list or delete them as you are inclined. You're not forced to recreate or forward the message just to send it to another person.

Administrative Features/Functions:

- **Yellow pages**: If you're using NetWare, you might as well save yourself a lot of trouble recreating the names of all the people that will be using e-mail. Some packages do the boring work for you—they automatically read the NetWare bindery (for pre-4.0 versions), or use NetWare directory services (for 4.0 and later versions) to see who works on your LAN.

  For other LAN environments, including UNIX, LAN Manager, NT Advanced Server, and others, such capabilities are sometimes available. Try to find a mail package that has this capability; it will make installation and adding new users much more convenient. Ask any prospective vendors about their plans for directory services tie-ins for their e-mail packages. Most should have good stories to tell, but few will offer usable functions today. By 1996 this feature will move into the "must-have" category.
- **Space-savers**: A few e-mail packages will let the administrator compress mail files after they've been read. This saves space on the file server and is a good idea.
- **Multiserver handling**: As networks grow, you'll want to be able to send mail among e-mail servers within an organization. Make sure the package you buy routes messages to other file servers on the internetwork and keeps a common directory of mail system

users. This will keep message traffic down, especially over frequently-traveled routes.

- **Forms handling**: For some applications, electronic forms can be a valuable addition to an e-mail package. For example, a receptionist might forward phone messages on phone forms and faxes on proper fax forms using e-mail. More important applications can include electronic paperwork replacements, forms-based database access, electronic order entry, funds transfers, and so forth.

While our list of features and functions is lengthy, it's by no means either exhaustive or complete. We've tried valiantly to hit the high points, but we ask you to think hard before consigning a feature or function to the "interesting," but unnecessary, category we introduced earlier. The best way to sanity-check your e-mail instincts is to invite the input of your power users, and to ask the e-mail vendor for reference accounts, and then to quiz them in great detail about how they use features whose significance isn't readily apparent. For e-mail, the proof of utility comes from actual use!

Basic E-mail Etiquette

The primary rule of e-mail etiquette is a general human principle, known as the golden rule: "Do unto others as they do unto you, " or "Don't do unto others what you would not have them do unto you." Whether your leanings are toward the positive or negative statement of this maxim, it applies to e-mail as much as it does other forms of behavior and communication.

When writing a message, always try to put yourself in your recipients' shoes. How would this look to you if you were reading it instead of writing it? Avoid composing messages, whether initiating communications or responding to communications from others, in the heat of the moment. If you're upset or passionate on a topic, it's wise to write your reply in the evening and then review it again the next morning, before sending it out.

Stay away from inappropriate references, whether joking or serious, and you'll lower the risk of offending readers. Be courteous, direct, and brief as well; you'll not only lighten your readers' burdens, you'll also lower the message traffic on your e-mail system.

In Chapter 20, we cover e-mail etiquette in greater detail, but if you stick with the golden rule, you'll be able to deduce the rest!

Managing Usage and Distribution

By making e-mail available to your users, you're virtually guaranteeing that the system will be used in some form or fashion. If you also establish a clear, understandable set of guidelines for usage at the time of introduction, you'll be that much better equipped to help your users get the best and most appropriate use out of that system.

The basic usage controls for e-mail are access and storage controls:

- **E-mail accounts**: Users should have individual e-mail accounts, to send and receive mail. Use passwords with those accounts to keep the uninvited from making life miserable for the unwary.
- **Space allocations**: Parkinson's Law dictates that users will always need "just a little more" disk space than you're willing to give them. Try to strike a balance between controlling costs and starving your user community—most of the sites we surveyed used disk allocations for e-mail in the three-to-twenty megabyte range.
- **Message aging and purging**: Set policies for how long e-mail messages will be kept on-line, whether read or unread. Let your users that purges are part of the e-mail maintenance routine, notify them beforehand when purges are to occur (regularly scheduled ones are best), and stick to your guns when the time to purge is at hand. For safety's sake always create a backup of the message database before purging, so that important messages that get deleted can be restored when the need arises.
- **Distribution list management**: Many organizations restrict creation and maintenance privileges for e-mail distribution lists to an authorized group of administrators; many others let users build their own, but limit the circumstances in which global addresses (e.g. "all" or "world" or "everyone") can be used. One way or the other, build a set of controls over how mail gets distributed, and you'll have an important handle on e-mail proliferation.
- **Limit anonymity**: Obscenity, harassment, or junk mail will be far less frequent if your users must identify themselves in all their

outgoing e-mail. For this reason, many companies eliminate anonymous sending of e-mail message.

- **Establish clear policy guidelines**: In Chapter 22, we provide information on the Electronic Mail Association's efforts to provide e-mail usage policy and guidelines for employees. Here again, we strongly recommend that you obtain these materials, familiarize yourself with them, and adopt those that make sense within your organization.

The best method of ensuring proper e-mail usage is to make sure the guidelines and restrictions surrounding the system are clearly understood. If everybody knows the rules, and understands their value, the chances that they'll be violated will be lower, and violations will more likely stem from ignorance than malice.

Summary

In this chapter we covered the features and functions that you should consider when buying an e-mail package, in terms of both those you shouldn't try to do without, as well as those that could make e-mail easier for your users and yourself as an e-mail administrator. We also covered the basics of e-mail etiquette and methods for managing e-mail usage and distribution. With this body of information in hand, you should be equipped to select an e-mail system and to prepare your organization and yourself to get the best use out of it.

chapter

24

MANAGING E-MAIL HUBS AND SERVERS

When it comes to dealing with e-mail, one of the more important decisions you'll need to make is how to set up and situate the store-and-forward services that make e-mail work. Typically, most packages require that a set of programs that run regularly, if not continuously, be installed on a machine somewhere.

This set of programs includes a process that watches for incoming e-mail messages and stores them appropriately for their intended recipients if those recipients are local, or forwards them to other such processes if the recipients aren't local. The set includes a notification process that waits for recipients to log into the network and make themselves known to be on-line, before it notifies those recipients that they have e-mail to pick up. It also includes a sending process that receives outbound e-mail messages and forwards them to other recipients if local, and to other e-mail processes elsewhere if they're not local. Finally, the set also includes one or more maintenance utilities to let e-mail storage be established and managed, and to handle user definitions, profiles, security, and other matters.

In case you haven't guessed, this set of programs or processes is what we've called an e-mail server throughout this book. Deciding how to situate this collection of e-mail capabilities is important, since it can dictate the purchase of additional equipment or may have a significant impact on existing servers to which e-mail is added.

Dedicated or Nondedicated?

For many e-mail packages, there is no choice for server installation: the only option is to dedicate a machine for e-mail services, which must be attached to the network and to any external connections required for wide-area, gateway, or remote access. In this case, life is simple but costly because the cost of the machine has to be reckoned as part of the cost of e-mail deployment. When selecting an e-mail package, make sure this cost is out in the open and figured into your plans. Since servers of almost any kind demand fair amounts of CPU power (486/50 or better), RAM (16 Mb or better), and disk storage (1 Gb or better), the costs will be higher than a typical power user's desktop machine.

If you're already using a network services environment of some kind, chances are good that you'll be able to find e-mail packages that can run in this environment. This means you may have to grapple with the dedicated versus nondedicated server issue. Let's examine these two options in terms of pros, cons, and costs:

1. **Dedicated e-mail server**
   Definition: e-mail services are installed on a dedicated, standalone server that fulfills no unrelated network services role.
   Pros: best possible performance, highest message throughput and capacity, least risk of loss of service due to problems with other applications or services, maximum availability of installed disk space on server.
   Cons: adds expense of additional machine and network connection.
   Costs: software, hardware, plus space, plus connection.

2. **Nondedicated e-mail server**
   Definition: e-mail services are installed on a server that provides other network services, which may include database, file and print, routing, or applications services.
   Pros: lowest additional cost, no additional space or connections needed.
   Cons: performance affected by other services and server traffic, vulnerable to loss of service due to problems with other applications and services, must share disk space with other consumers.
   Costs: software, plus reduced server bandwidth and availability.

In practice, the size of your organization and the amount of budget available for e-mail will have the greatest impact on your decision.

Budget may dictate whether purchasing a dedicated machine is possible or not, no matter what level of intended use or what size user community must be accommodated. The size of your organization may require one or more dedicated servers, simply because nondedicated ones cannot handle the required number of users or the anticipated message load.

Where possible, we recommend using dedicated e-mail servers simply because e-mail is so important to so many users. Except in the smallest organizations, where informality is the rule and where e-mail can be supplemented by yelling across the room, users will quickly come to depend on e-mail. By installing e-mail on its own server, you eliminate potential failures that other services and applications can cause, and you provide the greatest amount of potential access to that server. Our rule is: if you can afford to use a dedicated e-mail server, by all means do so!

Situating E-mail Servers

Situating e-mail servers is no different from situating other kinds of servers (we cover this topic extensively in another book in this series, *Network Design Essentials*), except that access to remote connections like telephone lines or WAN links must sometimes be factored into an e-mail server's location if it is also host to a gateway or remote access link.

Here's a quick review of the most salient situational imperatives for e-mail servers:

- **Access**: The e-mail server should be relatively secure, but accessible from the standpoint of letting you, or a service technician, access the hardware itself and the all-important cables that hook it up to the network, or other connections, to do its thing. This means leaving enough room to maneuver around and with the equipment in the event that cables or the equipment itself has to be swapped out or moved (this also gives the added benefit of ensuring sufficient space for air to circulate).
- **Convenience**: The e-mail server has to be close enough to its designated supervisor—this means you—to be workable. This means relatively convenient for you and any other network administrators to get at, and also, conveniently situated for the equipment to do its intended job.

In other words, some e-mail servers will need to reside where the network cabling comes together, be that in a telephone wiring closet or in a specially constructed wiring center. Similarly, servers need to be placed where you can get to them easily, whether it's to back them up, service them, or simply to start them back up after a power interruption. Likewise, e-mail gateways or remote servers have to be where the networking media and other connections they route come together.

- **Workability**: There's no point in putting any kind of equipment in the lobby, or any other common area where anybody can walk up and make off with it. Even if you have to convert a broom closet, it's better to put your gear where only co-workers can get at it, rather than leaving it completely unprotected. It's also important to make sure that the resources your equipment needs can be adequately met wherever you decide to put that gear: these necessities include adequate A/C power, sufficient heating and cooling, and enough space to set things up properly (even if this means putting in equipment racks to stack things up where you otherwise wouldn't have room).

As long as you can meet the spirit of these requirements, your e-mail server should end up situated acceptably, if not perfectly. The better you can adhere to these guidelines, the better your situation will work. Just remember: if your initial server situation proves unworkable, you can always move it—chances are, you'll end up moving sooner or later, anyway!

Naming E-mail Servers

If you followed our advice in Chapter 22 and started your development of a naming scheme with a full-blown X.400 exercise, this is one of the places where that exercise can pay off. One of the best ways to name e-mail servers is by the organization, or organizational unit, that they serve. Thus, the name of the marketing server might be 'mktg' if it merits its own server, or it might just be named after the site, 'aus' or 'Austin,' if multiple units within an organization are served by a single e-mail server at any given site.

On the other hand, if you've already established a naming convention for servers at your organization, try to fit your e-mail servers into that scheme if at all possible. At Novell, e-mail servers are named by a combination of location prefixes—PRV for Provo, Utah, AUS for Austin, TX, and SJF for San Jose, Fortune Drive, California—and according to functional and organizational elements, based on the size of the site involved. Austin supports only a relatively small number of users, so the sole e-mail server is named AUS-EMAIL. Both San Jose Fortune and Provo are home to nearly 2,000 employees, so a typical e-mail server name in either location is SJF-MKTG-EMAIL or PRV-ENGR-EMAIL.

It's important to strike a balance between uniqueness, intelligibility, and convenience. Uniqueness is required because that's what lets individual users be absolutely identified. Intelligibility means that the names have to make some kind of sense, so that end-users and administrators alike can learn what the names mean, and may even have a good chance of guessing at unfamiliar ones. Finally, convenience means that excessively long names will be as unpopular as ones that are too short; the former because they involve too many keystrokes despite their guarantee of intelligibility, and the latter because they involve arcane abbreviations that limit guessability.

SETTING UP E-MAIL SERVERS AND SERVICES

Again, the rules for setting up e-mail servers are similar to those for setting up servers of any kind. The basic ideas are to make sure e-mail has a better than average chance of working before installing it for real, to work around your users' schedules for a minimum of disruption to the workday routine, and to test your work at every step along the way to make sure that e-mail works properly for all its intended users.

The only way to make sure e-mail has any kind of chance of working is to install it in a test lab situation before going into production mode. This will let you isolate and identify potential hardware and software incompatibilities in advance. It will also let you practice installation in a pressure-free environment before taking on real users with real problems that you might not otherwise know how to solve. You'll also want to check on-line information resources and with the e-mail vendor's technical support staff to find out if more recent revisions, patches, or fixes to your proposed configuration will be needed to make things work. This is yet another case where prevention beats cure.

When it comes to the actual installation, be prepared to work evenings or weekends to disrupt your users as little as possible. If you're going to install e-mail on a nondedicated server, make sure you perform a backup immediately prior to installation just to be on the safe side. That way, if the unforeseen does occur, you'll be able to restore the pre-mail configuration so that the other services on your target server will still be available to your users on the next working day.

We also recommend that you install e-mail incrementally, to small groups of users at a time, rather than blanketing your entire organization in one fell swoop. There are two compelling reasons for this approach: early adopters will help you find problems that eluded your test lab without involving the whole user community, and by tackling new users in batches, you'll be better able to handle their questions and problems directly, rather than being overwhelmed by hordes of uninformed and possibly frustrated customers.

Finally, when it comes to installation, test both at the server and on your users' desktop machines; testing is the only way to be sure things are working correctly. This is especially important for e-mail names, e-mail access, and individual message storage capabilities. Just because the server is working flawlessly doesn't mean much for the users if their front-end installations don't work. Make sure each user can send and receive e-mail, and that the server can store and forward both local and remote e-mail messages. Remember the motto of the United States Postal Service: "The mail must go through!"

If you need more information on any of these topics, please refer back to Chapters 5, and 12 through 14, for more details about installation and preparation.

Managing Your E-mail Server

Keeping track of your e-mail server is an important part of the administrator's job. This means monitoring traffic, in terms of both incoming and outgoing messages, for individual users and for the server as a whole. The rule of thumb is that a well-managed server runs better and more reliably. As e-mail attains its proper degree of importance within your organization, staying on top of the underlying systems will only become more important as time goes by!

Here's a partial checklist of the kinds of management activities you'll want to perform regularly on your e-mail server:

- Operating system or network operating system upgrades: it's easier to get support if you're running the current software version of just about anything, so schedule time for regular upgrades. This will usually bring the server down, so make sure to work around your users' schedules.

- E-mail software upgrades: these apply to both server and client software. Be ready to handle at least one or two upgrades to your e-mail software yearly. It's a great idea to look into an automated software distribution package, especially if you have to service a large number of clients or servers, because such a tool can save you lots of time and walking around. Why not use the network? It's already there, and it's a lot faster to move files around on the wires than it is to walk floppies around the building or campus.
- Message database maintenance: it's a good idea to perform regular integrity checks and to compress already read messages as well, provided your e-mail system supports it.
- Directory maintenance: as employees come and go, and distribution lists change with the changes to your organization, it's imperative to keep the e-mail system up-to-date. It's a good idea to schedule such maintenance activities weekly to monthly, depending on how quickly your organization typically changes or grows.
- Usage monitoring: you'll want to compile usage trends, which means keeping track of daily/weekly/monthly message rates and disk consumption. This will be your most compelling argument when it comes time to add another disk drive or e-mail server, so it's worth keeping up with.

Managing an e-mail server is like owning a house: there's always something more to do to keep up with it. If you tackle these tasks, as well as other upkeep and maintenance activities on a regular basis, it'll never get away from you. The most important aspect of successful maintenance is regular walkthroughs of a well-thought-out checklist of activities. Use this list, and others that occur to you, to construct the routine that works best for you, but above all, make a schedule and stick to it!

Message Storage Management

If our case studies taught us anything we absolutely must tell you about e-mail maintenance, it's that you'll want to keep a constant eye on your storage space to make sure there's enough room to accommodate the ongoing and never-ending influx of e-mail. This will mean regular policing of message storage, regular purging of stale messages, and the occasional adjustment of individual users' mail storage allocations—up for those who can't cope with the current ceiling, and down for those who never get close to that ceiling.

You'll also want to perform regular backups of the e-mail server, especially before purging old messages, or whenever you schedule a software or hardware upgrade. Things break most commonly right after they change, so always be prepared to get back to where you started whenever making changes!

Please check Chapter 16 for a more detailed discussion of surviving upgrades and system or element replacements.

Gambling on Gateways

From an installation and maintenance perspective, gateways are like servers, only more so. Because they provide the link between different—and incompatible—e-mail worlds, there's a lot more that can go wrong with gateways than most other e-mail servers. Perhaps that's why they've garnered a reputation as balky and often cantankerous pieces of software, difficult to use and equally difficult to master and understand. We think it's because gateways are often written by third parties, that is, by an organization that's not part of the company whose e-mail system sits at either end of the gateway in question.

Whatever the cause of the difficulties that sometimes arise with gateways, they bear even more watching than do ordinary e-mail servers. We recommend that you become conversant with the details involved in restarting the gateway, since that's the most common fix for gateway problems. We also recommend that you learn whatever administrative tools a gateway provides and that you try to figure out a way to run those tools remotely (this beats driving to work at odd hours just to restart or reconfigure a balky gateway).

Stay on top of the bulletin boards that cover your gateways, and keep in regular touch with their vendors. That way, you'll be forewarned when version changes or patches or fixes to either e-mail package united by a gateway may be problematic, and you'll be in sync with changes and enhancements to that gateway that might do you some good. Because gateway options are often limited, it's wise to be even more careful with them than usual, paying close attention to them whenever possible.

Public Access Providers (Controlling Access Costs)

Your organization may decide to connect to a public access provider for e-mail, such as GEnie, CompuServe, or MCI Mail. Some companies use these public providers for all their e-mail needs, internal and external, while others use them only for remote access for staff and customers. Whatever the motivation, working with public access providers calls for extra attention to billing arrangements and for educating your users about getting the best bang out of your organization's bucks.

Your arrangement with an access provider will commonly be covered by some kind of site license or blanket agreement, so inquire as to the circumstances and familiarize yourself with the arrangement. By checking the details of billing, of prime-time versus off-hours rates, and of package deals specified in your contract or agreement, you may discover some techniques to maximize access while still controlling costs. If you can then pass this information on to your users, everyone may be able to benefit from this research.

Here are some things to look out for:

- Hourly rates for connect based on modem speeds can offer significant savings for faster modems. For instance, using a 19.2-kilobaud modem on CompuServe costs only twice as much as a 2.4-kilobaud modem today, yet offers eight times the bandwidth. The upfront costs of such modems may be higher, but the payback will typically occur in six months or less, depending on usage levels.
- For scheduled uploads/downloads of messages, off-hours connect costs can exceed half the cost of prime-time connections. If you can automate this activity, you'll be able to save some serious money.
- Navigation tools for end-users let them read messages and write replies while off-line, rather than while connected to the public access provider. This kind of software seldom costs more than $100 per user. Interactive public access users can spend as much as 80 percent of their on-line time reading and writing. At rates from

$5 to $16 per hour (in the United States), the payback for such software could be in as little as one month for a heavy user!

Since we can't know all the details of your particular arrangement with an access provider, we can't tell you all the little tricks and twists you can take to squeeze the most out of your on-line time. But we can and will recommend yet again that you read the contract: look for loopholes, and use the heck out of any that you can find.

Summary

In this chapter we examined the ins and outs of situating, managing, and maintaining e-mail servers and gateways. We tried to underscore the elements of an effective routine and the need to perform that routine regularly and devotedly. We also discussed some tips for getting the most out of the dollars you spend on public access providers that may provide your organization with e-mail services.

Message-Based Applications

As important as e-mail is to many organizations, messaging technology offers lots of possible applications above and beyond basic exchange of messages among users. When applications start taking advantage of messaging for information exchange or delivery, it's safe to think of them as message-based.

In Chapter 22, we mentioned a fairly simple extension of messaging technology, where a specific e-mail address provides access to a news/document server, and the subject field of a message to that server requests that the document named in that field be delivered in reply. This lets users browse an on-line catalog of available documents and request delivery of copies of those that they find interesting. This type of server is sometimes called a "library server" because it acts as a document repository from which copies can be extracted as needed.

Today, many organizations use this kind of technology to deliver monthly sales bulletins, price lists, news summaries, and a broad range of sales and information documents to their sales forces. It's perfect for people who are always on the move and hungry for new and current information to share with their customers.

Message-based applications work because they can supply information on demand, as with the library server example, or because they can deliver the right information frequently enough to their intended audiences to be useful. This kind of approach works very well for employees who use their computers occasionally and who can survive on information that may not be up-to-the-minute, but is fresh enough still to be worthwhile; salespersons are a good example.

Application Possibilities

If we examine the kinds of information that people use most frequently when interacting with one another, either inside or outside their home organizations, the possibilities message-based applications afford quickly become interesting.

Imagine, if you will, that once a week your e-mail contains a new company directory that includes the name and address of each employee, his or her e-mail and snail mail addresses, and other useful information (such as department, title, mailstop, etc.). Imagine further that this directory is in a format that's usable in an interactive search program, and that copying this file to the right directory is all you need to do to be able to query this newest version. What you've just imagined is a pretty straightforward message-based implementation of the standalone directory search capability we recommended in Chapter 23. It is available from some e-mail packages today and is on the drawing board for many more.

Now, think of other collections of data that don't change much over short periods of time that could fit the same model: price lists, product catalogs, training catalogs, sales reports, financial results, personnel records . . . the list is virtually endless. With the right software, all of these things become usable through message-based applications. These kinds of applications can be described as distributed databases, or loosely coupled databases.

Now, think of tasks that have to move from worker to worker in regular succession, such as claims processing at an automobile insurance company. A mail clerk will open incoming claims, create a case number for each one, and route cases by type to a particular claims processor. The claims processor will then assign a claims adjuster to the case to assess damage and determine liability. The case will then be forwarded to a payment processor, who will issue a check if the company is liable or else oversee payment from other liable parties. The paperwork will then be turned over to a records clerk, who files the materials for any future reference and annotates the claimant's records regarding the date, time, involved parties, payment status, and other circumstances related to the claim.

Workflow applications use messaging to route case information electronically and to monitor status on individual cases, case workers, and case types. Once the relevant documents are digitized, nothing keeps them from moving electronically rather than physically. Such applications typically accommodate digitized photographs and legal agreements, in addition to text and database records, to create electronic equivalents of the case files needed to process a particular case (in our example, an insurance claim). Likewise, all of the information needed to track policies, sales, and customer correspondence can be assigned, routed, and monitored using message-based technologies.

In fact, it looks as if a great deal of what passes for paperwork in organizations today might be amenable to message-based implementation on a network. All that's missing is a ubiquitous infrastructure (the plumbing), the right kinds of software, and a commitment to convert paper-based systems into message-based ones. This is indeed a formidable hurdle, but it appears to be in the process of being overturned.

Replication, or Distributing Data

One key to delivering useful information to its consumers is to ensure that what they're perusing is as consistent, accurate, and timely as possible. Whenever multiple copies of the same information exist, a well-known computer science issue called "the distributed data problem" rears its ugly head. Simply stated, here's the problem: "If you have more than one copy of a piece of information, and all the copies don't agree, how do you know which copy is the 'true' version?"

The answer can get pretty complicated at times, especially when multiple copies may be updated concurrently, and even more so when those copies might be updated simultaneously. In general, though, the rule is that the copy with the freshest time stamp (that is, the datum that's most recent) is the one that's assumed to be the true version. The real answer is to avoid the distributed data problem whenever possible, which is why the shared database examples we provided depend on servicing an arbitrary number of readers, who can only look at but not change the contents of the database, and only a small, tightly controlled number of writers, who are allowed to update the database under special circumstances and only after satisfying stringent access controls.

All of the directories, catalogs, reports, and other information we mentioned earlier as data that could be delivered by message-based applications fall into this category. The application acts to update replicas of the database, but doesn't concern itself with any changes that may have been made to a replica. The only changes that are propagated to designated recipients are those made to the master version from which all replicas are generated.

Even so, outlying users will have useful information to contribute to the master database. This will typically be handled through a series of special tools that include appropriate filters and data checks, both human- and machine-oriented. For example, the salesperson in the field may upload a sales order to the head office when he or she logs into the e-mail server, perhaps even while downloading the latest sales report or company directory. The results of that order won't appear in a sales report until accounts receivable verifies the order and confirms the customer's payment or their receipt of an invoice, which is essentially a timed promissory note. Only then can the results of that sale be incorporated into the sales figures for that salesperson, his region, her territory, and the division or company's quarterly results.

The same approach will be true for most filed information. It will be delivered, probably in the form of a text- or form-based message whose contents must be checked and verified before the master database will be updated to reflect its contents. This checking can range from mechanical inspection to make sure the kinds and ranges of data are appropriate (no alphabetic names in a dollar field, for instance) to running a credit check to establish a prospective buyer's creditworthiness and purchasing terms.

The key to the whole affair is to ensure the quality of the master database before any replication can occur. Then everything that proceeds from that master's contents can be assumed to be as accurate and reliable as the delivery mechanisms allow.

Frequency versus Volume

The freshness of data is always a concern in a loosely coupled database environment. Here, the most important tradeoff is the frequency of updates versus the volume of information involved in applying an update. Generally, there's an inverse correlation between the frequency and the volume, which is to say: the more frequent the updates, the smaller they will typically be; the less frequent the updates, the larger they'll become.

This tradeoff must also account for the time and energy required to perform an update and for the opportunity cost that an update incurs. In plain English, this means we don't want to waste too much of a valuable salesperson's time updating a database when he could be spending that time selling things to customers. If, however, the interval between updates is too long, what the salesperson sells may not correspond very well with what the organization has to offer.

Neither of these extremes is too palatable, so organizations must strike a balance that works to their best advantage. Where currency or market fluctuations cause frequent price changes, it's not unusual for salespeople to update price lists, bid forms, or other sales-related instruments daily. Most other kinds of information are amenable to longer update intervals, with weekly updates typical. Sometimes, updates will only be replicated after a specific volume of change has occurred—this is what we'd have to call a "change-driven upgrade" approach.

Whatever your choices regarding update frequency might be, you'll have to build an update mechanism and provide regular updates for the loosely coupled databases you purvey via message-based applications. Managing updates is critical and must be included as a cost of doing business in this type of environment.

Selecting Message-based Applications

Most organizations have their own way of doing things, and few are completely amenable to "plain vanilla" business forms, report structures, and other mechanisms for supplying and delivering information. This means that most message-based applications resemble a toolbox more than a completed project. In other words, when you buy a message-based application, you're buying the ability to customize and tailor sets of forms, activities, and information delivery mechanisms to your organization's needs.

Selecting message-based applications can be tricky, especially if you want to build something that no one else has tried before. Nevertheless, here are a few criteria to consider when selecting a message-based application:

- *Does it offer the necessary underlying database capabilities?*
  Can it accommodate the kinds of text information, graphics, images, or free-form data you need to include in your targeted sales reports, price lists, directories, or whatever?

- *Does it support the mix of platforms and connections you use?*
  If it supports only PCs and most of your users are on Macs, you have a problem. If so, don't give up right away—find out what the vendor's plans for Mac support might be, and try to figure out if you can build a suitable workaround in the interim (Insignia Solutions' SoftPC and PCAnywhere to let a Mac use the PC version for the time being, for instance).

- *Have any applications similar to yours already been built with this system?*
  Okay, so your personnel management application may incorporate digitized photographs of your employees but, other than that, are there some personnel records systems already built around this platform? Try to talk to reference accounts to find out how usable, flexible, and friendly the system is. Find out also how much consulting help for application customization is available, and how much such help might cost.

- *Does it support the kinds of forms and queries your users need?*
  Ad hoc inquiries are a database technologist's delight, but the real action comes from the order forms, parts lists, and other paperwork extravaganzas that make your organization so special and unique. The more you can make the new system look like what the users already know, the less they'll have to learn to do their jobs. Is this feasible? Straightforward? Easy? Does it look any good? Can you assign keyboard shortcuts? Ultimately, you need to use this tool to build a system that salespeople will use.

- *How does replication/update work?*
  Because change is a way of life for message-based applications, propagating changes should be simple and easy. Make sure the time and effort needed to handle changes fit within the frequency and volume you have to spare.

There's a great deal more involved in building high-quality message-based applications than we've been able to cover here, but if you carefully research the issues we've raised, they will lead you to the other issues that matter for your organization. If you take the step of locating and interviewing existing customers for any tool you're considering to build message-based applications, you'll also be able to determine if that tool is suitable for your needs. Doing your homework takes time and costs money, but it will clearly pay off if you invest heavily in making the right decision.

Using Message-based Applications

Delivering message-based applications to your users should employ a phased approach, much like the e-mail deployment method we advocate in Chapters 14 and 16. Start with a series of meetings with your prospective users to find out what they really want from the application, and how they'd like it to look and behave.

Move to the test lab to get the basics built, but proceed into a pilot test with real users as soon as you can. Pick some hotshots, and some not-so-hotshots, from your organization's target group to help you shake down the application. Expect lots of changes to come out of the pilot. Be prepared to pilot test until the cows come home, or at least until the users grudgingly accept what you've all built together (enthusiasm is a much better target to aim for, by the way).

You'll know you're ready for prime time when the application starts showing up on users' systems outside your pilot test group. When a tool is ready to use, people will try to use it, even if they have to bootleg it to make it work. Realistically, you'll find that word of mouth will precede your introduction of the production model and that training and delivery will be far larger problems than proselytizing to the unconverted or unconvinced.

The pilot group will be invaluable in helping to set your training agenda. If you've chosen your pilot team wisely, they'll also be able to help drive the description of the tips and shortcuts that real users can appreciate best. This group will also help identify common questions, and working through the pilot should help determine the corresponding answers. Use all this input to get the initial training built, and deploy across teams or workgroups incrementally.

Once you've got the application out there, you're in maintenance mode, where the real work begins. Commit yourself to staying in touch with the users and to responding to their questions, concerns, demands, and comments. Remember that 90 percent of an application's life cycle is spent in this mode, so learn to live with it comfortably. If you're lucky, your users will take the ball and run it all the way out of the precincts you've built for it, and everybody will learn a lot along the way!

Summary

In this chapter we examined the capabilities of message-based applications, with an eye to understanding the kinds of things they can do for a typical organization. Loosely coupled databases, forms-based information delivery, library servers, and workflow applications all appear to offer significant value to those organizations able to build and manage effective implementations. Selecting a toolset you can use and live with will be the key to a successful implementation, as will a careful and considerate approach to the design and customization process for message-based applications. As with anything else, with the right attitude and the right input, the sky's the limit for a properly built message-based system.

Workflow and Office Automation

Beating Back the Buzzwords

We've talked a bit about workflow at this point in the book, having defined it more or less as the electronic analog of how paperwork moves through a work environment. We've touted its abilities to automate repetitive business processes, to track work as it moves through an organization, and to capture and convert collections of paper-based information automatically into highly organized, easily accessible databases.

While all of this is true, there's a major problem with the term "workflow" in today's software marketplace. A 1993 survey of workflow products (*The Workgroup Computing Report*, November 1993) indicates that well over 100 vendors that claim to provide workflow support offer such products in the marketplace. Presumably, this number is even higher as you're reading this, but the problem remains intact: these products range all the way from electronic mail distribution list management tools to systems capable of modeling entire business processes like order entry, purchasing, or customer service. Which ones are workflow? Which ones aren't?

This state of affairs leads us to an important caveat for all would-be workflow technologists: just because a vendor claims that a product supports workflow, automates workflow, or whatever it does relates to workflow, doesn't actually mean that the product does what you might need or expect it to do for you.

In turn, this requires that anyone wishing to investigate workflow technology must understand what workflow technology is, and what it can and can't do. Even more important, such an investigator must have a good working knowledge of his or her organization's work processes in order to understand which ones might be amenable to workflow implementations. The same knowledge will also help to determine the degree of customization necessary to take an off-the-shelf workflow package and turn it into something your colleagues and co-workers can actually use.

In this chapter we try to dig down into workflow technology by providing a more detailed definition of this buzzword. We also try to explore the kinds of processes that are well suited to workflow implementations, and describe how a suitable process might be modeled for a workflow implementation. We also examine how you might go about selecting a workflow package and use it in your organization.

What Is Workflow, Really?

What workflow really represents is an attempt to take business processes and computerize them in a way that makes workers more efficient, more productive, and better equipped to complete the tasks they're asked to do. From this broad viewpoint, any use of computing that's work related qualifies as workflow.

There are still several elements missing from our definition thus far:

- A network is required to support electronic routing of "work" from one worker to another within an organization and to let workers communicate with one another while stepping through a process.
- A model of the business process is required to diagram the "flow" and to establish the steps that must be completed before the work flows from one worker to another.
- Methods for entering "work" into the workflow system, tracking its current assignment and status, and reporting on completion and contents, have to be defined and implemented.

Therefore, our working definition of a workflow application is as follows: networked software that accurately and completely models a specific business process and includes routing, tracking, and reporting capabilities about individual tasks belonging to the modeled process.

Limitations to Workflow Implementation

At this stage, our definition requires that a process be accurately and completely modeled in software. This requirement strictly limits the kinds of processes that can be implemented as workflow applications, because many of the tasks we do in the workplace are too free-form, or too tenuous, to be completely modeled. Also, many tasks are too complicated to model accurately or completely, because they require major decisions to be made at regular intervals to get a job completed. Maybe that's why nobody has yet built a wedding planner as a workflow application!

The sad truth is that workflow today resembles the industry's hope for Artificial Intelligence (AI) technology back in the early 1980s. At that time, AI was viewed as a panacea, able to transform computers from brute hunks of logic and circuitry to sensitive, intelligent agents capable of freeing humans of the drudgery and humdrum side of work. In the same vein, it's easy to see workflow as the magic bullet that will transform the humdrum tasks of running an organization into a smoothly functioning information management mechanism.

The limitation that brought AI technology to earth is the same one that's bringing workflow technology down from the heavens: in order to be suitable for workflow implementation, a business process must meet a tight set of constraints, all of which serve to describe and circumscribe exactly the process and all the steps it contains:

- It must be a frequently repeated task, or it won't be worth automating.
- The task must consist of a number of well-documented, well-understood steps.
- The contents of each step must be well understood and well bounded (no cosmic thinking allowed, no tricky decisions needed).
- Individual assignments for each step must be possible, if not customary.

- The transfer of tasks, and the points at which transfer occurs, must be easy to accomplish and easy to understand for all workers involved.

- The work that is accomplished, or the tasks that must be performed, must be easy to document and record (preferably, on a computer).

Taking all these factors into account helps to explain why the most common examples of business processes that have been successfully implemented as workflow applications are forms-driven.

One thing that workers everywhere more or less understand how to do these days is filling out a form. Tasks that require forms, whether simple or complex, to be filled out and routed with a "work package" are easy for all of us to relate to. The act of engineering the form already requires an understanding of the steps that must be completed, and the information that a form gathers together documents the work that gets performed as the form gets completed. In fact, it's hard to say if the process drives the form, or the form drives the process in many cases.

Figuring How the Work Flows

Therefore, when the time comes to select the kinds of processes that should be implemented as workflow applications, the presence or absence of a form governing the process (or at least a well-established, well-documented set of steps, rules, and procedures for the process) should be pivotal to your go-ahead decision.

Once you've decided that a particular process is worth reengineering as a workflow application, it's essential to observe that process in its current form as many times as you can stand it. The idea is to capture all of the steps involved in completing the process, to understand all of the decisions that must be made to complete each step, and to determine when and how a task that belongs to the process is handled. This latter determination includes the following critical observations:

- When does a task begin? What information describes a task at its inception? How is this information recorded?

- How does a task get assigned? Who decides? How does it get delivered to its designated recipient or recipients? How is this transfer tracked?

- Who are the workers involved in completing a task? What roles do they play? How is their management involved? Where do people go for help when they get stuck, delayed, or when circumstances conspire against them?
- What are the exceptions that occur for each step? How are exceptions handled? How do workers distinguish "a tough job" from "an easy job"?
- When is a step complete? How is this completion recorded? What's a normal completion time for the step? What happens to tasks that aren't completed within that time? How time-sensitive is this step?
- When is a task complete? How is this completion recorded? What kinds of notifications occur upon completion? What's a normal completion time for a task? What happens to tasks that aren't completed within that time? How time-sensitive is this task?
- What records are kept about the task? What information is specific to individual steps, and what information stays with the task? What reports are generated about the participants, the task volume, the step volume, etc.?

Only if you can obtain clear, unambiguous answers to all these questions should you be willing to proceed with implementing the process under observation as a workflow application. Processes that aren't well documented by this kind of analysis often prove to be too slippery to implement as well. There are plenty of processes that do fit within the kind of modeling our questionnaire can support—if you run into one that's intractable, our advice is to try another!

Workflow Options

When it comes to actual implementation, the kinds of products available today range from tools built for specific applications, like sales tracking, customer service, or inventory control, to general-purpose workflow automation tools. The rules that apply to selecting such a tool are as follows:

- The more general-purpose the workflow package, the more kinds of processes you'll be able to model, but the more modeling work you'll have to do.

- The more specific the focus of a workflow package, the more important it is to establish a good fit between the tool and the process it's trying to model.
- The more a workflow package costs, the more things you should expect it to do for you (remember, the converse is also true).
- Only those tools that support your chosen platforms, networks, and existing software are usually worth considering (unless you're willing to replace every desktop and the network to get what the tool can provide).
- How easy it is to tune or tweak an application built with the tool will ultimately be important, because all business processes change as markets and technologies change. If a particular package doesn't support small, incremental adjustments to the data or the workflow model, it probably won't stand up well to the test of time and repeated use.
- Only tools that are usable get used; ask for references and check with existing users about their use experiences; also, ask for a "trial use" period before committing to a particular workflow package and use that package during the trial to see if it can do what you really need it to do.

Unless your organization is large or sophisticated enough to have an in-house programming staff at your disposal, you shouldn't try to be too ambitious in your use of workflow technology. In that case, you'll be best served if you find a package that models the kinds of processes you want to automate, and stick to customizing the package to meet your organization's particular needs.

While more ambitious projects may be appealing, only those that get finished ever get any recognition! For that reason, we also suggest that you look for modest, small-scale projects to pilot your use of workflow technology, and move to the bigger, more complex processes after you've climbed the learning curve. Just as we've recommended a test lab for your e-mail, and stepwise installation for your network, we recommend that you start small and learn before trying to reinvent your entire organization all at once.

SUMMARY

In this chapter we take a closer look at workflow. Because it can help to automate your organization's business processes—at least the tractable ones—it offers the hope that you can work more efficiently and understand your processes better. But it's wise to proceed with caution when considering a technology that's not consistently understood or represented, even among its proponents and purveyors. If you understand your requirements thoroughly, you'll be able to decide if this technology can meet them, and you'll be well equipped for implementation should you decide to proceed.

chapter 27

Lotus® Notes™ and Related Applications

Lotus Notes Overview

Notes is a program that defies description, using more traditional software categories like spreadsheet, e-mail, database, and word processor. Yet it has become a paradigm for an emerging software category, known as groupware. Notes offers many different capabilities, but it can best be described as an inherently distributed document database with an exceptionally rich set of front-end database and interface design tools that let end-users manipulate and distribute shared information.

In the next few paragraphs, we try to elaborate on what all this means, but the explosive growth of Notes in the marketplace indicates that seeing is believing for many of its users. While the product may be hard to describe, it's neither hard to grasp nor terribly hard to use, and it has become a software development platform of choice for organizations ranging from government agencies, to the Fortune 1,000, to a host of small and medium-sized companies around the world as well.

Notes Is a Database . . . No, It's an Infrastructure . . . No, it's . . .

When we say that Notes is inherently distributed, this means that the program understands how to manage multiple users in multiple locations. Even more important, Notes is imbued with an understanding of how to manage multiple copies of the same information.

On the surface, managing multiple copies of data sounds like nothing special, but it's actually a fairly thorny problem (see our discussion of the "distributed data problem" in Chapter 25 for more details). Lotus Notes uses a mechanism called replication, where a copy of all or part of a database is sent from a master repository to whoever needs the information.

Furthermore, Notes is capable of tracking who's got copies of what, and can issue messages to keep remote users synchronized with the master. Such messages contain the database updates, changes, and deletions necessary to bring the copy back into full agreement with the master, and get applied automatically whenever users send or receive Notes messages.

The ability to keep multiple copies in agreement lets the users of those copies stay in tune with one another. While it sounds completely obvious, Notes pioneered this kind of technology for PC users, and it is still fairly unique today. Replication is the key mechanism that lets Notes serve distributed user communities.

Distribution also comes into play for Notes in its ability to inform users about what information is available on any accessible Notes server. All it takes to obtain a copy of that information is a request, which is answered with a reply that contains the requested data.

Electronic mail is Notes' primary delivery mechanism and therefore completely essential to its operation. In fact, most Notes applications are mail-focused: forms and documents travel the network attached to electronic mail, traveling to and from the databases in which the information they contain resides.

Here's a possible example: the accounting department can develop a Notes-based expense report form that gets filled in by employees (perhaps on laptops while they're on the road). These forms will be automatically routed to their managers for approval and, when approved, forwarded to the accounting department for reconciliation and payment. When the payment is issued, Notes sends a message informing the recipient that a check has been cut, with all the relevant information.

As delivered, Notes includes over 20 such applications, ranging from project tracking, to group conferencing, to account management, that are ready to use as is. Or, the Note administrator can customize any of them to meet special organizational requirements not already covered in the ready-made versions.

Notes from Underground

In order to understand better what Lotus Notes can do, let's examine some of its more typical uses. Besides e-mail, which Notes does very well, electronic meetings or discussions, and call-tracking are two other common applications.

Electronic meetings will be familiar to anyone who's ever joined an interactive discussion on-line, but for those unfamiliar with the genre, here's how one works: two or more users log into a shared display application, where everything each user types at his or her keyboard is displayed simultaneously to all participants. By itself, this requires no special Notes capabilities. What Notes brings to the party is the ability to select or solicit the participants, to schedule the time that the meeting will occur, and to notify invitees (repeatedly, if necessary) when the meeting will take place and how to join in. Notes also maintains a journal of the meeting, which it can supply to all participants (and any other designated recipients) via e-mail.

Notes also supports discussion databases, which work something like electronic meetings, except that they maintain a set of ongoing topics to which access can be individually controlled. The value of a discussion database is that participants can communicate asynchronously, but discussions can continue over time. Documents can be drafted, agreements negotiated, and projects designed, all among a virtual community of e-mail users. Of all the popular Notes applications in regular use, discussion databases appear to provide the biggest benefits for the least amount of effort. By adding structure and shared access to what otherwise might look like a random collection of e-mail messages, discussion databases let widely distributed groups of individuals get serious work done.

A call-tracking system is a database that contains an entry for every phone call made or received by a particular organizational unit, be it telemarketing, technical support, product information, or some other group that does important business by telephone. Over time, information about known problems, patches and fixes, customer data, or typical product orders will accumulate. This data is a treasure trove of useful information that can be searched and perused by the members of the group's staff, and by others inside or outside the organization; also, common questions and their answers can regularly be tabulated and distributed via e-mail to customers, salespeople, or support engineers.

This approach not only gathers valuable data, but makes sure it's available to any and all who need it.

Finding the Fit: Is Notes What You Need?

The range of applications built around Notes today is staggering: it's being used to cover information handling that ranges from processing sales orders and deliveries, to forwarding job interview data among designated interviewers, to providing access to news and trend information from customer databases for financial analysts.

Lest Notes sound like it's ready for anything, or that it can do everything, it's important to remember that Notes is message based. Because sending and receiving messages takes time, and may even be asynchronous (senders may be on-line, but receivers off-line), this means Notes isn't suitable for high-volume transaction processing applications, like an airline or rental car reservation service. This is particularly true because Notes isn't built to handle lots of simultaneous requests quickly; it's built to handle moderate numbers of requests that occur randomly, and to link requests to specialized database searches and reports. Nor is Notes a replacement for a full-blown relational database like Oracle or Sybase, in that its query and reporting mechanisms are deliberately limited by being focused on narrow, specialized uses rather than broad, generalized ones.

Notes is subject to the limitations we covered for workflow applications in Chapter 26: it works best for well-defined, narrow collections of data that correspond to a particular set of well-understood activities, processes, or communications needs.

Notes-worthy News Items

Within its limitations, however, Notes offers significant value to its users. Today, supported Notes clients include Windows, OS/2, Macintosh, and several varieties of UNIX (SunOS 4.x, SCO, Solaris 2.x, HP-UX, and AIX). Servers supported include NetWare, Windows NT, all the flavors of UNIX mentioned above, and OS/2. Networking protocols supported include NetBEUI, NetBIOS, TCP/IP, and SPX/IPX.

All of these things position Notes as an excellent cross-platform communications tool.

Notes also offers a good collection of predefined on-screen forms, with databases to stand behind them, and an equally strong forms and database-definition toolset to extend what's already there. Lotus stands behind the product too, with on-site training and additional consulting services for application customization or outright application development available to those willing to pay for it.

Finally, the marketplace is starting to embrace Notes in its own unique ways. Several third-party vendors have announced their intentions to use Notes to build products for their customers that range from trouble-ticketing applications to custom new services. As more vendors stake their businesses on Notes, it should continue to gain credibility and market share.

Summary

In this chapter we examined Lotus Notes. Its unique combination of messaging, database services, and replication management makes it well suited for distributed information routing and delivery. As a harbinger of potential message-based applications to come, it's interesting technology; as a platform for automating business processes, it's gaining significant mind share as many industries try to leverage their technology investments further. We think Notes is a worthwhile candidate for investigation if message-based technologies appear to offer value to your organization.

USING COMPUSERVE FOR E-MAIL

As the world's largest and most heavily used public information provider, CompuServe Information Services (CIS) offers an unimaginably broad range of public and private services, all available at a modest cost with a single, usually local phone call. Covering CompuServe in-depth is the focus for an entire book (and many are available on the subject—please consult the Resource Guide.

In this chapter we skip over most of what CIS has to offer and concentrate on its e-mail services more or less exclusively. As an e-mail user of the service, the following things are necessary for you to know:

- A CompuServe account is required to let you access the service, to send and receive e-mail; CompuServe also bills for access time, and for some e-mail related services, so the account will also have some associated costs (more on this later in the chapter).
- A modem and telephone hook-up for your computer will be required, but CompuServe access is possible from just about any kind of PC or other computer that you might have.
- An understanding of basic CompuServe commands to interact with e-mail, or a front-end CIS navigation program, will be needed for you to compose and send e-mail, and to pick up waiting messages.

Fortunately, none of these things is terribly difficult to set up, nor prohibitively expensive. With a small amount of effort on your part, you can begin using CompuServe and gain direct access to e-mail communications with more than two million CIS users worldwide. Because CompuServe also offers fee-based access to gateways to public e-mail services like the Internet, MCI Mail, and others, its reach is incredibly broad.

Obtaining a CompuServe Account

Because of its widespread use and popularity, there are many more ways to get a CompuServe account than we can document here. Therefore, we suggest some places to look, and conclude by providing a direct contact to CompuServe Information Services itself.

Most of the books on CompuServe, most modems, and most telecommunications software packages come with introductory sign-on usage credits for CompuServe. These promotional packages will provide mail-in coupons or a toll-free phone number to set you up with an account, and typically provide $15 to $25 (U.S.) in free connect time and usage credits for that account once it's established. CompuServe itself offers such credits for direct sign-ups and for purchasing its *CompuServe Starter Kit*, which includes on-line documentation and a services overview, or for purchasing one of its on-line navigation software packages.

You can obtain an account over the phone, or by writing CompuServe and requesting a membership. For telephone inquiries, ask for Representative 200. Here are the numbers to use:

- Within the United States. (except Ohio), including Alaska, Hawaii, Puerto Rico, and the American Virgin Islands, call toll-free at (800)848-8199.
- Outside the United States, or in Ohio (CompuServe's home state), call (614)457-8650.

Telephone hours are from 8 A.M. to 10 P.M. Eastern time from Monday through Friday, and from noon to 5 P.M. on Saturday. Written inquires for a CompuServe account should be directed to:

CompuServe, Inc.
Attn: Customer Service
P.O. Box 20212
5000 Arlington Centre Boulevard
Columbus, OH 43220 USA

CIS E-MAIL OVERVIEW

One of the basic and most frequently used features of CompuServe is its electronic mail facility, eponymously named CompuServe MAIL. You can access CompuServe MAIL with the GO MAIL command, and use other commands to compose, send, receive, forward, and delete CompuServe e-mail messages. We strongly recommend that you purchase and use a CompuServe navigation tool, because it will let you compose and read e-mail messages off-line, and thereby save you significant amounts of connect time (and its associated charges, which range from $3.00 to as high as $9.60 per hour at current U.S. domestic rates).

CIS User Addresses

CompuServe MAIL messages are addressed to user IDs, which are sequences of octal digits (all numbers are between 0 and 7). Ed Tittel's CompuServe ID is 76376,606 and Margaret Robbins' is 75730,1451. These identifiers have no inherent significance, except that some number ranges indicate special status; they're assigned by CompuServe and associated with a specific user account, much like a telephone number is assigned to a branch exchange and a street address by the phone company.

CompuServe does supply a yellow pages utility that can be accessed with the GO DIRECTORY command. As long as you can supply the first and last names, and city and state of residence, of any individual whose CompuServe ID you need to obtain, CIS will be happy to supply you with the requisite ID, providing that the individual or business whose ID you've requested has a valid CompuServe account. Because the IDs are long (8 to 10 digits) and arbitrary, you'll want to build an address book that lists user names and associated IDs. Here again, most of the CIS navigation packages include an address book facility that lets you store name–ID pairs and retrieve them by name (yet another reason to get some navigation software!).

CompuServe MAIL Capabilities

CompuServe MAIL can send and receive text messages up to 64 kilobytes in length. Typically, users correspond with one another on a variety of subjects, in much the same way they'd use a business or personal letter, but with more of the spontaneity and speed of a fax or telephone call. Most correspondence via CompuServe MAIL can be readily handled through the exchange of such messages.

CompuServe MAIL messages have three parts:

1. an address section, which provides the IDs for the sender and for intended recipients.
2. a subject field, which provides up to 24 characters to describe the contents of the message, or the name of a file to be transferred from sender to receiver(s). Together, parts 1 and 2 comprise the header of a CompuServe MAIL message.
3. a body which includes the text of the message, or a file sent as an attachment to the message header.

It's possible to include text generated from another program on your computer as the body of a CompuServe message, but it must be true ASCII text. This means if you want to use a file created in a word processor or some other kind of advanced text editor as the body of a CompuServe MAIL message, you'll need to save that message as "plain text" or "text" before including it as the message body in MAIL. If not, there's a good chance the message will either be totally unreadable, or at least garbled when it's picked up by its recipient(s).

CompuServe MAIL is typically available to its recipients within 15 to 30 minutes of being sent, provided that they log into CompuServe to retrieve their e-mail at that time. MAIL messages can be addressed to individual recipients, or to multiple recipients, but there is a ten-cent ($0.10 U.S.) charge for each additional recipient beyond the first one for mail addressed to more than one ID. For short messages (under 3 or 4 pages), you'll be better off sending individual e-mail messages to each recipient; for longer messages and files, the costs of transfer time will probably exceed the surcharge, making the surcharge preferable.

CompuServe will allow ordinary users to transfer files up to 1 Mb in length in MAIL messages. Even so, the costs involved are directly related to the size of the file, which is why most CompuServe users employ file compression software to reduce the files they send as much as possible before exchanging them. This is also why most file libraries on CompuServe store their contents in compressed form because it likewise reduces the costs of downloads. We recommend packages like PKZip for the PC and StuffIt Deluxe for the Macintosh, because they will afford CompuServe users significant connect time savings if used.

Sending a file via MAIL is just a matter of supplying a filename (with full PATH or disk location information) as the subject field of a message, and of indicating a communications protocol for CompuServe to use when receiving that message. For the same reasons we recommend fast modems, navigation software, and file compression software, we recommend using more modern protocols like CompuServe B or CompuServe B-plus for file transfers: they are more efficient, save time, and therefore reduce connect costs. When selecting navigation software for CompuServe, make sure it supports a broad range of advanced protocols including the ones just mentioned, as well as protocols like YModem and Zmodem.

CIS Gateways: Tie-Ins to Other E-mail Services

In addition to providing direct access to CompuServe's own considerable user community, MAIL also supports a number of gateways to other public e-mail services, including:

- America Online
- AT&T EasyLink
- AT&T Mail
- BIX
- cc:Mail
- CIX
- GEnie
- the Internet
- MCI Mail
- Novell MHS
- Prodigy
- SprintNet
- X.400 systems like Advantis, Deutsche Bundespost, Infonet

There are some limitations to using gateways from CompuServe MAIL: not all of them support file attachments, they require independent access to recipients' external e-mail addresses (CompuServe doesn't yet offer access to X.500 or other external directory services), and messages sent to some gateways may be assessed an extra handling charge.

Each of the e-mail services accessible through a gateway remains subject to its own particular limitations—for example, Internet mail messages are limited to 50,000 characters in length—so you'll also have to learn how to play the e-mail game by the rules that pertain to the other side of the gateway. Yet many users find that a CompuServe account is all that's needed to meet their e-mail needs, including contact with other e-mail systems.

CompuServe MAIL also offers alternative delivery services for messages, including fax, TELEX, postal letters, and telegrams to members of Congress called CONGRESSGrams. Each of these services is assessed a handling charge, in addition to the costs of the underlying services for fax, TELEX, postage, or telegram.

Given its ease of use, broad reach, and the range of services it can provide, we think CompuServe MAIL is worth considering, especially for smaller organizations that don't have immediate needs for workflow or other message-based applications. This tool provides a great way to keep remote users, contractors, vendors, suppliers, and customers linked together in an affordable and usable electronic mail environment.

Summary

In this chapter we focused on the e-mail services available from CompuServe. Because of the broad range of information and other services that CompuServe offers in addition to e-mail, we believe it's worthy of consideration. However, as the number of gateways to public information and e-mail services indicates, there's no dearth of choices when selecting a public e-mail service provider. If CompuServe doesn't fit your bill, for whatever reason, any of the others are also worth investigating. Whatever choice you make for yourself, public e-mail access is a great tool for communicating, both inside and outside your organization.

Breaking in the Users

If your users ever give you a case of heartburn, remember that they're the reason you're using e-mail in the first place. If you're able to be objective about it, you might even be able to look past the complaints to see that the users are only trying to do their jobs, and that against some unlikely odds. Chances are if they only knew more about what they were doing, they'd have less reason to complain and more ways to solve problems that you wouldn't even have to know about.

The key to good user relationships is information: lots of high-quality, hands-on, useful information about how to get the best bang for their networking and e-mail activities. As an e-mail administrator, you can be a powerful pipeline for progress if you arm your users with the information they need to do their jobs.

Tell Them What's Coming

In many ways, we're all creatures of habit, slaves to what might seem to be a mindless routine. As a network administrator, you'll have occasion to alter the routine every now and then. Woe betide you if your efforts to maintain the network and your e-mail system make it uncomfortable for users, or if it takes their e-mail access away during prime-time work hours. The element of surprise may be essential for combat, but it's anathema to maintaining a good relationship with your users.

We recommend that you warn them in advance of anything that could impact network or e-mail use, even if it's scheduled to happen at midnight. You might think that no one will be the wiser, but we guarantee you that anybody who feels like she has to be using e-mail at that hour will be mighty irked if it slows to a crawl or disappears altogether at that time!

That's why we recommend the "tell 'em three times" approach to spreading the word about potential network impacts:

- Send out a message to users at least three days in advance of the event, preferably a week ahead.
- Resend the message the day of the event, early in the morning, so that everybody gets reminded that day.
- Send notice again 15 to 30 minutes before the event to give your users fair warning that it's just about to happen.

It's also recommended that you follow up with a message immediately after the event to inform your users about what's happened, and to notify them about what has changed, particularly if they have to do things differently as a consequence of whatever changes you've made. If major changes result, let them know that they're coming in your pre-event messages, and plan a training class to review those changes as soon as possible (at the very least, pass around a handout explaining what's changed, how it impacts them, and why the change occurred).

Give Them the Details

Change can be scary, but mostly it's the fear of the unknown or unexpected that provokes user anxiety. When you install upgrades or replacements on your network or e-mail system, or add new capacity or capability, it's time to fill in your users about exactly what this means to them.

The best time to inform them about changes is before they actually occur. If you can hold a training class ahead of the installation of new features and functions, or replacement of a familiar program or version, you'll earn your users' gratitude for arming them before they're faced with something new and different. If you can't beat the changes to the starting gate, you don't want to lag behind by too much, because you'll be inundated with questions and complaints unless you can tell your users what they need to know.

Make sure you provide materials that capture the essential details of what they need to know, and that your training or handout doesn't go into the kinds of information that they're not interested in. Even if you have no choice but to hand out user manuals as your only form of training and documentation, you can earn a lot of kudos by taking the time to go through the materials and compiling a list of the things they should pay attention to the most. A simple road map like this will save them from wasting time on things they would rather not have to skim.

Offer Constant Training

When it comes to first-time e-mail users, nothing helps to ease the technology transition as access to information about what they're going to face and how this mysterious stuff really works. As an e-mail administrator, you should be armed with materials to welcome the uninitiated to the wonderful world of networking and e-mail. A classroom encounter is nice but not necessary, as long as you can provide some gentle guidance into a new kind of information environment for your neophytes.

Even the technologically savvy can benefit from training though. It's a good idea to keep an ongoing series of brown-bag seminars on the network to review new or changed applications for the folks who have been around for a while. It's also a good idea occasionally to provide subject overviews for new or inexperienced users—things like "Basics of Electronic Mail," "Introduction to Workflow," and "Using the Order-Entry System" are always bound to attract an audience, especially if your organization has a regular influx of new employees.

The basic value of ongoing training is that it sends a message to your users that you want them to know what's going on and that you care enough about their skills to want them to continue developing. As you perform upgrades and replacements, don't forget to ask your vendors if they can't help organize a class—many of them are thrilled at the opportunity to get in front of their customers—and try to work with everybody concerned to find a suitable place and time to continue your training efforts.

When it comes to messaging-based applications, don't forget that knowledgeable users are the best source of insight as to what kinds of applications might work, and how the applications they use should work. This means educating your users on what their e-mail and messaging systems can do, about workflow and business process modeling, and about automating work tasks. If you can arm them with sufficient information and supply them with the right tools, they can make your job easier (and in some cases where real enthusiasts get involved, they can even help to build the kinds of applications they'll need).

Don't forget that your job is a challenging one, too. E-mail administrators have to work with more technologies, equipment, and software than most people know about. You should plan on getting some training yourself, just to keep your skills sharp, and to keep learning more about how to use and run the network.

Ask for Feedback

It's important to provide your users with information, but even more important to tell them what they need to know. The only way to find out if you're hitting or missing this all-important target is to ask them how well equipped to deal with the network they feel that they are. This could be in the form of a training questionnaire, a suggestion box, or a question-and-answer period, and it should be part of your repertoire of questions as you walk around your network, checking in with the users.

The best ways to assess your users' comfort level with the network is to gauge their questions and complaints, to see if they point at missing information; to ask them how they're doing point-blank; and to provide as many opportunities for continuing network education, to see who's biting!

Summary

Informed users are the best kind to have, from the standpoints of lightening your workload and of arming them to do their best with the network for your organization. Make sure you stay in touch with their needs and their feelings about the network, and try to offer them training that gives them the biggest return for the least amount of effort. If you can stay ahead of them, you'll be able to tell your users everything they need to know!

part

E-MAIL IN THE REAL WORLD

IV

OVERVIEW

In the first three sections of the book we've given you all the background you need to understand, design, and install your own e-mail system. They say experience is the best teacher, and we believe it, having learned from some experiences of our own! In this section we'll give you the opportunity to learn from other people's experience, to help augment your own.

Here we look at three different networks and e-mail installations of very different sizes, and discuss what the installation was like for each one, what kinds of problems they had (and sometimes still have) with their e-mail system(s) up and running, and what they plan for their e-mail futures. We look at what worked and what didn't, and what they're doing about it. These examples should illuminate some pitfalls for you to avoid, and may also suggest some interesting new ways of handling e-mail details that you might be able to apply to your own network.

A Smallish Network

Ozz Research Computing, Inc., of Austin, Texas, is a high-end computer graphics and multimedia firm with a fairly small network. It has fewer than 30 PCs networked together, with a combination of Apple Macintoshes (the favorite machine of graphic designers), IBM-PC clones, and the odd RISC-based UNIX workstation along with a plethora of specialized graphics creation and recording equipment. This organization has settled on Microsoft Mail for its e-mail needs.

The Mid-Sized Model

The second network we look at belongs to Vtel Corporation, a manufacturer of video conferencing systems, also based in Austin, Texas. Vtel has about 300 employees and its network has about the same number of PCs. In addition to IBM-PC clones, it has a group of UNIX workstations and some Apple Macintoshes, plus several types of remote connections. Vtel uses a mix of cc:Mail and UNIX-based SMTP mail, as befits its mixed-platform population.

An Industrial-strength Network

For an example of a large network, we turn to MD Anderson Cancer Center in Houston, Texas. The center is part of a hospital and medical school complex and is linked to the statewide University of Texas system. Their network has more than 5,500 PCs and representatives of just about every possible network technology, PC type, and networking format, along with many different types of medical equipment. Their environment also includes a mainframe that plays host to their e-mail hub, and includes six other varieties of e-mail, all of which are tied together through a set of host gateways and an ingenious common e-mail naming scheme.

Case Study
Smallish Co., Inc.

About the Corporation

Our first case study is of a fairly small network, one that links together about 25 workstations and other computers. It belongs to a graphics imaging and multimedia company called Ozz Research Computing, Inc., based in Austin, Texas.

Ozz Research, 9420 Research Boulevard, Austin, TX 78759, can be reached at (512) 794-8590. Ozz Research is a specialty graphics software development and image production firm, with a pronounced emphasis on high-resolution digital imaging, multimedia, and hypertext authoring tools.

Ozz Research is a company that small affordable microcomputers made possible, because the introduction of sophisticated imaging systems in the early 1980s, along with PCs, created the technology that continues to support the company's business. The company's origins in 1983 nearly coincide with the introduction of the PC, but its earliest efforts actually predate the PC, based around special-purpose systems from Datapoint and Superset Technologies. Likewise, Ozz Research was ahead of its time in that it has been networked since its inception, using technology included with Datapoint's pioneering ARCnet networking technologies built right into its workstations.

Today, Ozz Research runs its business on a network that features a combination of PCs and Macintoshes, but to a large extent Macintoshes are its workstations of choice. Ozz Research uses an IBM-PC clone as its network server, running Novell's NetWare network operating system, with file and print services for both Macintosh and PC clients. The networking technologies in use include ARCnet for the PCs, and a combination of LocalTalk and Ethernet for the Macintoshes. Here again, NetWare acts as the focal point, uniting the multiple networking technologies in use.

Thus, the company's business is completely built around networking. Even though Ozz Research continues to depend on ARCnet for office automation, it is looking at higher bandwidth technologies (primarily Thomas-Conrad's TCNS 100-Mbps token-passing networking scheme) to accommodate its high-end graphics and multimedia efforts. Today, the bulk of its network runs over coaxial ARCnet, but it is planning to expand into fiber-optic and coaxial-based high-bandwidth networking in the second half of 1994.

The five full-time employees at Ozz Research regularly use the network, and everyone uses a PC or a Macintosh in the course of their jobs. The network server acts as the principal repository for all incoming jobs, along with a collection of esoteric image-recording and processing equipment that includes a LaserDisc and a CD-ROM recorder. Customers typically work with Ozz from the concept stage, through design and implementation, to the delivery of a finished product that can range from an interactive training manual or press release on diskette, to a comprehensive multimedia encyclopedia for advanced technologies.

Ozz Research also offers in-house graphics, layout, and live and animation studio services, and has a broad international clientele that ranges from law firms needing animation and hypertext services to make complicated events or high-technology cases accessible to juries, to a mix of high-technology and manufacturing companies with hypertext creation or multimedia needs.

Bruce Hahn is the founder and "technology steward" for Ozz Research and has been involved with the company since its inception in 1983. He has been instrumental in introducing the current network server, in managing the conversion from LocalTalk to Ethernet on the Macintosh side, and in expanding the capabilities of its ARCnet network. As with many startup companies, Ozz Research has had the difficult task of balancing technology acquisition needs against ongoing expenses, but it has been fortunate enough to build the kind of equipment collection and networking capacity that it needs to meet its customers' sophisticated imaging and data-handling needs.

THE NETWORK LAYOUT

Figure 30.1 shows a diagram of the Ozz Research network. Note that the network has three segments. The segment on the right in the diagram contains most of the Macintosh systems, which are primarily used for graphics creation and simple animation tasks. It is linked into the network through a 486 PC that supports a Miramar Systems Macintosh-PC gateway. In the middle of the diagram is the segment that connects the PC systems for office automation, additional graphics, and illustration work. The segment on the left is the production segment, with some of the older Macintoshes and the Sony LaserDisk recorder linked via LocalTalk using Sitka TOPS, and scanners and other production equipment. The Novell server acts as a file and print server for all the three network segments.

The only remote connection in the network is a single dial-up line to a PC that offers users outside the office access to PC-based network workstations using Symantec's PC Anywhere remote control software. Ozz Research uses this capability to let its employees access e-mail, files, and specialized applications while they're on the road, sometimes

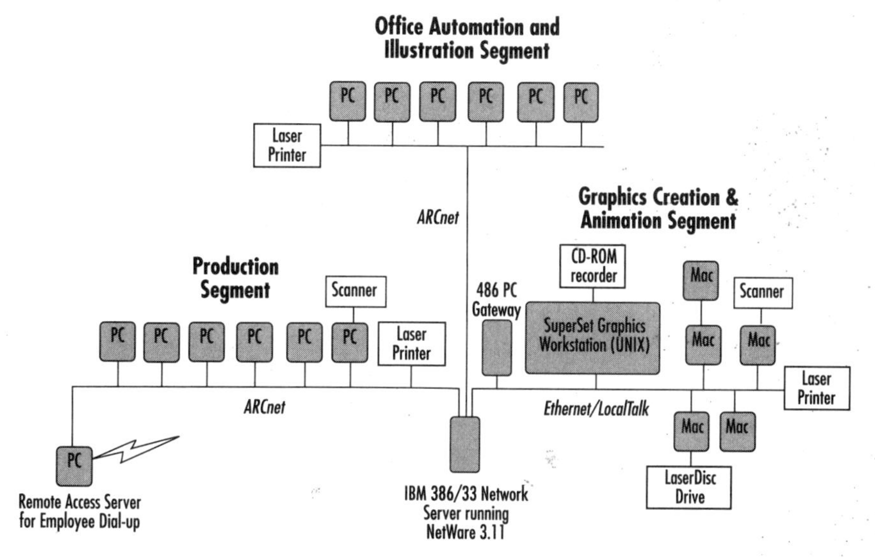

Figure 30.1. *The Ozz Research network.*

even for access to demonstrations or presentations for display at customer locations.

The Current E-mail System

Ozz Research is currently in the process of implementing e-mail for its employees and outside contractors. It has chosen Microsoft Mail (MS-Mail), primarily because its PC interface of choice is MS-Windows, and because MS-Mail offers a broad range of gateways that can accommodate both Ozz's own eclectic mix of systems (which include PCs running DOS and Windows, Macintoshes of many vintages, a small number of UNIX-based workstations, and the occasional special-purpose system like its SuperSet Technologies SuperSet graphics engine).

The network links 13 IBM-clone PCs and 5 Macintoshes. The IBM clones are running DOS 5.0 and 6.2, along with MS-Windows, while the Macintoshes are all running System 7.1.

The network server is an Austin Computing 386/33 PC with 16 megabytes of RAM and 1 gigabyte of hard disk space. It's running NetWare 3.11 with NetWare for Macintosh 3.011.

E-mail Benefits

As a firm that services many specialized clients, Ozz Research has developed an interesting employment model. "Basically, we run the company around a core of five people, all of whom have broad technology experience and know how to work with our customer base," says Bruce. "We have access to a pool of very talented people in a range of specialized fields, from law to a number of engineering specialists to a team of highly skilled video and film production people." Rather than trying to keep all of this expensive and diverse talent always on the payroll, Ozz Research has opted to draw from an ever-shifting collection of consultants and contractors who can bring the skills needed for a particular project to bear whenever they're needed.

Bruce opines: "In a project-oriented business like ours, we want to have access to the best talents, and to exactly the experts that we need to meet our clients' needs. This means that communication is critical, and for us, e-mail is becoming an increasingly important tool in forging effective teams out of our staff and our outside contractors." Simply put, e-mail helps to make Ozz Research's business model possible, because it lets geographically dispersed teams of individual contributors communicate easily and effectively.

For Ozz Research, other e-mail benefits include elimination of phone tag for co-workers who may not work the same schedules, or even be in the same locations, as well as the ability to circulate work schedules job bids and contracts, and job-related files and information readily among project team members. "You could say that e-mail provides the glue that ties everything together at Ozz," says Bruce, as he explains how a constant stream of complex graphics production, studio work, and animation makes for long hours and very tight schedules.

The Problems

As in any living network environment, Ozz Research has its share of problems related to its network in general, and to e-mail in particular. It encountered some issues during the initial installation of MS-Mail related to multiple versions of NetWare client software creating previously unimportant incompatibilities, and it has a lot of maintenance issues with the huge volume of data generated by the graphics production process. The combination of network types leads to some incompatibilities, as well.

"The expense of adding all the right gateways to support Internet access, UNIX SMTP mail, Macintosh clients, as well as DOS and Windows users was greater than we expected, too," adds Bruce, as he goes on to describe a series of trial-and-error experiments needed to put all the pieces in place and to get them working properly. "We liked the idea that Microsoft was bundling e-mail [Microsoft Mail] with its new Windows products, and when we looked at the product, we liked its gateway offerings and ease of use. As we got further into installation, we learned that just because it's bundled doesn't mean it's free, especially when it comes to hooking up to the external e-mail systems we want to use to service our clients."

Nevertheless, Ozz Research is happy with its e-mail system. "We've been around high-tech and the software business long enough to know that nothing is as easy as the vendors try to make it sound, so we weren't too surprised when we hit some snags along the way."

Future E-mail Plans

In future expansions, Ozz Research plans to consider some of the capabilities promised by e-mail systems like those offered by Lotus Notes and Beyond Mail. "We've heard a lot about messaging-based applications," says Bruce, "but we're still not sure how to weigh the costs against the possible benefits. However, we recognize that workflow support, and some of the forms- and database-related capabilities of these systems could help our project focus at Ozz." Right now, the costs are still too high for Ozz to want to commit funds to these kinds of systems, no matter how interesting they might be.

Because the technologies involved don't directly apply to Ozz Research's core businesses—graphics, animation, and multimedia—Ozz is presently content to sit on the sidelines and wait. "With technology—and it doesn't seem to matter what kind," Bruce muses, "you can count on at least two things: it gets cheaper over time, and you can tell if its benefits make it useful by how broadly it's adopted." Given that this statement typifies the attitude of many small businesses, even those that are technologically sophisticated like Ozz Research, it looks like the costs are a significant barrier to wholesale adoption of message-based applications today. It also appears that these applications could explode if this hurdle is overcome, or if the benefits prove to be too good to pass up, based on the experience of early adopters.

chapter 31

Case Study A Medium-sized Corporation

The Corporation

In this chapter we look at a medium-sized network with fewer than 300 nodes spread across two sites in the same city.

Vtel Corporation (formerly VideoTelecom Corp.), at 108 Wild Basin Road, Austin, Texas 78746, can be reached at (512) 314-2700. It makes video conferencing equipment, and designs, develops, and manufactures the video conferencing systems out of its two sites in Austin. The development and administrative branches of the company are housed at the Wild Basin address, while the manufacturing division is in a separate building on Technicenter Drive, also in Austin. In addition, the company has a sales and support office just outside of London, UK, and several sales offices throughout the United States. Company employees, vendors, and other contacts all use the network regularly.

Vtel uses its network for three major purposes: to share files, especially engineering plans and software source code files; to provide messaging between employees and groups via e-mail; and to save money by using networked copies of software, by buying licenses for only the number of users who use a particular software package at any time rather than buying a copy for everyone who might ever use it. It also uses it to share printers, modems, and Internet access, and possible future uses include shared CD-ROM drives and interactive video over the network.

The network management group at Vtel has grown dramatically in the last year, from one to six people. Sal Lozano, the director of the group, has over two decades of experience in group computing management, primarily in the mainframe world. Sal's staff members' responsibilities include server administration, PC support, video network maintenance, and general troubleshooting, and they have between two and five years of experience each.

The Network Layout

As you can see in Figure 31.1, the Vtel network extends between the two Austin sites via a high-bandwidth, high-speed T1 link. Half of the bandwidth of the link is used for video transmissions, the other half for network data. It has one server at the Technicenter site and three more at the Wild Basin site. A pair of Cisco routers provide the main link between the two sites, and the Cisco router at Wild Basin also links the other segments of the network. One of these segments is the T1 connection to the Technicenter site, another attaches to the Internet link, a third connects the group of UNIX workstations, and the other segment

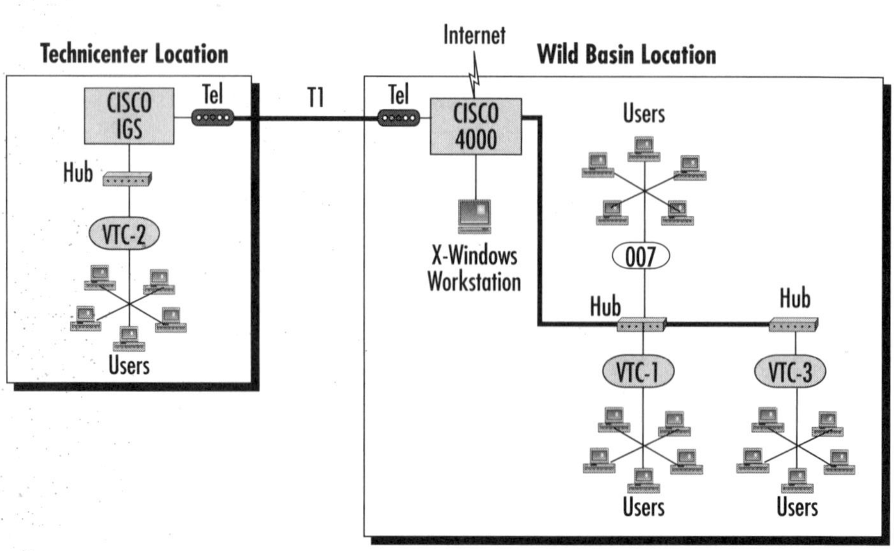

Figure 31.1. *Vtel's present network layout.*

connects to the three servers and workstations that comprise the bulk of the network.

The network operating system is NetWare 3.11. As Vtel brings new servers onto the network, it is currently installing them with the latest 3.X version of NetWare. Because it will have six servers on the network by the end of 1994, Vtel would like to upgrade to NetWare 4.X so it can take advantage of its centralized management capabilities. It's wary of moving to version 4.0; Vtel would prefer to wait until it's had a chance to stabilize. Furthermore, the move to 4.0 will be very time consuming. Taken together, these factors mean that Vtel will probably not move to NetWare 4.X until the end of 1994 at the earliest.

E-MAIL PROFILE

Since one of Vtel's self-professed primary reasons for using a network is for e-mail, it should come as no surprise that 100 percent of its employees use one or more of its e-mail systems, and that it's been using e-mail for nearly the same amount of time it's had a network in place—namely, six years.

Vtel started out with the DOS version of cc:Mail and has begun to use more and more MS-Windows–based cc:Mail in the past two years, along with a general shift toward Windows on Vtel's users' desktops. In late 1993, Vtel added an Internet to cc:Mail gateway that is broadly used within the company. The engineers in the company use the gateway to exchange information with colleagues at other companies, while other employees use the gateway to exchange e-mail with various Vtel business partners. An important perceived benefit here is a reduction in express mail usage and related costs.

In early 1994, Vtel began to use Microsoft's Scheduler+ for managing company schedules. Although this application is based around Microsoft Mail, the scheduler is the only use that Vtel currently makes of Microsoft's messaging products. Scheduler+ is used to issue invitations to meetings and to handle replies and track meeting attendance. "This has made the headache of scheduling meetings—and conference rooms—much less painful," says Sal. "We'd rather let the computer wrestle with all the coordination that's required to get a roomful of people together, than have to do things the old-fashioned way."

In addition, Vtel uses a cc:Mail to SMTP gateway to distribute mail between its PC-based users and its UNIX-based workstations users—primarily engineering or software development staff. "A few hardy PC users will occasionally log into a UNIX machine over the network and use *elm*, an elementary UNIX-based e-mail package," says Sal, "but most of our PC users prefer to go through the gateway instead."

With over 300 e-mail users in the company, Vtel is committed to continued use of messaging technology. At present, Scheduler+ represents its main foray beyond basic e-mail, but it is keeping current on emerging messaging applications and is also concerned to make sure its own products can take appropriate advantage of such technologies, if and when that's needed.

E-mail Deployment

The first introduction of cc:Mail is too deeply buried in the past for Sal to remember any significant issues surrounding e-mail deployment at Vtel, but on the whole he believes that the initial rollout was uneventful. "cc:Mail has been very good to us," he continues, "We've expanded our use of the product over the years without encountering too many glitches, and our users continue to be satisfied with its capabilities."

The only e-mail–related glitch that Sal can recall occurred during the installation of the cc:Mail to Internet gateway, when some of the installation details weren't immediately apparent. Sal admits to going live without building a test lab version first, but adds that the problems were routine and easily resolved with a few calls to Lotus Technical Support, which helped them tweak a few installation parameters and quickly get up and running.

In addition to caring and feeding for Vtel's network, Sal's IS staff also handles all of Vtel's e-mail needs. This additional responsibility has not proved too taxing, and Sal believes that his group will continue to manage all aspects of the network and its software for the foreseeable future. "Our company builds complex networked communications systems," says Sal. "If we can't cope with e-mail, given what we do, there's not much hope that our customers can cope with Vtel's video teleconferencing gear. So far, we haven't hit anything we can't handle."

The Problems

One of the most challenging problems that cropped up during e-mail deployment at Vtel related to e-mail names. Because mail routing between UNIX users and cc:Mail users requires that every user have matched UNIX and cc:Mail e-mail names, Sal's group had to make sure that all users had UNIX IDs and that every UNIX user name was mapped to the correct cc:Mail ID.

Vtel's UNIX e-mail names also work as Internet IDs and consist of first initial plus last name, while cc:Mail names consist of each user's full name with first name first, followed by a space, followed by the last name. In many cases, the first name is all that's used for a cc:Mail user name, tracing back to the company's small-group, informal naming convention in the days when it was staffed by only a handful of people. "Right now, we haven't had too many problems with cc:Mail names, even with three or four hundred users," says Sal, "but we recognize that when the company grows, users with common names like 'Joe' or 'David' will have to enter more keystrokes to properly identify themselves." (Even though cc:Mail stores full names for each user, they need only identify themselves with enough keystrokes to uniquely specify their particular mail names.)

Keeping up with a constant influx of new employees has also proved to be a challenge for Sal's IS group at Vtel. They typically create 10 to 20 new e-mail name sets per month and have worked to automate as much of the process as possible. "We've tried to build scripts and tools to help us speed up adding new users to the network, and to our e-mail systems," says Sal. "Because e-mail is so important to our users, we can't make them wait on our convenience to get them set up; we have to get them up and running as quickly as possible." Keeping up with departing employees—deleting accounts and disk allocations—is just as important, adds Sal, because his group tries to keep Vtel's exposure to network and e-mail infiltration as low as possible, and to keep precious system resources as available as possible.

Day-to-day e-mail use is typically smooth, but it also poses some interesting problems for Sal and his group. E-mail can sometimes become a forum for heated and public arguments ("flaming"). Some users hoard e-mail messages forever, and this ultimately requires Sal's group to police e-mail disk usage and to purge and compress their e-mail databases regularly. The amount of administrative activity that the e-mail systems require can sometimes become a burden to Sal and his group, but overall he considers these costs mild, especially when compared to the undeniable benefits that e-mail has delivered to Vtel and its users.

Vtel also supports two remote e-mail servers on its network. These service remote employees, field personnel, vendors, business partners, as well as members of Vtel's board of directors. Vtel's U.K. office has also been automated to dial one of the remote e-mail servers on the hour to exchange e-mail messages on a regular basis. A similar setup exists with Price-Waterhouse (Vtel's accounting firm) and with Dell Computer (a major Vtel customer). "We try to stay in touch with our customers, our partners, and our vendors," says Sal, "and for that purpose, e-mail has proved to be invaluable."

Vtel's E-mail Wish List

Whenever you get to know a system well, there are always things about it that you wish it would do differently, or features missing that you would like it to supply. Sal's wish list for e-mail reflects both of these tendencies. First and foremost, he wishes that Vtel would set message lifetimes to only one month (they're currently set at three months). "A month is plenty of time for a user to decide if he or she want to keep a private copy of a message, and get it out of the system," says Sal. "I wish we'd set a hard and fast policy about the amount of disk space allocated to each user." Vtel's monthly disk consumption for e-mail currently runs at about 50 MB, and anything that could help to limit and reduce this consumption would be welcomed with open arms.

Along the same lines, Sal also wishes that disk monitoring and consumption could be better automated, and possibly even tied into a network management console of some kind. He and his group have to struggle with multiple management consoles, utilities, and special, program-specific interfaces, all of which increase the slope of the learning curve.

Creating and maintaining mailing lists are other administrative chores that Sal would like to see improved. Handling mailing lists is restricted to designated list administrators in cc:Mail, and Sal's group monitors this activity closely. He would appreciate a good process to identify which mailing lists a particular user should participate in, and tools to help automate that process.

Sal would also like to see the user definition utilities improved to make it as easy to move a user from one post office to another, as it presently is to define one within a particular post office, and then to advertise their creation to other post offices in cc:Mail. Today, users must be transferred to a new post office one at a time in a tedious process that requires redefinition of that user, running a utility to transfer that user's mail files to the new post office, then finally, manually checking the user's drive mappings to make sure they reflect the new post office definitions. He'd like a utility that automates this entire process to be simply driven by the list of users to be moved from a source post office to a destination post office.

E-mail Policy

Vtel has a loose policy regarding e-mail. Its only guidelines are to inform employees that e-mail is a form of public communication, and that the contents of e-mail reflects on the company as well as on its author. While Vtel does believe that e-mail is not a private form of communication, and that it reserves the right to examine e-mail messages, the company practices no censorship, nor does it actively monitor e-mail contents.

Vtel is currently working with its personnel department to formulate an official e-mail policy. It will stipulate that e-mail cannot be used by employees for personal gain, so that one can't run a side business through company e-mail, nor advertise a garage sale on e-mail. It will also state that discriminatory language and use on Vtel e-mail is prohibited, so that messages cannot include text that could be construed as discriminating against individuals or groups on the basis of sexual preference, religion, gender, or race. Vtel's intended policy is that e-mail is exclusively for business use, but it is intended as a legal posture to protect the company from liability, not to prevent users from sending each other lunch invitations via e-mail.

Vtel has, however, found it necessary to eliminate anonymous e-mail access from its system, because an e-mail "suggestion box" was consistently abused when mail senders couldn't be identified. An alternative anonymous suggestion mechanism has been instituted, but it has not been subject to the same abuse.

Vtel's e-mail policies are similar to those of many mid-sized and larger companies. They have proved effective in controlling inappropriate usage and in protecting the company from liability, without unnecessarily limiting user enthusiasm for e-mail use. We think this is just what a good policy should ensure.

Future E-mail Plans

Vtel's future e-mail plans are fairly modest: "We want to keep doing more of the same," says Sal. While it has followed the development of messaging-based applications with some interest, its interests in distributed technologies are currently focused at the operations side of Vtel's business. It is currently investigating broader use of database technology to integrate accounting, inventory, manufacturing, and order management. "Ultimately, we'd like to tie all this into e-mail somehow," says Sal, "but this project is still very much in the early research stage."

Vtel's senior management staff currently uses VisionQuest planning software. This package allows users to hold remote meetings, and includes decision-support capabilities to support brainstorming and planning. "It's a distributed package that runs over the network," offers Sal, "but it's not really message-based. That's about as advanced as we get right now."

As for workflow, forms-based messaging, or groupware, Vtel has yet to find compelling reasons—or compelling products—that could justify their use. While it can't rule such things out, they have not yet become a part of the IS planning that Sal Lozano manages for Vtel. Sal concludes: "In the meantime, there's plenty to do while the promises start to catch up with reality."

chapter 32

Case Study
A Large Institution

The Organization

Finally, let's look at an example of a large network. This one has thousands of nodes and users and contains examples of just about every possible networking compatibility test you might imagine.

The University of Texas MD Anderson Cancer Center is located at 1515 Holcombe Boulevard, Houston, TX 77030, and can be reached at (713) 792-2121. MD Anderson is one of the preeminent cancer treatment centers in the world and is located in the Houston Medical Center, a large medical campus near downtown Houston that also includes the Baylor Medical Center, the University of Texas Medical School, and a variety of hospitals and other teaching and medical establishments.

MD Anderson typifies many larger organizations in that its computing roots go back into the 1950s and it still boasts a major installation of IBM mainframes and related computing equipment. MD Anderson's network has been 12 years in the making, however, and currently supports over 5,500 individual PCs, of which 3,800 are IBM-PC clones, 1,500 are Macintoshes, and the remainder are high-end RISC- or SPARC-based workstations. Our contact at MD Anderson is Dan Kohner, manager of the Network Services department, whose group oversees networking technologies.

Most of the major commercial networking technologies are in use at MD Anderson, including a dwindling arrangement of ARCnet and some LocalTalk, with the bulk of the networked nodes attached via Ethernet, which can be found in 10BaseT, 10Base2, 10Base5, and 10BaseF formats. MD Anderson is also connected to a campus-wide FDDI ring that encompasses the entire Houston Medical Center.

Because of the large number of laboratories, clinics, and operations at MD Anderson, networking is a crucial element in many aspects of the organization, from processing and forwarding patient records, to providing campus- and system-wide communications for networked employees. This organization's size also helps explain why three separate organizations plus all of the functional MD Anderson departments, taken together, share responsibilities for various aspects of the network. These organizations and entities are as follows:

- The MIS department manages the mainframes and all organizational information assets and owns the campus internetwork and infrastructure.
- Each operational unit at MD Anderson that has a network has a designated network administrator to manage the network locally, and each unit also has its own backup administrator. This group is the first line of support for e-mail as well.
- The Network Services department provides overall network management and design, and works to define networking hardware, equipment, and software standards. This group also provides a second layer of support and expertise for networking configuration, software, and system issues. This group provides second-level e-mail support, and also coordinates campus-wide distribution lists and manages all e-mail gateways.
- The cabling department manages all wiring installations and handles the purchase and installation of routers and hubs.

The network services group is currently composed of seven individuals, each of whom is an expert in one or more areas of networking. The average number of years of industry experience in this group is over 10, and most of the individuals have advanced computer training and/or degrees in a computer-related field. Dan Kohner has been in the group for 12 years and has been responsible for most of the networking deployed at MD Anderson. He is a widely sought speaker for industry events and participates in several committees that oversee networking standards and events. He is also an enthusiastic proponent for e-mail and messaging applications, as you'll shortly see for yourself.

The Network Layout

It's helpful to look at the MD Anderson network as a three-level hierarchy, consisting of an intracampus backbone, a set of intrabuilding feeder trunks, and the distribution networks that bring connectivity to users' desktops (see Figure 32.1).

Each NetWare server acts as a router among its local cable segments. The feeder trunks are served by Cisco routers that provide segmentation of intrabuilding networks, and Cisco routers also manage access to the intracampus FDDI backbone.

The Servers

Across the campus, MD Anderson has about 80 NetWare servers, about half of which are running NetWare 4.01. The rest are still running NetWare 3.11, but the company expects to upgrade all of them by the end of 1994. It also has 20 or 30 UNIX servers, whose users typically access TCP/IP protocols and applications. Of course, it still has a significant cache of mainframes, which the users access via terminal emulation programs and NetWare For SAA, or through Telnet-based emulation.

The Network Hardware

At the time of our interview the MD Anderson network was using five Cisco routers to tie the entire internetwork together, and planned to add four more during the course of 1994. In addition, it has a number of Cabletron and Synoptics hubs for the twisted-pair wiring, with a preference for the Synoptics hubs because of their superior manageability, with Synoptics Optivity management software.

The PCs

On the PC side of things, the numbers are equally impressive. To start with, MD Anderson has 3,800 IBM-PC clones of various types as desktop machines, with about 300 portables or laptops. About 65 percent of these are running Windows 3.1 as the primary operating environment, 25 percent use some flavor of DOS, version 3.31 or higher, with the

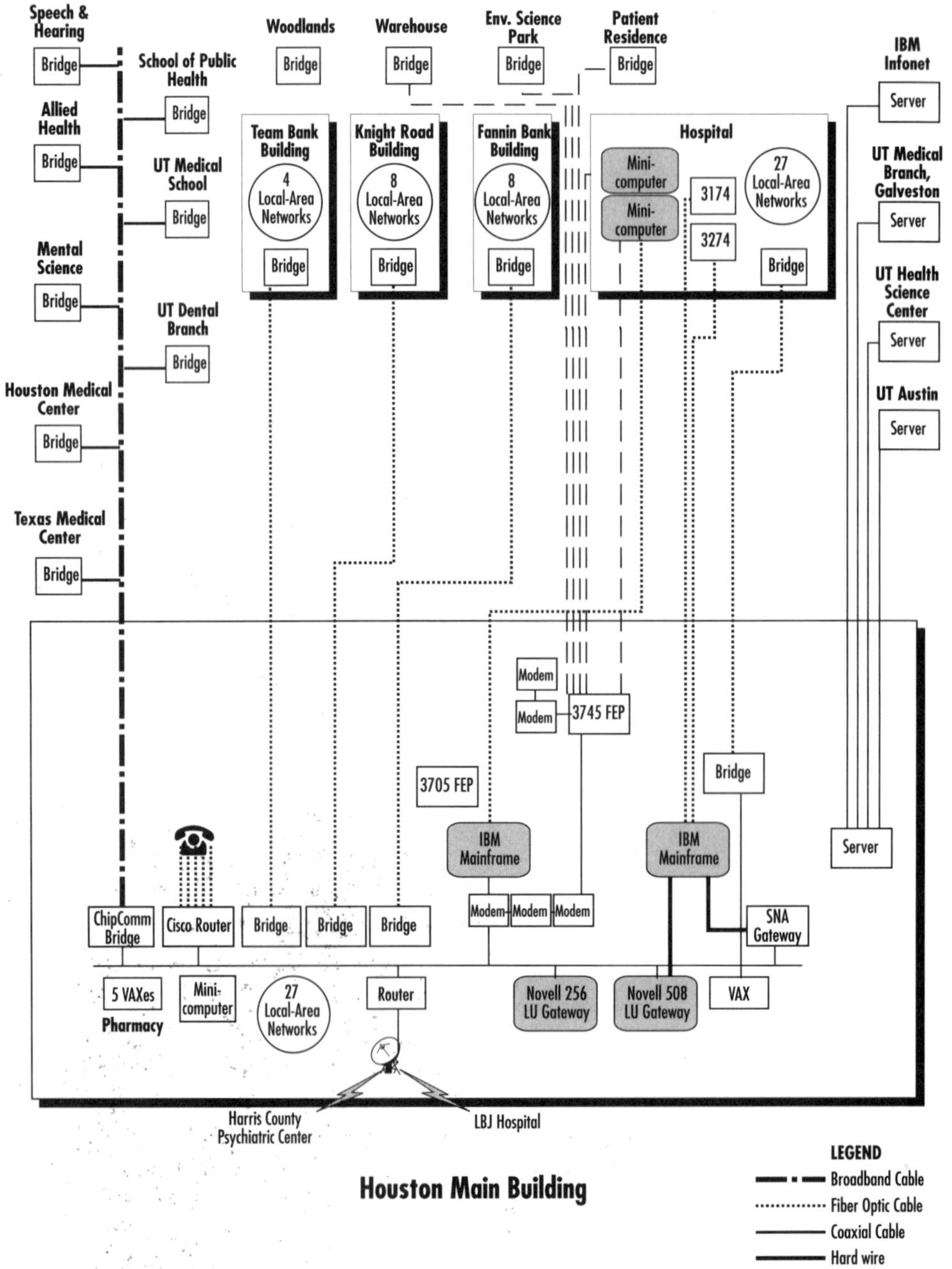

Figure 32.1. *A diagram of the MD Anderson intrabuilding and intracampus network.*

remaining systems split between UNIX and OS/2 operating systems. In the DOS and Windows community, e-mail use is split among QuickMail, cc:Mail, and Lotus Notes; in the UNIX community SMTP mail is the norm; OS/2 users typically emulate a terminal on the mainframe and read their e-mail there.

MD Anderson also has about 1,500 Macintoshes of varying ages and capabilities, from old Mac SEs to newer Quadra 950 models. The older ones run version System 6.0.8, while the newer ones are running System 7.0.1 and 7.1. Besides these machines, it has about 300 portable or laptop Macintoshes (PowerBooks of various makes and models). All of the Macintosh users are on CE Software's QuickMail package.

Finally, it has around 100 RISC- or SPARC-based workstations, typically running some variant of the UNIX operating system. Like their PC-based UNIX colleagues, these users also run SMTP mail.

In addition to the PCs and workstations, the MD Anderson network links a wide variety of specialized equipment, from MRI to ultrasound. Since most of this gear is not workstation oriented, it typically does not play host to e-mail. However, MD Anderson still supports a sizable population of dumb terminals, all of which attach to a host of some kind to read e-mail. Mainframe-attached terminals use an e-mail package called Parimation; VAX-attached terminals use VAXmail or AlisaMail.

MD Anderson's E-mail Profile

Given its user population, and the number of e-mail packages in use—at least five that Dan knows of—it should come as no surprise that Dan's group includes a dedicated group of four analysts whose job is to manage e-mail for all of MD Anderson. Dan estimates that 85 to 87 percent of his 8,000-plus user community regularly uses one form of e-mail or another.

E-mail plays a critical role at MD Anderson, according to Dan. "I see e-mail used for everything from setting meetings, to business communications, to exchanging research information and test results," he says. "It's amazing what e-mail has done for MD Anderson, not just within our organization, but to facilitate communications with other research and teaching institutions as well."

Whatever any individual user's e-mail profile might be, Dan's staff has done a terrific job of making e-mail accessible from any platform, anywhere on MD Anderson's far-flung network. Their secret has been to set up consistent e-mail names across all the packages in use, based around the IBM mainframe e-mail application, called Parimation, that they use.

"The [mainframe] host is our e-mail hub. It acts as the central repository for all messages and user database information, so we maintain gateways from the host to all of the other e-mail systems we support [total of six altogether: cc:Mail, AlisaMail, QuickMail, SMTP, Lotus Notes, and VAXmail]. We establish a host e-mail ID for every user, based on their initials and a three-letter department code [there are over 300 unique department codes defined for MD Anderson's user community], that we use consistently on each and every e-mail package on campus. This keeps us out of trouble with name conflicts, and we've yet to have a problem maintaining consistent e-mail directories across all of our gateways."

In addition, users can log into whatever e-mail system they can access most easily, even if they're not at their desks, and still get access to the same messages and e-mail information as if they were at their home workstations. "We've tried to set our e-mail systems up so that there are pathways to everything. Users can even forward their e-mail from one e-mail environment to another, so that they can read their e-mail from inside their preferred e-mail application," says Dan.

MD Anderson also maintains multiple remote e-mail servers, including a Notes server with database replication capabilities, as well as dial-back access to either the mainframe or a VAX for e-mail access. cc:Mail remote access is currently under review, and because MD Anderson also offers a variety of remote LAN access options to its users, contractors, vendors, and other outside users, all of the e-mail packages can be accessed remotely, allowing users to dial in from the platform of their choice.

All in all, MD Anderson has one of the most complex but best-engineered e-mail systems we've ever seen anywhere. It's a testament to the hard work and design skills of its teams of e-mail analysts that this system works across as many different e-mail packages, through as many gateways, and on as many different hardware platforms as it does.

E-mail Problems

Dan allows that all this perfection wasn't achieved without some frustration along the way, nor without the occasional system glitch.

"Everything we've encountered so far we've been able to handle with routine vendor technical support, even when we've been struggling with our own ignorance, and not problems with the software."

Dan's most galling experience in getting the many gateways up and running came when he realized that AlisaMail required DEC Pathworks, not the Interconnections NetWare for VMS product that he was already using. "We had to bite the bullet, and go out and buy Pathworks for our AlisaMail users on the VAX. Other than the expense, it went without a hitch, but that taught us to evaluate all of the software requirements for e-mail completely and carefully before we agreed to support any more packages."

The LAN-based e-mail packages also handle a significant number of electronic forms, which require specially formatted text files to be filled in and mailed off to a receiving database built around MD Anderson's SMS Distributed Medical Systems application on the mainframe. "It was a pain designing and testing all the templates for the system, not to mention time consuming," adds Dan, "but we think this use of e-mail is one of the best benefits of our overall system."

MD Anderson's use of electronic forms equivalents allows clinics, pharmacies, doctors' offices, labs, and other operations at MD Anderson to convert what might ordinarily be paperwork into electronic equivalents. E-mail messages can move across the network, and into their medical records database, much more quickly and efficiently than paper can. "This approach also lets us do immediate data-checking and verification," adds Dan, "so the work is more accurate as well as more timely. This application, by itself, has made all the time, money, and effort we've spent on e-mail worthwhile."

MD Anderson's E-mail Policies and Training

Like many large institutions, MD Anderson has enacted a formal e-mail policy. In principle, it strongly resembles the policy under development at Vtel. But it's much more elaborate and more strictly enforced at MD Anderson, primarily because of the volume of e-mail generated by an 8,000-plus user community.

"When the system was first rolled out," says Dan, "junk mail overloads were common on the system." MD Anderson devised a creative and effective solution to this problem: they restricted distribution list creation capability only to the e-mail analysts, and forced the user community to make formal requests for new distribution lists to be built. The analysts also did away with the e-mail name for "everyone" (sometimes known as "world" or "all" because it reaches all the users on a system), to keep the number of global messages to a minimum.

MD Anderson also enacted a policy that prohibits use of the e-mail system for advertisements of any kind—what Dan calls "junk e-mail"—and enforced this policy through training, in employee handbooks, and as a part of its management culture. "Our systems also time and date stamp when recipients read their e-mail and report that information back to the sender," adds Dan, "so users know their responsiveness is a matter of public record." This has fostered frequent e-mail use on campus and has made e-mail a normal communications tool for the whole user community.

In addition to policy, MD Anderson also offers lots of user support in the form of regular training. The e-mail analysts offer regular user classes—at least once a month for beginning, intermediate, and advanced users for each e-mail package—that run from a half day to a whole day in length. The analysts themselves are also required to attend at least two weeks' worth of training yearly, to keep them abreast of new tools and technologies for the systems they manage.

E-mail Plans and Wish Lists

"We're just starting to get into some of the more advanced Lotus Notes e-mail application. Currently this includes a variety of native Notes databases, and an electronic meeting program based on Notes." Dan's e-mail analysts are also investigating a possible DB2 to Notes database link that would permit them to maintain Notes databases on the mainframe, where they would be accessible to other e-mail users as well.

"What we're trying to do is to figure out ways to save time and travel by using e-mail more effectively," he continues. For example, the Notes electronic meeting software has saved hundreds of hours of walking time for its management members, simply because it lets everyone "meet" from their own desktops without having to walk across MD Anderson's 20-plus acre campus.

The folks at MD Anderson are very excited about the future possibilities that e-mail and message-based applications might hold. They're currently investigating workflow automation, image-delivery, document-tracking, and advanced scheduling and meeting management applications, all with an eye to improving communications and cutting down on-campus (and off-campus) transit times.

"We haven't got this all figured out yet," says Dan, "but we've already learned that e-mail is a powerful tool that we want to use as much as we can. Besides, getting there is half the fun!" With that kind of attitude, we can count on seeing some interesting applications of this technology from MD Anderson in the future.

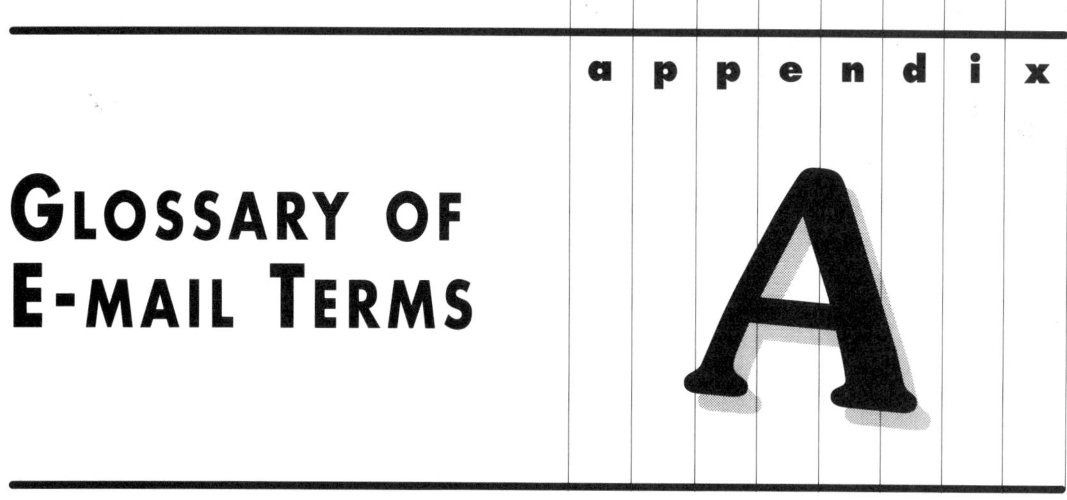

Appendix A: Glossary of E-mail Terms

14.4 kbps (and other typical modem speeds): the rated speed at which a modem can send bit patterns across the line (14.4 kbps = 14,400 bps). Other common modem speeds include 300, 1200, 2400, 9600 and 19,200 bps. In general, faster is better when it comes to modems. (See also: **bps**, **kbps**)

3270: a model number for a family of IBM computer terminals; one of the most common of mainframe terminal types.

acronym: an abbreviation formed by taking the first letter of each word of the phrase you want to abbreviate. Since e-mail terminology is loaded with long wordy phrases, it's also loaded with acronyms. Some technologists talk about TLAs, which stands for three-letter acronyms, as being essential for legitimacy amongst nerds!

AFAIK: e-mail acronym for "as far as I know."

America Online: a public information service that offers e-mail and gateway delivery services (see the Vendor List for contact information).

ANSI: computer acronym for American National Standards Institute; one of the primary standards-setting bodies for computer technology in the United States.

archives: in general, a place where obsolete or unused records are stored; in computerese, a place where backed-up files are kept.

ARCnet: token-passing type of network technology; inexpensive but rather slow by current standards (ARCnet is an acronym for "Attached Resource Computer, networked").

ASAP: e-mail (and general) acronym for "as soon as possible."

ASCII: computer acronym for "American Standard Code for Information Interchange"; an eight-bit code for data transfer that was adopted by ANSI to ensure compatibility among data types.

bandwidth: a measure of the capacity of any type of transmission medium; computer networks and telephone links (a.k.a. asynchronous connections) are typically measure in bits per second—bps). Most network links are measured in megabits per second (Mbps) or gigabits per second (Gbps); most telephone links are measured in kilobits per second (kbps) or Mbps.

baud: a unit of signaling speed defined as cycles per second. This equals bits per second (bps) only if one bit is transmitted per cycle. Bps is more accurate for rating modem speed, but baud is more commonly used when discussing modems.

BBS: computer acronym for "Bulletin Board System"; a computer-operated dial-in service that typically supports file uploads and downloads and that often offers electronic mail services. BBSs may be either private or public.

bit: the smallest unit of computer information—a 1 or a 0—as represented in binary (Base 2) form.

blind copy: an e-mail message that does not list the names of all the other recipients, or of the other individuals to whom it was copied. Blind copies are useful if you want to send e-mail without telling individual recipients the names of all the other recipients for a message.

bps: computer acronym for "bits per second"; a measure of the number of ones and zeros that a computer or telephone connection can handle in one second.

BTW: e-mail acronym for "by the way."

bug: computerese term that indicates an error in programming is present in a software program.

byte: eight bits of computer data; kilobyte (1,024 or 210 bytes), megabyte (1,048,576 or 220 bytes) and gigabyte (230 bytes) are common measures of computer capacity.

carbon copy: often abbreviated as "cc:". For e-mail, creating a carbon copy is a way of sending additional copies of a message to designated individuals other than the primary recipients named in the To: field of an e-mail address.

cc:Mail: a popular electronic mail package sold by Lotus Development Corporation that runs on DOS, Windows, Macintoshes, UNIX, and OS/2 machines.

CCITT: computer acronym for Consultative Committee for International Telegraphy and Telephony; a group within the International Telecommunications Union (ITU) that defines telecommunications standards.

client: a PC when it is in the position of requesting a service from a network server; also, an e-mail user or his or her workstation can be called an e-mail client.

coax: nickname for coaxial cable.

coaxial cable: a type of cable that has one "strand" inside, the other surrounding it, separated by an insulating layer. They both have the same axis, so they are coaxial. You'll recognize this as similar to the cable that attaches your TV to your VCR.

CompuServe: a very large bulletin board. This is a great source of information about e-mail; nearly all computer equipment and software vendors maintain forums here. See the Vendor List for more information.

database: a computerized and heavily indexed collection of organized information; common database examples: a library's electronic card catalog, information about an organization's employees, and order and purchase information.

DaVinci Mail: a popular electronic mail application offered by DaVinci Systems Corporation (see Vendor List for details).

debug: a computerese verb that describes the act of locating and correcting bugs in software programs.

decrement: to deduct by a fixed increment; as used in this book, it describes lowering the count of e-mail messages as they are read (which decrements the count of waiting messages) or deleted from the e-mail system (which decrements the count of messages stored in that system).

decryption: the act of turning an encrypted message into its plain-text equivalent by the application of a special decoding algorithm. Decryption reverses encryption, which is used to make e-mail messages unreadable to anyone who does not possess the information needed for decryption (which is most commonly called a key).

desktop: shorthand for desktop computer (see below).

desktop computer: a computer used by an individual user, most commonly a personal computer (PC) or a workstation.

directory synchronization: the act of comparing the contents of two address databases, with overlapping (and sometimes identical) contents to resolve any disagreements, and to bring the two databases into conformance with one another.

distribution list: a named list of recipients for an e-mail message (synonym: mailing list).

DNS: TCP/IP acronym for Domain Name Service; a distributed name/address database used on the Internet, and in other private TCP/IP-based networking and e-mail environments.

domain: in the Internet world, a domain is part of a naming hierarchy. Syntactically, an Internet domain name consists of a sequence of names separated by periods (as discussed in explaining Internet addresses in Chapter 2). In the OSI world, a domain is generally used as an administrative partition of a complex distributed address space.

DOS: computer acronym for Disk Operating System, now synonymous with the operating system used for IBM PCs and clones controlled by Microsoft (flavors of this particular DOS include Microsoft's MS-DOS, IBM's PC-DOS, and Novell DOS, formerly known as DR-DOS).

DWIM: e-mail acronym for "do what I mean" (usually directed at a computer).

e-mail: shorthand for electronic mail, e-mail refers to any of a number of software systems that let multiple users exchange messages electronically, via some kind of connection (LAN, WAN, asynchronous, or otherwise).

EBCDIC: computer acronym for Extended Binary Coded Decimal Interchange Code; an IBM data encoding format (similar to ASCII in intent, but different in actual physical format).

EDI: computer acronym for Electronic Data Interchange, EDI refers to a system for electronic exchange of invoices, purchase orders, shipping instructions, and other paperwork related to vendor–customer relationships between companies.

Electronic Document Interchange: see **EDI**.

electronic mail: see **e-mail**.

encryption: a process of making data unreadable by applying complex mathematical transformations to that data; encryption usually requires one or more special bit patterns called keys in order to work. Encrypted data is generally not readable without possession of the proper key; its intent is to limit readability of the data to authorized recipients only. Encryption is an option for the contents of e-mail messages on some systems.

envelope: the "wrapper" that goes around data being sent over a network (synonymous with packet or datagram in this context) or around a message being sent by e-mail (synonymous with message header in this context).

Ethernet: a very common network technology; inexpensive to install but its age is showing, primarily in its speed limitations. Faster than ARCnet, though.

facsimile: see **fax**.

fault tolerance: the resiliency of a system, when faced with component or software failures, measures its degree of fault tolerance. The more fault-tolerant a system, the better it can cope with failure, but the more it costs. We recommend using fault-tolerant systems for all critical applications, including e-mail.

fax: a telephonic form of electronic document exchange that allows paper documents to be scanned and transmitted over the phone from sender to receiver. Fax requires sending and receiving equipment, but is widely used worldwide. Many e-mail systems can send faxes as well as more conventional electronic messages.

FDDI: Fiber Distributed Data Interface, the fastest of the four major network technologies (the others are ARCnet, Ethernet, and token-ring), and also the most expensive.

filing cabinet: a place where documents are stored; in computer-speak, this sometimes refers to a file server or a hard drive where documents, programs, mail messages, etc., would be kept in electronic form.

fix: see **patch**.

folder: a container for files; folder is computer terminology taken from paper filing systems and acts as a named container for related individual files. Folders can sometimes occur within other folders, in which case they are said to be nested (arranged in a hierarchy).

forms: in this book, forms generally refer to the electronic analog of a paper-based form, usually a graphical on-screen depiction of a form, with an underlying database or record management application to store, retrieve, and organize the underlying data (e.g., to handle the stuff that would normally get written on a paper form).

forms-based application: an application that's driven by completing on-screen forms, which are usually sent as messages to update an underlying database.

FWIW: e-mail acronym "for what it's worth".

FYI: e-mail acronym "for your information".

gateway: generally, a gateway is a special-purpose software program that knows how to move information from one kind of system to another; for e-mail, this means a program that knows how to move messages between two incompatible messaging applications.

ground address: the address on earth used to situate someone on the planet, but most often used to send snail mail.

groupware: a special kind of application built around a network, and possibly around messaging technology, to facilitate the interaction among individual workers in a group. Scheduling and calendaring programs are two classic groupware examples.

host: synonymous with computer, usually a mainframe or a minicomputer that acts to provide ("host") services for other users on PCs or terminals.

host-based mail: any electronic mail system that runs on a minicomputer or mainframe.

IM(H)O: electronic mail acronym for "in my (humble) opinion" (the parentheses around humble mean it's optional, so you could write IMO or IMHO).

image: in this book, the term image is used to refer to a complex type of computer data that represents a high-resolution picture, or image, of some document or other visual data. For example, image data for a signature card in a bank lets a teller look at a customer's signature at his or her terminal without having to retrieve the signature card from a paper filing system.

increment: to add to a count or a measurement, typically by one. Each message that arrives for a particular user on a mail server increments the count of waiting messages by one.

Internet: the name for a worldwide, TCP/IP-based networked computing community with over two million users worldwide that links government, business, industry, and education together. Sometimes also called "the Internet."

internetwork: a network of networks; an internetwork is therefore a collection of individual media segments linked together by special equipment built for that purpose (e.g., bridges and routers are types of internetworking equipment).

IP: acronym for Internet Protocol, this protocol name actually acts as shorthand for TCP/IP, which is the name of the protocol suite used on the Internet and which consists of a collection of protocols and related networking applications including e-mail.

IP-connectivity: the ability to internetwork with an IP-based network.

kbps: kilobits per second (kilo is a special binary counting prefix for computers and amounts to 2^{10} or 1024 bytes).

LAN: acronym for local area network, supplied by many types of networking technology used to allow computers to communicate within a more-or-less confined geographical area (usually 2–4 square miles or less).

LAN-based mail: is a kind of electronic mail system that runs on a local area network.

local application: an application that runs purely on a desktop machine, be it a PC or a workstation, without involving the network in any way, shape, or form.

login/logon: login is the activity required to establish a working connection to a network and the resources it provides; a logon is the set of keystrokes or information that must be provided to make a successful login.

logout/logoff: logout is the activity required to break a working connection to a network; a logoff is the set of keystrokes or other information that must be provided to log out successfully from a network.

Lotus Notes: a powerful message-based application from Lotus Development Corporation that offers advanced message delivery and document handling capabilities, including database replication. See the Vendor List for more information on this product.

machine: PC, computer, workstation.

Macintosh: Apple's Motorola-based microprocessor machines; Macintoshes are popular in today's marketplace because they're graphically organized and easy to use, and provide a broad array of software and capabilities.

mail server: a PC, workstation, or other computer that stores and forwards electronic mail messages on behalf of senders and receivers (see also **post office**).

mailbox: the name of a particular e-mail recipient, be it a user (for normal e-mail delivery), a device (for automatic fax or TELEX services), or a program (for delivery of workflow and forms-based message application data).

mailing list: a named list of recipients for an e-mail message (synonym: distribution list).

mainframe: a large, expensive computer—typically, made by IBM—that is invariably managed by a dedicated information systems staff.

Mbps: computer acronym for Megabits per second ("mega" is a special binary counting prefix for computer terms that means 2^{20} or 1,048,476 bytes).

megabyte (Mb): term for 1,048,476 bytes, commonly used as a measure for memory or disk capacity.

memory address: a specific collection of computer storage elements can only be located by its address; the memory address of a datum typically acts as the sender or recipient address when that datum is in use by the computer's central processing unit (CPU).

message: a formatted collection of electronic information built for use in a particular electronic mail application.

message database: the set of messages maintained by a particular messaging application, or on a specific messaging server, is called a message database. In most cases, it consists of all unread messages, saved messages, templates, and other e-mail documents that users and administrators have decided to keep on-line.

message-based application: any application that uses e-mail messages to communicate information among a user community, or to manage distributed data collections, is a message-based application. Lotus Notes is a prime example of such an application.

MH: see **Rand Message Handling System**.

MHS: electronic mail acronym for Message Handling System; context is important to this term, because Novell MHS is completely different from OSI MHS, even though the acronym is the same in both cases. If the context isn't clear, the most commonly used MHS is Novell's, but the most commonly referred to is OSI's.

Microsoft Mail: an electronic mail application developed by Microsoft and used for its Scheduler+ message-based groupware application.

modem: modem is actually an acronym, standing for **mo**dulator/**dem**odulator, and refers to the kinds of equipment used to translate (modulate and demodulate) digital computer signals into analog telephone signals. Simply put, modems let computers "talk" on the telephone.

MS Windows: see **Windows**.

MS-DOS: see **DOS**.

multitasking: refers to the apparent or actual ability of a computer to handle more than one activity at a time; multitasking is important because it lets a computer communicate over the network or the telephone at the same time it's doing other things.

network: a collection of computers linked together in order to share resources, including devices and information.

network interface card: sometimes abbreviated as NIC, a network interface card provides the link between a computer and the networking technology and topology it wishes to use.

network operating system: the software that runs on your network server and moderates the clients' access to the server resources.

NIC: see **network interface card**.

notification: a message sent to a designated recipient to indicate that a specific event has occurred; the most common usage of the term is to indicate successful delivery of an e-mail message, but all kinds of other notifications are routinely issued by messaging software, including appointment reminders, meeting information, etc.

off-line: in an environment where a computer can participate on a network or take part in a telephonic connection, a computer that isn't participating is said to be off-line. Off-line also means that a device is unavailable (e.g., a printer or other peripheral device can also be off-line).

on-line: the opposite of off-line; that is, on-line means that a computer or device is participating on a network, part of an active telephone connection, or available to prospective users.

operating system: the software that runs in your PC, whether you're on a network or not, and manages access to such resources in the PC as your PC's diskettes, hard drive, and memory.

OS: acronym; see **operating system**.

OSI: computer acronym for Open Systems Interconnect, a collection of networking and communications standards defined and managed by the International Standards Organization (ISO).

OTOH: e-mail acronym for "on the other hand".

paperless office: the ideal computing environment to which businesses supposedly aspire, this term refers to an unattainable goal of converting all paper-based information into its electronic equivalent.

patch: a change to an application or software system that gets applied to an existing program. Patches are applied most often to fix bugs, or to provide minor enhancements (that's why they're sometimes called fixes).

PC: computer acronym for personal computer, PC usually refers to an IBM-PC or its clone equivalent, even though any microprocessor-based computer that sits on a user's desktop could rightfully be called a "personal computer."

post office: a place where mail gets stored and forwarded (applies to both snail mail and electronic mail); because of the analogy, post office is another term for mail server, and in fact is the term used for mail server in e-mail systems like Microsoft Mail and cc:Mail.

Prodigy: a public information system jointly funded and operated by IBM and Sears (see also **America Online** and **CompuServe**).

PROFS: acronym for IBM's PRofessional OFfice System, an e-mail environment built around IBM mainframes and minicomputers. PROFS is designed to assist users in creating, communicating, and managing job-related information.

protocol: a set of networking rules. Unless they share a protocol, two computers cannot talk to one another.

protocol set: a collection of protocols that provide network access for users and applications. AppleTalk and TCP/IP are two common protocol suite examples.

protocol suite: same as protocol set, except that the suite is usually a complete collection of all the protocols of a particular type, whereas a set might only include some, but not all, of those protocols.

queue: a computer data structure that lets items be stored in the order of arrival (first-in, first-out); a queue is the computerized equivalent of standing in line, and lets users issue requests for service (e.g., printing, and faxing) that will be handled in the order they are received.

RAM: computer acronym for random access memory. High-speed data storage in a computer. Usually anything stored in here vanishes when you turn off the computer.

Rand Message Handling System: addressing scheme developed at Rand Corp., on which Internet addressing was based (sometimes abbreviated as RMHS).

real-time systems: computer systems that are designed to react to service demands or reported events as quickly as possible; the term "real time" means that the system is expected to react to demands immediately, if not sooner.

receipt requested: a form of electronic mail delivery that sends a notification back to its sender when the message is opened by or delivered to its intended recipient (works like return receipt delivery for snail mail).

RFC: computer acronym for Request for Comment, a document controlled by the Internet Activities Board (IAB), the governing body for the TCP/IP protocol suite (all TCP/IP protocols, interfaces, and applications are governed by related RFCs).

RFC822: standard for the format of Internet text messages (updated by RFCs 1138, 1148).

RFC987: standard that describes mapping X.400 messages and formats (the one everyone believes in) into the RFC822 format (the one everyone actually uses).

ROTFL: e-mail acronym for "rolling on the floor laughing."

router: an internetworking device capable of decoding network addresses and of forwarding packets to the destination network, or at least to another router that is "closer" to the destination.

scanner: a computer imaging device capable of turning paper-based documents into electronic equivalents, a scanner is essentially a device that takes a picture of a document page and turns it into digitized form.

scheduling: a type of message-based application that coordinates the schedules of individual group members.

seamlessness: the characteristic whereby discrete, disparate system components function together as a tightly integrated system.

server: a PC whose function is to provide access to network resources.

smiley: a special sequence of ASCII characters designed to look like a particular facial expression, and to signify the emotion that such an expression denotes (e.g., ":)" is a basic smiley face, and indicates a cheerful grin).

SMTP: e-mail acronym for Simple Mail Transfer Protocol, SMTP is the basic TCP/IP e-mail application.

SNADS: e-mail acronym for IBM's Systems Network Architecture Distribution Services, which provides a generalized architecture for asynchronous distribution services that are used to implement office information architectures and a comprehensive document interchange architecture for exchanging documents among systems.

snail mail: a euphemism for regular mail delivery, emphasizing its speed relative to electronic mail.

standard: set of guidelines and rules, as stated by some standards-setting body (an official standard) or some vendor (a de facto standard).

sticker shock: the emotion that follows reading the price tag on a new vehicle, or computer system, when it's higher than expected.

store-and-forward systems: a software system that can retain incoming information and forward outgoing information to the designated system (a good behavior description for how e-mail servers work).

sysop: computerese abbreviation for systems operator, the individual responsible for monitoring one or more message forums on a BBS system.

telex: a text-based asynchronous data transfer system similar to, but older than, facsimile systems. Telexes are most popular in Europe and use teletype equipment over phone lines to transfer text messages at relatively low expense.

terminal: a display device for a computer system—usually a cathode-ray terminal (CRT), most often with an attached keyboard, that has little or no local processing power (which is why terminals are often called "dumb terminals"). Most minicomputer and mainframe systems originally used terminals as their only devices for human interaction (today, PCs can act like, or emulate, terminals, in addition to performing other tasks).

twisted pair (TP): a type of wiring that contains even numbers of copper wires, twisted together by twos.

UNIX: the name of a specific type of computer operating system, originated at Bell Labs in the 1970s. Because it is widely taught in colleges and universities worldwide, UNIX is one of the most familiar OSs in the computing community.

Usenet: a BBS accessed via the Internet, Usenet may be the most active BBS in the world today.

user ID: abbreviation for user identifier, a unique name or bit string that identifies a system user to a particular software system.

voice message: a stream of audio signals left as a verbal message, usually on some kind of answering machine or voicemail system. Many e-mail systems accept voice messages as attachments to text messages today.

WAN: computer acronym for wide area network, a network whose span exceeds 2–4 square miles, that usually depends on some kind of specialized high-speed access technology, or which uses a high-bandwidth asynchronous connection between individual LANs.

WAN-based mail: an electronic mail system that works over a wide area network.

Windows: Microsoft Corporation's graphical user interface software, MS-Windows is one of the best-selling PC software systems in the world.

workflow: a type of message-based application that automates some kind of business or organizational process, especially as it relates to how work materials and assignments move among members of a work team and across an organization.

workgroup: a collection of individuals who work together and are interconnected via a network of computers.

workstation: a desktop computer, usually a more powerful machine than an ordinary IBM-PC or clone, often with a high-speed Reduced Instruction Set Computer (RISC) processor, often running UNIX as its OS.

X.400: the ISO standard governing e-mail systems, X.400 describes message formats, protocols, and message exchange technologies.

X.500: the ISO standard governing synchronization of multiple directory service environments, X.500 describes name and address requirements and defines a method to map between multiple directory services.

YMMV: e-mail acronym for "your mileage may vary"; indicates that individual experiences may not live up to the claims made for a particular system feature or function.

appendix B

Top-Level Internet Domain Names

Electronic Postmarks

Recall from our discussion in Chapter 2 that Internet addresses have two parts, a user name and a domain. The user names are assigned by people at the domain site and can be completely arbitrary, but the domain names do provide some information if you know what to look for. For instance, from the top-level component of the domain, you can usually tell in which country the site is located. This portion of the domain name is usually the rightmost element in the name.

The table below lists many of the most common top-level names. This list is not exhaustive, because new countries are coming on-line every day, but it does cover the majority of top-level domain names. You might not get mail from all of these places right away, but scanning the list is a fascinating way to see that Internet e-mail connectivity is truly global!

Table B.1. *International Internet domain names.*

AD	Andorra	AM	Armenia
AE	United Arab Emirates	AN	Netherland Antilles
AF	Afghanistan (Islamic State of)	AO	Angola (Republic of)
AG	Antigua and Barbuda	AQ	Antarctica
AI	Anguilla	AR	Argentina
AL	Albania	AS	American Samoa

(continued)

Table B.1. *International Internet domain names (continued)*

AT	Austria
AU	Australia
AW	Aruba
AZ	Azerbaidjan
BA	Bosnia-Herzegovina
BB	Barbados
BD	Bangladesh
BE	Belgium
BF	Burkina Faso
BG	Bulgaria
BH	Bahrain
BI	Burundi
BJ	Benin
BM	Bermuda
BN	Brunei Darussalam
BO	Bolivia
BR	Brazil
BS	Bahamas
BT	Bhutan
BV	Bouvet Island
BW	Botswana
BY	Belarus
BZ	Belize
CA	Canada
CC	Cocos (Keeling) Island
CF	Central African Republic
CG	Congo
CH	Switzerland
CI	Ivory Coast
CK	Cook Islands
CL	Chile
CM	Cameroon
CN	China
CO	Colombia
CR	Costa Rica
CU	Cuba
CV	Cape Verde
CX	Christmas Island
CY	Cyprus
CZ	Czech Republic
DE	Germany
DJ	Djibouti
DK	Denmark
DM	Dominica
DO	Dominican Republic
DZ	Algeria
EC	Ecuador
EE	Estonia
EG	Egypt
EH	Western Sahara
ER	Eritrea
ES	Spain
ET	Ethiopia
FI	Finland
FJ	Fiji
FK	Falkland Islands (Malvinas)
FM	Micronesia
FO	Faroe Islands
FR	France
FX	France (European Ter.)
GA	Gabon
GB	Great Britain (UK)
GD	Grenada
GE	Georgia
GH	Ghana
GI	Gibraltar
GL	Greenland
GM	Gambia
GN	Guinea
GP	Guadeloupe
GQ	Equatorial Guinea
GR	Greece
GS	South Georgia and South Sandwich Islands
GT	Guatemala
GU	Guam (US)
GW	Guinea Bissau
GY	Guyana
HK	Hong Kong
HM	Heard and McDonald Islands
HN	Honduras
HR	Croatia
HT	Haiti
HU	Hungary
ID	Indonesia
IE	Ireland (Republic of)
IL	Israel
IN	India
IO	British Indian Ocean Territory
IQ	Iraq
IR	Iran
IS	Iceland

(continued)

Table B.1. *International Internet domain names (continued)*

IT	Italy
JM	Jamaica
JO	Jordan
JP	Japan
KE	Kenya
KG	Kyrgyz Republic
KH	Cambodia
KI	Kiribati
KM	Comoros
KN	St. Kitts Nevis Anguilla
KP	North Korea
KR	South Korea
KW	Kuwait
KY	Cayman Islands
KZ	Kazakhstan
LA	Laos
LB	Lebanon
LC	Saint Lucia
LI	Liechtenstein
LK	Sri Lanka
LR	Liberia
LS	Lesotho
LT	Lithuania
LU	Luxembourg
LV	Latvia
LY	Libya
MA	Morocco
MC	Monaco
MD	Moldavia
MG	Madagascar (Republic of)
MH	Marshall Islands
MK	Macedonia
ML	Mali
MM	Myanmar
MN	Mongolia
MO	Macau
MP	Northern Mariana Island
MQ	Martinique
MR	Mauritania
MS	Montserrat
MT	Malta
MU	Mauritius
MV	Maldives
MW	Malawi
MX	Mexico
MY	Malaysia
MZ	Mozambique
NA	Namibia
NC	New Caledonia
NE	Niger
NF	Norfolk Island
NG	Nigeria
NI	Nicaragua
NL	Netherlands
NO	Norway
NP	Nepal
NR	Nauru
NU	Niue
NZ	New Zealand
OM	Oman
PA	Panama
PE	Peru
PF	Polynesia
PG	Papua New Guinea
PH	Philippines
PK	Pakistan
PL	Poland
PM	St. Pierre and Miquelon
PN	Pitcairn
PR	Puerto Rico (US)
PT	Portugal
PW	Palau
PY	Paraguay
QA	Qatar
RE	Reunion
RO	Romania
RU	Russian Federation
RW	Rwanda
SA	Saudi Arabia
SB	Solomon Islands
SC	Seychelles
SD	Sudan
SE	Sweden
SG	Singapore
SH	St. Helena
SI	Slovenia
SJ	Svalbard and Jan Mayen Islands
SK	Slovakia (Slovak Republic)
SL	Sierra Leone
SM	San Marino
SN	Senegal
SO	Somalia

(continued)

Table B.1. *International Internet domain names (continued)*

SR	Suriname	UG	Uganda
ST	St. Tome and Principe	UK	United Kingdom
SV	El Salvador	UM	US Minor Outlying Islands
SY	Syria	US	United States
SZ	Swaziland	UY	Uruguay
TC	Turks and Caicos Islands	UZ	Uzbekistan
TD	Chad	VA	Vatican City
TF	French Southern Territory	VC	St.Vincent and Grenadines
TG	Togo	VE	Venezuela
TH	Thailand	VG	Virgin Islands (British)
TJ	Tadjikistan	VI	Virgin Islands (US)
TK	Tokelau	VN	Vietnam
TM	Turkmenistan	VU	Vanuatu
TN	Tunisia	WF	Wallis and Futuna Islands
TO	Tonga	WS	Samoa
TP	East Timor	YE	Yemen
TR	Turkey	YT	Mayotte
TT	Trinidad and Tobago	YU	Yugoslavia
TV	Tuvalu	ZA	South Africa
TW	Taiwan	ZM	Zambia
TZ	Tanzania	ZR	Zaire
UA	Ukraine	ZW	Zimbabwe

If you've been active at all on the Internet, you're probably wondering by now why the most common formats you're familiar with are not represented in Table B-1. The domain names in Table B-2 below mostly predate the country code convention, but all indicate United States organizations of various types. For most Internet users, these top-level domain names will be encountered regularly in "domestic e-mail" messages.

Table B.2. *Old-Style U.S. domain names*

ARPA	Old-style Arpanet	MIL	US military
COM	US commercial	NATO	Nato field
EDU	US educational	NET	Commercial network provider
GOV	US government	ORG	Non-profit organization
INT	International field (used by NATO)		

appendix C

Addressing E-mail across Gateways

Getting from "A" to "B"

As we mentioned in Chapters 2, 12, and 24, getting e-mail from one system to another requires a special piece of software called a gateway, which knows how to translate message formats and how to forward mail from a sender in one messaging environment to a receiver in another, incompatible messaging environment. The key to a successful transition is proper addressing, which tells the gateway where to send the message, and may often indicate which gateway must be used as well.

Table C-1 covers some of the more common formats for moving messages across gateways, both public and private. We indicate the messaging system of origination with a "from" and the destination system with a "to" at the head of each entry. We also use the word user to indicate an arbitrary username for the destination in some cases (in order to make this work properly, you'd have to substitute a real username, so that user@mcimail.com actually becomes jdoe@mcimail.com or 360-0756@mcimail.com if the user hasn't created a symbolic name for him- or herself).

Because there are so many different e-mail systems in use today, we couldn't document all of them in this appendix. If your particular gateway formats aren't covered here, don't despair—you should be able to work out the details by reading the manuals for your gateway software, or by contacting the gateway vendor's technical support. For most public messaging systems, you'll also be able to get help from the system's support staff as well.

Table C-1: *Common Gateway Address Formats*

From	To	Format Example	Notes
from Internet	MCI Mail:	user@mcimail.com	
from Internet	CompuServe;	75935.1234@compuserve.com	Example uses CompuServe user ID 75935,1234. You must replace the comma in the customary numeric CIS ID with a period. CIS charges extra for these messages.
CompuServe	Internet	INTERNET:mrobbins@bga.com	Example internet ID mrobbins@bga.com. CIS charges extra for these messages.
Internet	Prodigy:	47Q3X@prodigy.com	Prodigy charges extra for this. You must enable a configuration feature in your Prodigy software for this to work.
Internet	America Online:	user@aol.com	
AppleLink	Internet:	user@domain@internet#	Total must be less than 35 characters long.
Internet	AppleLink:	user@applelink.apple.com	

appendix

D

Resource Guide

This appendix includes several sources of information that we hope you will find useful in your search for information on electronic mail. The first section is the Vendor List, which includes contact information for all of the companies we mentioned in the book, with product information for specific products that might have been mentioned. The second section, called Information Resources, includes references and other information about e-mail and related topics that we believe you will find of interest in your further explorations into the subject. The third section is a list of relevant publications that you might find worthy of reading in the search for current information about e-mail and other networking-related computing topics.

Vendor List

This list is presented in alphabetical order, by vendor or organization name. The index at the end of this book will help you locate information in this listing by product name and by technology area. Readers outside the United States who wish to contact these organizations should use a non-800 number and dial the country code for the United States before the area code for those numbers (plus 1, in most cases).

Action Technologies
1301 Marina Village Parkway, Suite 100
Alameda, CA 94501
Phone: (510) 521-6190; Fax: (510) 769-0956
Product: Action Workflow Analyst and related tools (workflow application development toolset; contact Action Technologies for pricing information).

Alisa Systems, Inc.
221 East Walnut Street, Suite 175
Pasadena, CA 91101
Phone: (818) 792-9474; Fax: (818) 792-4068
Product: AlisaMail (general-purpose e-mail gateway and e-mail services). Prices start at $10,000.

America Online, Inc.
8619 Westwood Center Drive
Vienna, VA 22182-2285
Phone: (703) 893-6288 or (800) 827-6364
Product: America Online Software (free to qualified subscribers; for more information on AOL, please consult Tom Lichty's excellent book: *America Online ... Tourguide,* Ventana Press, Chapel Hill, NC, 1993, $19.95)

American Telephone & Telegraph (AT&T) EasyLink Division
400 Interpace Parkway
Parsippany, NJ 07054
Phone: (800) 242-6005 or (314) 291-8580 (customer service can direct you to the right AT&T outlet); Fax: (214) 778-4235
Product: messaging products and services, including AT&T Mail

Banyan Systems, Inc.
120 Flanders Road
Westboro, MA 01581
Phone: (508) 898-1000
Products: Banyan VINES (network operating system with integrated e-mail), Banyan ENS for NetWare (StreetTalk services for NetWare)

Beyond, Inc. (Beyond is in the process of being acquired by Banyan Systems)
38 Sidney Street
Cambridge, MA 02139

Phone: (617) 621-0095; Fax: (617) 621-0096
Product: BeyondMail (advanced e-mail software)

Byte Magazine, a McGraw-Hill Publication
One Phoenix Mill Road
Peterborough, NH 03458
Phone: (603) 924-9281; Fax: (603) 924-2550
Product: BIX (Byte Information eXchange, BBS service available to computer owners with modems at (800) 695-4882 or (617) 491-5410)

Brightwork Development, Inc.
Jerral Center West
766 Shrewsbury Avenue
Tinton Falls, NJ 07724
Phone: (800) 552-9876; Fax: (908) 530-0622
Products: LAN Automatic Inventory, LAN Server Watch, NETremote+ (networked remote control software)

CE Software, Inc.
1801 Industrial Circle
West Des Moines, IA 50265
Phone (515) 224-1995 or (800) 523-7638; Fax: (515) 224-4534
Products: QuickMail, QuickMail MHS (e-mail server and client software for Macintoshes, PCs, etc.; from $100 per client)

Cisco Systems
1525 O'Brien Dr.
Menlo Park, CA 94043
Phone: (415) 326-1941 or (800) 553-6387; Fax: (415) 326-1989
Products: Asynchronous communications servers (dial-in, dial-out for network users), multiprotocol, multitopology routers

CompuServe Information Services
Attn: Customer Service
P.O. Box 20212
5000 Arlington Centre Boulevard
Columbus, OH 43220
Phone: (800) 848-8199 or (614) 457-8650
Product: CIS (on-line information and research services, electronic mail)

DaVinci Systems
4200 Six Forks Road
Raleigh, NC 27609
Phone: (919) 881-4320 or (800) 328-4634; Fax: (919) 787-3550
Product: DaVinci eMail (e-mail servers and client software); pricing from $80 per person and down, depending on volume

Digital Equipment Corporation
146 Main Street
Maynard, MA 01754
Phone: (508) 493-7161 or (800) 332-4636
Products: VAXmail (e-mail software furnished with VAX VMS and Ultrix systems; contact Digital for pricing); PathWorks (network operating system extension for VAX clients; contact Digital for pricing)

dtech, Inc.
15 West Sixth Street, Suite 1500
Tulsa, OK 74119-5455
Phone: (800) 800-4278 or (918) 583-7446; Fax: (918) 583-0560
Product: Heaven Nodes (network inventory and management software)

Electronic Messaging Association
1655 North Fort Meyer Drive, Suite 850
Arlington, VA 22209
Phone: (703) 524-5550; Fax: (703) 524-5558
Product: EMA membership and e-mail policy information (available by written request; see Chapter 22 for complete details on e-mail addresses for this organization)

GEnie (General Electric network for information exchange)
401 North Washington Street
Rockville, MD 20850
Phone: (800) 638-9636 or (301) 251-6475; Fax: (301) 251-2516
Product: on-line information services and e-mail

InterConnections
14711 Northeast 29th Place
Bellevue, WA 98007
Phone: (206) 881-5773 or (800) 950-5773; Fax: (206) 867-5022
Product: Leverage for NetWare (supports DOS and Windows NetWare clients on VAXs; pricing available from InterConnections).

Internet Activities Board (IAB)
Internet Engineering Task Force (IETF)

These are the two groups that govern the Internet protocols and related applications. The IAB is the parent body and concerns itself with usage, access, and rules and regulations; the IETF handles the technical side of things and controls the contents of the RFCs. Both groups can be reached through

DDN Network Information Center
14200 Park Meadow Drive, Suite 200
Chantilly, VA 22021
Phone: (703) 802-4535 or (800) 365-3642; Fax: (703) 802-8376

Internet

Dial services to the Internet are available from a number of vendors, including:

Performance Systems International, Inc.: world-dial Internet access service
510 Huntmar Park Drive
Herndon, VA 22070
Phone: (800) 827-7482 or (703) 620-6651

Product: world-wide research and information access

Lotus Development Corporation

2141 Landings Drive
Mountain View, CA 94043
Phone: (415) 961-8800; Fax: (415) 961-8400
Products: Lotus Notes, cc:Mail (e-mail front ends, engines, gateway; call Lotus for pricing information)

MCI Mail

1133 19th Street NW, Suite 700
Washington, DC 20036
Phone: (800) 444-6245 or (202) 833-8484; Fax: (202) 416-5858
Product: MCI Mail electronic mail services

Microsoft, Inc.

1 Microsoft Way
Redmond, WA 98052
Phone: (206) 882-8080; Fax: (206) 936-7329
Products: Microsoft Mail (e-mail package), MS-Windows (GUI interface for PCs), MS-DOS (PC operating system), Scheduler+ (message-based scheduling application bundled with Workgroup for Windows).

Miramar Systems
121 Gray Avenue, Suite 200B
Santa Barbara, CA 93103
Phone: (805) 966-2432 or (800) 862-2526; Fax: (805) 965-1824
Products: MacLAN Connect, MacLAN Connect for NetWare (pricing from $495 to $695)

Novell, Inc.
122 East 1700 South
Provo, UT 84606
Phone: (801) 429-7000 or (800) 638-9273; call for appropriate division fax number.
Products: NetWare MHS, Global MHS, Personal MHS, SMF 71 (electronic mail protocols, servers, and services; contact Novell for product and pricing information)

Pegasus Mail
Current versions:

Program	*Archive Filename*	*Version*
Pegasus Mail for DOS:	(PMAIL301.ZIP)	3.0 (R1a)
Pegasus Mail for the Mac:	(PMMAC204.HQX)	2.0 (R4)
Pegasus Mail for Windows:	(WINPM102.ZIP)	1.0 (R2)
Mercury Mail transport:	(MERC111.ZIP)	1.1 (R1)
PMPOP POP3 Gateway:	(PMPOP100.ZIP)	1.0 (R0)

Availability:
Pegasus Mail and Mercury can be obtained as follows:
Via anonymous FTP on the Internet—
from risc.ua.edu, in /pub/network/pegasus, or tyr.let.rug.nl, in pub/pmail
From CIS (CompuServe Information Service): in the "NOVUSER" library forum. To get to NOVUSER, type "GO NOVUSER" at any CIS "!" prompt. After entering the forum, choose "Library" from the menu, or type "lib" to get to the library files. Search for the keywords "David" "Harris" or "Pegasus" to find the most recent files.
By sending a diskette, a self-addressed envelope, and US $10 (postage and handing) to:
Pegasus Mail, Box 5451, Dunedin, New Zealand.
Products: Pegasus Mail, Mercury Mail Transport

Prodigy
445 Hamilton Avenue
White Plains, NY 10601
Phone: (800) 776-3449 (available in United States only; no fax number available)
Product: Prodigy on-line information and e-mail services

SprintNet (a subsidiary of U.S. Sprint)
12490 Sunrise Valley Drive
Reston, VA 22096
Phone: (800) 877-5045 or (703) 689-6300; Fax: (703) 689-6066
Products: e-mail and public packet-switched network access services

Thomas-Conrad Corporation
1908-R Kramer Lane
Austin, TX 78758
Phone: (512) 836-1935 or (800) 332-8683; Fax (512) 836-0286
Products: TCNS (100 Mbps high-speed networking interfaces, hubs; pricing available from Thomas-Conrad)

WordPerfect Corporation (being acquired by Novell, Inc.)
1555 North Technology Way
Orem, UT 94057
Phone: (801) 225-5000 or (800) 451-5151; Fax (801) 222-5077
Products: WordPerfect Office, InForms (integrated office automation, forms-based messaging application; WPO from $295 per user, no pricing currently available for InForms)

Information Resources

Internet References

The references in this section will get you information about BITNET, Usenet, UUCP, SMTP, and a whole host of other UNIX- and Internet-related e-mail and applications information. Because there are so many Internet titles out there, with more coming daily (ours to be among them in the second half of 1994), we don't cover all the available literature. These books will provide a good place to start, though.

Daniel P. Dern
The Internet Guide for New Users, McGraw-Hill, New York, 1994 (List price: $27.95).

This is an excellent starting point for Internet beginners, and covers access, information resources, Internet facilities, and basic Internet etiquette.

Susan Estrada
Connecting to the Internet, O'Reilly and Associates, Sebastopol, CA, 1993 (List price: $15.95).

This short book includes the best information about how to get Internet access from school, home, or office we've ever seen anywhere. It also covers the costs and contracts involved in signing up with a commercial access provider versus setting up access for oneself.

Donnalyn Frey and Rick Adams
A Directory of Electronic Mail Addressing and Networks, O'Reilly and Associates, Sebastopol, CA, 1993 (List price: $24.95).

This book includes exhaustive coverage of all of the networks that connect to the Internet, and the pathways between them. It provides an address guide for all the many Internet participants, and can help to resolve issues surrounding delivery of e-mail from one network to another, within the global Internet community.

Seth Godin
The Smiley Dictionary, Peach Pit Press, Berkeley, CA, 1993 (List price: $6.95).

This reference helps decode e-mail inflection through punctuation, better known as smileys.

Ed Krol
The Whole Internet Guide, O'Reilly and Associates, Sebastopol, CA, 1993 (List price: $29.95).

This book does the best job of covering Internet access, resources, trivia, and applications of any Internet-focused book we've ever seen. If you can afford to buy only one book on the Internet, this is it (Ed Krol also writes regularly about the Internet for Network World and is "in the know" on most things going on there).

David W. Sanderson
Smileys, O'Reilly and Associates, Sebastopol, CA, 1993 (List price: $7.95).

This reference helps decode e-mail inflection through punctuation, better known as smileys.

OSI References

The references in this section will get you information about OSI standards like X.400 and X.500, and related e-mail and applications information.

American National Standards Institute (for the International Standards Organization)
OSI Specifications, Vols. 1–12, New York City, 1985–1993 (some volumes may be updated; List price: $1795.00 for the complete set).

All of the standards information and documentation is controlled (and copyrighted) by the ISO, whose U.S. affiliate member is ANSI. This is some of the most expensive documentation in the world (a recent article in BYTE indicates that it costs about $345.00 per inch!), but it is the only place to go for the official word on the OSI protocols and services. This is the technical resource for OSI, and is of interest primarily to designers and programmers.

Peter Judge
Open Systems: The Guide to OSI and Its Implementation, QED Information Sciences, Inc., Wellesley, MA, 1988 (List price: $29.95).

This is an extremely useful book, because it gives an excellent overview of OSI technology and protocols, talks about how it can be used, and then goes on to discuss how the different profiles and implementations (GOSIP, UK GOSIP, MAP, TOP, etc.) differ in their views and requirements for OSI technology.

B. Plattner, C.Lanz, H. Lubich, M. Müller and P. Walter, trans. by Stephen S. Wilson
X.400 Message Handling, Addison-Wesley, Reading, MA, 1991 (List price: $49.95).

This book covers X.400 messaging, addressing, and related mail delivery services. It also includes valuable information on vendors that offer X.400 public and private messaging services.

Marshall Rose
The Open Book, Prentice Hall, Englewood Cliffs, NJ, 1990 (List price: $40.00).

Marshall Rose, a widely-recognized authority on networking, wrote this book as an exposition of what's inside OSI, what the standards-making process is like, what the important components and APIs are most likely to be, and what it has been and will be like to do business playing the OSI game.

Adrian Tang and Sophia Scoggins
Open Networking with OSI, Prentice Hall, Englewood Cliffs, NJ, 1992 (List price: $44.95).

A thorough review of OSI standards, protocols, applications, and services. This book is an excellent reference for those concerned with understanding the details of the OSI environment, and for those interested in future directions for networking technologies.

TCP/IP References

The references in this section will get you information about TCP/IP, NFS, SMTP, SNMP, and a whole host of other IP-related e-mail and applications information.

Douglas Comer
Internetworking with TCP/IP, Vols. 1, 2 , 3: Principals, Protocols, and Architecture, Prentice Hall, Englewood Cliffs, NJ, 1990, 1991, 1993 (List price: $50.00 each).

Comer's books are the most exhaustive and informative discussion of TCP/IP around, and include information about network management, name domains, along with lots of technical information about how to build local and wide-area internetworks on top of the TCP/IP protocol suite. For technophiles, this is a must-have resource on TCP/IP.

John Davidson
An Introduction to TCP/IP, Springer-Verlag, New York, 1988 (List price: $20.00).

Davidson's book is a concise (under 100 pages) but detailed description of the entire TCP/IP protocol suite itself, but it doesn't say much about how it gets used, who's using it, etc.

Defense Data Network (DDN) Network Information Center
DDN Protocol Handbook, Vols. 1–3, U.S. Government Printing Office, Menlo Park, CA, 1985 (some volumes may be updated; List Price: $110.00)

Most of the technical information necessary to fully understand and implement the TCP/IP protocol suite is specified in the three volume DDN Handbook, which can be ordered from:

Government Systems, Inc.
Attn: Network Information Center
14200 Park Meadow Drive, Suite 200
Chantilly, VA 22021
Phone: (703) 802-4535 or (800) 365-3642; Fax: (703) 802-8376

Updates and enhancements to the TCP/IP protocol suites are handled via documents managed by the Network Information Center (NIC) called Requests for Comment, known to TCP/IP junkies as "RFCs." Contact the NIC for a current list (if needed). This is **the** technical resource for TCP/IP, and is of interest primarily to designers and programmers.

Marshall Rose
The Simple Book, Prentice Hall, Englewood Cliffs, NJ, 1990 (List price: $50.00).

Marshall Rose, a recognized networking maven, wrote this book as an exposition of what the TCP Simple Network Management Protocol (SNMP) is all about. It includes a lot of useful history, comparison with OSI Common Management Information Protocol (CMIP) and Services (CMIS). This is by far the most illuminating and useful network management and SNMP resource in the list, from the standpoint of business and practical implementation issues.

William Stallings
Local Networks, Third ed., Macmillan Publishing Company, New York, 1990 (List price: $40.00).

This is possibly the best general introduction to LANs available, and includes lots of information about TCP/IP, albeit in a somewhat scattered form.

Handbook of Computer Communications Standards, Volume 3: DOD Protocol Standards, second ed., Macmillan Publishing Company, New York, 1990 (List price: $34.95).

A detailed description of the current TCP/IP standards in effect, including specifications for protocols and services for each of the layers that comprise the TCP/IP protocol suite (starting at the network layer—TCP/IP adheres to the IEEE 802 family of standards for Physical and Data Link layers, with additional support for X.25, satellite communications, and packet radio). This is a very technical reference and need only be consulted when detailed technical issues must be resolved.

Andrew Tanenbaum
Computer Networks, second ed. Prentice Hall, Englewood Cliffs, NJ, 1988 (List price: $50.00).

Tanenbaum's book has been the principal text for undergraduate and graduate networking courses at universities around the world since the first edition appeared. This latest version is pretty up-to-date, and includes the best all-around technical reference on networking. Like Stallings' *Local Networks,* this book scatters its discussion of TCP/IP around various chapters and headings; also like Stallings' book, don't use this one as a primary TCP/IP reference.

K. and J. T. Washburn
TCP/IP: Running a Successful Network, Addison-Wesley, Reading, MA, 1993 (List price: $49.95).

This is an excellent, up-to-date reference on designing, installing, and using TCP/IP protocols and applications in a networked environment.

Publications List

There are a great many more networking- and computer-focused magazines available than those listed here. If we've overlooked one that you particularly like, forgive us (and drop us a line to let us know). These are the ones we read regularly and that seem to provide the most balanced network-related news and information. Most of them are free to qualified subscribers, so nothing should stop you from getting them. Just be sure to indicate that you have technical and budget responsibility for a network on the qualification forms, and you'll get what you deserve from these publications!

Computer Shopper is published 12 times a year by Coastal Associates, a division of Ziff Communications Company. The address is One Park Avenue, New York, NY, 10016, and its subscription department can be reached at (800) 274-6384 (inside the United States) or at (303) 447-9330 (outside the United States). The magazine costs $29.97 inside the United States, and an additional $39 for postage outside the United States. *Computer Shopper* is primarily a PC-focused advertising supplement—a normal issue looks like an oversized phone book—but it includes ads and contact information for hundreds of mail-order dealers who carry networking equipment and software. It's a great place to shop around and to establish the floor for pricing on any items you might need to purchase.

Computerworld is published 53 times a year by IDG Publications, P.O. Box 9171, 375 Cochituate Road, Framingham, MA, 01701-9171, and can be reached at (800) 669-1002 for subscriptions, (508) 879-0700 for editorial information. The magazine costs $48 inside the United States, and between $95 and $295 outside the country, depending on exact location. *Computerworld* covers the computer industry in general, but gives networking issues good coverage as well. It's a good counterpoint to the Ziff-Davis *PC Week*, in that its focus includes coverage of non-PC systems as well.

Infoworld is published 51 times a year by Infoworld Publishing Company, a subsidiary of IDG, at 155 Bovet Road, San Mateo, CA, 94402, and can be reached at (415) 572-7341. The magazine is free to qualified subscribers, but otherwise costs $130 inside the United States, and $145 in Canada (other subscription costs available upon request). *Infoworld* covers the computer industry in general, but gives networking issues good coverage as well. It also publishes Rich Tennant's cartoons in every issue (our personal favorite nerdy form of entertainment).

LAN: The Network Solutions Magazine is published monthly by Miller Freeman, 600 Harrison Street, San Francisco, CA, 94107, who can be reached at (415) 905-2200. An annual subscription costs $19.97. This magazine provides coverage on a broad range of networking topics, including technology overviews, user tutorials, and product reviews. For an excellent source of network product and vendor information, be sure to check out its annual *Buyers' Guide* (published in September of each year).

LAN Times is published 25 times a year by McGraw-Hill, Inc., 1221 Avenue of the Americas, New York, NY, 10020, who can be reached at (212) 513-6800. The magazine is free to qualified subscribers. *LAN Times* also provides coverage on a broad range of networking topics, including technology overviews, network industry news, product reviews, and includes editorials from networking industry leaders and personalities. For an excellent source of network product and vendor information, be sure to check out its annual *Buyer's Directory* (published in August of each year).

Networking Management is published 12 times a year by PenWell Publishing Company, 1421 South Sheridan, Tulsa, OK, 74112, who can be reached at (918) 831-9424 (subscriptions) or (508) 692-0700 (editorial inquiries). The magazine is free to qualified subscribers, and costs $42 inside the United States, and $65 outside the country, for nonqualified subscribers. *Networking Management* provides coverage on a broad range of network management topics, including technology overviews, network industry news, and standards information.

Network World is published 51 times a year by IDG Publications, 161 Worcester Road, Framingham, MA, 01701-9172, and can be reached at (508) 875-6400. The magazine is free to qualified subscribers, and costs $95 inside the United States, and between $95 and $245 outside the country, depending on exact location, for nonqualified subscribers. *Network World* provides weekly coverage on a broad range of network management topics, including technology overviews, network industry news, and offers special departments for enterprise internets, local networks, global services, and client-server applications.

Open Systems Today is published 28 times a year by CMP Publications, Inc., 600 Community Drive, Manhasset, NY, 11030-3875, (708) 647-6834 (subscription). The magazine is free to qualified subscribers, and costs $79 inside the United States and Canada, and between $179 and $200 outside the country, depending on exact location, for nonqualified subscribers, per year. *OST* provides semimonthly coverage on a broad range of computer industry topics, including technology overviews and industry news, and offers special departments on networking, that is primarily focused at the open systems side of the computer industry, with a strong emphasis on UNIX. It offers a valuable complement to most of the other magazines mentioned here, which devote most of their networking coverage to PC-related topics.

PC Week is published 51 times a year by Ziff-Davis Publishing Company, a division of Ziff Communications Company, One Park Avenue, New York, NY, 10016, 609-786-8230 (subscriptions). The magazine is free to qualified subscribers, and costs $160 inside the United States, and between $200 and $350 outside the country, depending on exact location, for nonqualified subscribers, per year. *PC Week* provides weekly coverage on a broad range of computer industry topics, including technology overviews, industry news, and offers special departments on networking. It also publishes a weekly network-focused supplement, called *PCWeek Netweek*, that will be shipped to readers who express interest in networking.

The Workgroup Computing Report is published 12 times a year by Patricia Seybold's Office Computing Group, 148 State Street, Boston, MA, 02109, (617) 742-5200 (Fax: (617) 742-1028). Like many specialty-focus publications, this one is expensive at $385 yearly, but well worth it to those seeking information on workgroup computing, messaging-based applications, and related technology and industry trends. Some of its articles are republished on the CD-ROM–based computing database published monthly by Ziff-Davis called *Computer Select* (subscription is $1195 yearly, plus applicable local and state taxes).

INDEX

C

D

E

F

G

H

I

K

L

M

N

O

P

Q

S

T

T

V

W